GOOD FAITH IN CONTRACT AND PROPERTY

GOOD FAITH IN CONTRACT AND PROPERTY

Edited by

A. D. M. Forte

·H A R T·
PUBLISHING

OXFORD – PORTLAND OREGON
1999

Hart Publishing
Oxford and Portland, Oregon

Published in North America (US and Canada) by
Hart Publishing c/o
International Specialized Book Services
5804 NE Hassalo Street
Portland, Oregon
97213-3644
USA

Distributed in the Netherlands, Belgium and Luxembourg by
Intersentia, Churchillaan 108
B2900 Schoten
Antwerpen
Belgium

Distributed in Australia and New Zealand by
Federation Press
John St
Leichhardt
NSW 2000

Hart Publishing Ltd is a specialist legal publisher based in
Oxford, England.
To order further copies of this book or to request a list of other
publications please write to:

Hart Publishing Ltd, Salter's Boatyard, Oxford OX1 4LB
Telephone: +44 (0)1865 245533 or Fax: +44 (0)1865 794882
e-mail: mail@hartpub.co.uk

British Library Cataloguing in Publication Data
Data Available
ISBN 1 84113-047-8

Typeset by Hope Services (Abingdon) Ltd.
Printed in Great Britain on acid-free paper
by Biddles Ltd, Guildford and Kings Lynn.

CONTENTS

EXPANDED TABLE OF CONTENTS

TABLE OF CASES

TABLE OF LEGISLATION
AND
DELGATED LEGISLATION

TABLE OF INTERNATIONAL
CONVENTIONS AND PRINCIPLES

PREFACE

Cicero tells the story of Orata, a dynamic entrepreneur, who owned a house over which, as he knew, there was a servitude. He sold the house to Gratidianus who sold it back to him a few years later without mentioning the servitude, as the law required of sellers. Of course, Orata was well aware of the existence of the servitude, but, even so, he rather cheekily sued Gratidianus for his failure to mention it. The action was based on the contract of sale and the judge required to decide it by applying the standard of good faith. Cicero does not expressly tell us the outcome and modern scholars, also applying the standard of good faith, conclude that Orata lost since it would have been outrageous for a seller to be held liable for his failure to mention something which the buyer knew all about. In fact, however, Orata won. The judge clearly took the view that, by omitting to mention the servitude, the seller had failed to live up to the requirements of good faith in that situation.

I happen to prefer the old judge's decision, since he would have been right to be suspicious of the good faith of anyone who chose not to comply with his duty to mention a servitude affecting a house which he was selling. But the difference between the judge's view and the reaction of modern scholars to the same facts illustrates how people from different backgrounds, applying the standard of good faith, can reach diverse conclusions. Gerhard Beseler once remarked that it was the "high calling" of the Roman jurists to work out the detailed rules. The room for differences of view among their modern successors emerged very plainly at the Aberdeen conference, the papers from which make up this volume. And indeed none of the participants suggested that the mere invocation of the concept of good faith could dictate a single right answer to any particular problem. Rather, the central issue seemed to be whether, even at this late stage in the development of English and Scots law, the explicit recognition of some underlying principle of good faith would give the judges a useful tool for shaping the law in accordance with the relevant standards recognised by the community or by some particular group, such as bankers or insurers. Or have we achieved by other means, such as implied terms, all that codified systems have accomplished by invoking good faith, so that a principle of good faith would now be a destabilising rather than a creative force?

You may not find the answers to these questions in the papers which follow, but you will find much vigorous discussion of the issues. That discussion is timely, if only because the concept of good faith has already entered our law in various ways, such as the Directive on Commercial Agents, and may yet make further progress through other European initiatives touching areas of our private law.

2 November 1998   Alan Rodger

1

Introduction

A.D.M. Forte*

In late October 1998 a number of judges, law commissioners and schol-ars, both Scots and English, met in Aberdeen for a one-day symposium on good faith in contract and property law. The objective was to stim-ulate the process of debate on a topic which has commanded consider-able attention in England, Continental Europe, South Africa, and the United States in recent years. Curiously, however, for a legal system which prides itself upon the development of general principles, and in contrast certainly to English law which exhibits something of an aver-sion to these, the lively debate on good faith in other jurisdictions appeared to have passed by unnoticed in Scotland. Unnoticed that is until the decision of *Smith* v. *Bank of Scotland* was reported.[1] In that case, reference was made to a general principle of good faith which appeared to be regarded as underpinning the Scots law of contract. The decision provoked a flurry of comments (largely hostile), both to the decision and to the concept, and it was these which suggested to me that the time was ripe for some detailed consideration of good faith in con-temporary Scots law. There are, of course, certain international models dealing with contracts which cannot be ignored when discussing the role of good faith from an English perspective. But recent internal changes in both the governance of Scotland and in the domestic agenda for legal reform, have now combined to give added impetus to the need to explore the role (and some would add the very existence) of a general principle of good faith.

The Scotland Act 1998 provides that the new Scottish Parliament, opened on the same day that this brief introduction is being written, will have within its legislative remit the power to develop and change, *inter alia*, the law of obligations and the law of property in Scotland.[2] In my

---

* Professor of Commercial Law, University of Aberdeen.
[1] 1997 SC (HL) 111.
[2] See ss 29(4), 126(4), and Sched. 4 para. 2(3).

opinion it will be suggested, formally or otherwise, that the Scottish Parliament should consider the desirability of codifying particular areas of Scots law, such as the law of contract. In any event, the Parliament will receive proposals for reform of the law of contract from the Scottish Law Commission; and current proposals by the Commission in this area have advertised the importance of ensuring that Scots law remains congruent with a number of international models, of which the 1980 United Nations *Convention on Contracts for the International Sale of Goods*,[3] the 1994 UNIDROIT *Principles of International Commercial Contracts* and the *Principles of European Contract Law* prepared by the Commission on European Contract Law, are the most important.[4] These models lean as much in the direction of civilian legal ideas as they do towards the common law tradition and, of course, it is the civilian tradition which places the greater emphasis on the need for overt articulation of a general principle of good faith in a contractual context. Furthermore, any reforms in the area of private law generally, will be carried out against the background of the European Parliament's stated resolution that the development of the Single Market is, to some degree, contingent upon unification of private law throughout the European Union.[5] Even if a general principle of good faith in contract law does not already exist, and many would deny that proposition, it appears to be very likely that the factors referred to above will combine to ensure that it may soon become part of Scots law.

It is, of course, possible that we already do have just such a general principle at work in the law, though lacking perhaps in cohesive force at this time. Certainly the reception of good faith into Scots law as a substantive, legislative provision will be the easier to accommodate if the system as a whole is prepared to accept, in advance, its present existence therein. Furthermore, the parameters of the principle may be easier to establish if we begin the process of objective discussion in advance of the movement for reform. Most of the essays in this volume, which are based on the papers delivered at the symposium or commissioned thereafter, accept that good faith does exist in some form or in some partic-

---

[3] *Report on Formation of Contract: Scottish Law and the United Nations Convention on Contracts for the International Sale of Goods*, Scot. Law Com. No. 144 (1993). Note, in particular, para. 1.7.

[4] For example, see *Report on Penalty Clauses*, Scot. Law Com. No. 171 (1999). Note, in particular, paras 1.7–1.9. See also, *Discussion Paper on Remedies for Breach of Contract*, Scot. Law Com. Discussion Paper No. 109 (1999). Note, in particular, paras 1.10–1.13.

[5] Resolution of 26 May 1989, OJEC 1989 C 158/401; Resolution of 6 May 1994, OJEC 1994 C 205/518.

ular application. Even where this is denied, however, and the need for a general principle is rejected as Thompson advocates, there is, nonetheless, a certain fatalism in the belief (and it is one shared by English lawyers) that international developments will render the incorporation of the principle into domestic law inevitable.

To this extent, the incipient debate in Scotland exhibits something in common with that which has taken place in England: and an English perspective should not be ignored.[6] There are, however, certain marked divergences between the Scottish and English approaches to good faith, not least in the fundamental conceptualisation of its role. To the outside observer of the English debate on good faith (and the Scots lawyer must be considered an outside observer), there appears to be a reluctance to move from those rules devised to promote fairness to a general principle of which the specific instances are merely examples of its application. This is brought out clearly by McKendrick's essay which, although it suggests that the English law of contract can accommodate good faith, nonetheless betrays an ultimate reluctance to accept it as a construct of general application. In fairly sharp contrast, however, Blackie, Forte, MacQueen, and Styles, consistent with the legal culture in which they operate, argue for recognition that there are advantages, if not imperatives, to interpreting good faith as a unifying principle across the field of both contract and property law. Even Willett, who examines the concept against a consumerist background and within the broad context of European Union developments, sees good faith as having a central role to play in the evolution of an adequate, substantive law of consumer protection: a role not restricted to the soft law regulation of consumer contracts. Equally consistent with the mixed nature of Scots law, is the extent to which some of the essays, particularly those of Carey Miller and Styles, look to mixed legal systems, particularly South Africa, and continental systems, particularly the German, as reference points in the current debate. Indeed, although the good faith debate has profound contemporary relevance, the central core of essays dealing with the issue from a Scottish perspective all exhibit an approach rooted in doctrinal, historical analysis which has begun to characterise so much scholarship within the law of property and that of obligations in Scotland today. In some instances, this methodology places the exercise centrally in the wider contemporary debate within the civilian legal systems of continental Europe regarding the creation of a new, European, *ius commune*:

---

[6] Much of which is referred to in the following chapters.

a debate which one may characterise as fundamental to future progress on the construction of a uniform European private law.

Much work remains to be done on the Scottish contribution to the wider debate on good faith. Many issues remain to be explored, and the ideas presented here may require to be redeveloped, refined, and possibly even abandoned. But it is important to make a start and it is hoped that the essays presented here will continue that process of dialogue begun in Aberdeen last Autumn.

As organiser of the symposium it remains for me to thank publicly the Faculty of Law and also the Centre for the Study of the Civil Law Tradition in the University of Aberdeen for generous financial assistance which permitted the symposium to take place. I must also thank the Lord President, not only for his Preface to this volume, but also for chairing one of the sessions at the symposium, and the participants whose observations forced many of us to re-think our arguments. Finally, I must thank the contributors (two of whom expressed views so strongly and cogently after the symposium had ended that they were immediately pressed into service) who have had to put up with my many importunate demands on their time and patience over the past several months.

2

Good Faith in the Scots Law of Contract: An Undisclosed Principle?

Hector L. MacQueen*

"There is also an underlying principle of good faith in the Scottish law of contract although it is difficult to find a clear and comprehensive statement of it".[1]

Introduction

The above comment appeared in 1995 in the first published part of the *Principles of European Contract Law*, as one of the notes on national systems attached to the article of the *Principles* providing that each party to a contract must act in accordance with good faith and fair dealing.[2] The comment can almost certainly be attributed to the late Professor W.A. Wilson, who was the Scottish representative on the European Contract Commission responsible for the 1995 publication. Wilson was perhaps an unlikely champion of a good faith principle in Scots contract law, an idea which prior to 1995 had been associated with the neo-civilian work of Sir

* Professor of Private Law, University of Edinburgh. My thanks are due to Professor M. Bridge, University of Nottingham, and to Martin Hogg and Parker Hood, University of Edinburgh, for their helpful comments on an earlier draft of this essay. The discussion at the Aberdeen Symposium on good faith in October 1998 also proved invaluable in assisting me to collect my thoughts, as did an earlier presentation at a seminar on negotiations organised by the Royal Bank of Scotland in August 1997. Responsibility for the views expressed here, however, is mine alone.

[1] O. Lando, H.G. Beale (eds), *The Principles of European Contract Law. Part I: Performance, Non-Performance and Remedies* (Dordrecht, Boston and London, 1995), p. 58. The second part, which will also contain a revision of Part I, should be published in 1999.

[2] Article 1.106 (Article 1:201 in the revised version). The duty may not be excluded or limited. Article 1.107 (Article 1:202 in the revised edition) provides in addition that "each party owes to the other a duty to co-operate in order to give full effect to the contract".

Thomas Smith,[3] and which had otherwise been passed over largely in silence in modern writings and judicial decisions.[4] But in 1997, when as Wilson's successor on the Commission for European Contract Law I had begun to consider revision of and addition to the Scottish notes in preparation for the publication of the second version of the *Principles of European Contract Law*, the House of Lords pronounced on the case of *Smith* v. *Bank of Scotland*.[5] *Smith* extended to Scotland the previous decision of the House in the English case of *Barclays Bank plc* v. *O'Brien*,[6] and in the leading speech, Lord Clyde remarked at one point upon "the broad principle in the field of contract law of fair dealing in good faith".[7] The decision in *Smith* is focused upon the requirement of good faith as between creditor and debtor in a cautionary obligation, underpinning a duty of disclosure to the cautioner and also a duty to warn the cautioner of the consequences of the obligation and to urge upon him or her a need to take independent advice on the transaction. Lord Clyde saw this requirement of good faith as a better basis for the introduction of *O'Brien* in Scots law than the English Equity concept of constructive notice. Nearly all of Lord Clyde's remarks about good faith were therefore focused on the contract of cautionry, but it is apparent that he did not see the requirement as limited to that particular context.[8]

This essay is first an attempt to explain why, following this case and some further research, I decided to leave the note in the European Principles as it stood, adding only a reference to *Smith*. But it also seeks to pursue some of the implications of that conclusion in greater depth, in particular with regard to liability for pre-contractual negotiations.

---

[3] T.B. Smith, *A Short Commentary on the Law of Scotland* (Edinburgh, 1962), 297–8, asserts without much analysis or reference to authority that "in the Scottish law of contract bona fides is a general concept", and is mainly concerned to deny that *uberrima fides* is anything other than a synonym for good faith. The implications are not pursued in his later treatment of voluntary obligations other than in a discussion of concealment, *mala fides* and insurance: *ibid.*, 835–7.

[4] W.M. Gloag, *The Law of Contract* (Edinburgh, 2nd edn, 1929) has "good faith" as an index heading, but there is no general discussion other than the observation (at 400) that "it is a general rule that contracts are to be construed on the assumption of honest dealing". There is no relevant heading in the contents of or indices to W.W. McBryde, *The Law of Contract in Scotland* (Edinburgh, 1987); D.M. Walker, *The Law of Contracts and Related Obligations in Scotland* (Edinburgh, 3rd edn, 1995); S.E. Woolman, *Contract* (Edinburgh, 2nd edn, 1994); and *The Laws of Scotland: Stair Memorial Encyclopaedia*, vol. 15.

[5] 1997 SC (HL) 111.

[6] [1994] 1 AC 180.

[7] See n. 5 above, 121B–C.

[8] For a detailed analysis of this case see the essay by A.D.M. Forte in this volume.

What is Good Faith in Contract Law?

This question has been the subject of much debate in recent times. The background is that the existence or otherwise of such a principle in contract law is one of the major divisions between the Civilian and Common Law systems in Europe. Where the great Continental civil codes all contain some explicit provision to the effect that contracts must be performed and interpreted in accordance with the requirements of good faith,[9] English and Irish law are almost equally explicitly opposed to such broad concepts. This is not to say that the Common Law is happy to countenance bad faith in contracts; but the approach is, to paraphrase some well-known remarks of Lord Bingham, to avoid any commitment to over-riding principle in favour of piecemeal solutions in response to demonstrated problems of unfairness.[10]

Martijn Hesselink has provided an invaluable general analysis of what good faith has been taken to mean in the Continental systems.[11] First a distinction is drawn between subjective and objective good faith. Subjective good faith is concerned with knowledge of facts or events, or absence of knowledge, and affects mainly property law and possession. In this sense good faith is perfectly familiar in English and indeed Scottish law, both of which offer substantial protection to the *bona fide* possessor and to the good faith purchaser of goods from a seller without title while denying it to the acquirer in bad faith.

It is objective good faith, however, which is chiefly relevant to contract law. Objective good faith is about external, or community, norms and standards imposed upon contracting parties. Over time these norms and standards have been distilled into particular rules, notably in Germany. But the content of good faith is not fixed or static, and the existence of the general principle in the Codes enables the Continental judge to innovate and develop the law in response to circumstances without infringing upon the territory of the legislator. (It may be noted

---

[9] French *CC*, art. 1134; *BGB*, ss 138, 242; *NBW*, arts 6:2, 6:248; Italian *CC*, arts 1175, 1337, 1366, 1375; Portuguese *CC*, art. 762(2); Spanish *CC*, art. 1258; Greek *CC*, arts 200, 281, 288, 88; Swiss *CC*, art. 2.

[10] *Interfoto Picture Library Ltd* v. *Stiletto Visual Programmes Ltd* [1989] QB 433, 439 per Bingham LJ. For documentation of this statement, see J. Cartwright, *Unequal Bargaining* (Oxford, 1993); J.W. Carter and M.P. Furmston, "Good Faith and Fairness in the Negotiation of Contracts" (1994–5) 8 *Journal of Contract Law* 1, 93 (2 parts).

[11] "Good Faith", in A. Hartkamp *et al*, *Towards a European Civil Code* (Nijmegen, 2nd edn, 1998).

parenthetically at this point that in *Smith* v. *Bank of Scotland* Lord
Clyde drew upon two property law cases to support the principle of
good faith in Scots contract law;[12] if, however, the distinction between
subjective and objective good faith is sound, then it would seem that
good faith in property should be kept clearly apart from good faith in
contract)[13].

Three major functions of contractual good faith as interpreted on the
Continent are identified by Hesselink: (1) interpretation; (2) supplementation (i.e., the insertion in the contract of duties to be loyal, to protect,
to co-operate, to inform); and (3) correction or limitation, to prevent
abuse of right. And Hesselink goes on to show how these functions have
operated in a number of areas of contract law on the Continent, namely:
(a) in respect of pre-contractual negotiations, where there may be a duty
to inform or disclose, and a liability for breaking off negotiations in bad
faith; (b) as a ground of invalidity, especially in relation to standard form
contracts; (c) as a basis for the interpretation of and gap-filling in contracts; (d) as a way of dealing with unforeseen or changing circumstances
and hardship; (e) as a basis for contractual remedies such as the *exceptio non adimpleti contractus* under which a party who has not received the
contractual performance to which it is entitled may withhold its own
performance; and (f) as a control on the exercise of contractual remedies, in particular those of terminating the contract or of seeking implementation.

The debate about good faith in the Common Law world has been
triggered by various stimuli.[14] In England and Ireland there has been
the impact of European Community Directives touching upon contract

[12] I.e., *Rodger (Builders) Ltd* v. *Fawdry* 1950 SC 483; *Trade Development Bank* v. *David W. Haig (Bellshill) Ltd* 1983 SLT 510: see n. 5 above, 121B–C. On *Rodger (Builders)*, see K.G.C. Reid, *The Law of Property in Scotland* (Edinburgh, 1996) paras 695–700.

[13] See further Reid, n. 12 above, paras 131–137: "Scots law makes no clear choice between subjectivity and objectivity but takes something from both. Thus, on the one hand, the law inquires into the actual state of mind of the possessor . . . objectivity is allowed to manifest itself in two ways. For first, actual knowledge is in certain circum-stances supplemented by constructive knowledge; and secondly, knowledge, whether actual or constructive, is deemed to be interpreted by the possessor in a manner which is in all the circumstances reasonable. . . . Absence of actual knowledge of lack of title is in almost every case an indispensable condition of bona fide possession". See also the essay by D.L. Carey Miller in this volume and D.N. MacCormick, "General Legal Concepts" in *Stair Memorial Encyclopaedia*, n. 4 above, vol. 11, paras 1128–31.

[14] Notable contributions include J.F. O'Connor, *Good Faith in English Law* (Aldershot, 1990); the forum on good faith in contract published in (1994–1995) 7–9 *Journal of Contract Law*; J. Beatson, D. Friedmann (eds), *Good Faith and Fault in Contract Law* (Oxford, 1995); and R. Brownsword, N.J. Hird, G. Howells (eds), *Good Faith in Contract: Concept and Context* (Dartmouth, Brookfield USA, Singapore, Sydney, 1999).

law and deploying the concept of good faith. By this means the lawyers and courts of both systems have been forced to confront directly the meaning of good faith against a background in which a harmonious Community approach is required. The most striking example is the Unfair Terms in Consumer Contracts Directive 1993,[15] under which a term in a consumer contract which has not been individually negotiated may be struck down if, "contrary to the requirement of good faith", it causes a significant imbalance in the rights and duties of the parties, to the detriment of the consumer. The Commercial Agents Directive 1986[16] also makes a number of references to good faith.

This leads on to the possible European harmonisation of contract law at a much more general level, one of the underlying but more long-term objectives of the European Contract Commission. It seems almost certain that a general principle of good faith would be part of such harmonisation.[17] I have already quoted the relevant article of the *Principles of European Contract Law*, and a virtually identical provision can be found in Article 1.7 of the other great recent restatement of contract rules, the UNIDROIT *Principles of International Commercial Contracts*. Both sets of *Principles* find their roots in the Vienna Convention on Contracts for the International Sale of Goods 1980 (CISG), which the United Kingdom appears to be on the verge of ratifying and thereby at last moving into line with its European and other international trading partners. CISG avoids an outright commitment to a principle of good faith, but Article 7(1), the product of a compromise between the Civilian and the Common Law traditions represented in its creation, does say that in the interpretation of the Convention "regard is to be had to . . . the observance of good faith in international trade".[18]

[15] Council Directive 93/13/EEC, OJ 1993, L95/29: implemented in the UK by the Unfair Terms in Consumer Contracts Regulations 1994, SI 1994/3159.
[16] Council Directive 86/653/EEC, OJ 1986, L382/17: implemented in the UK by the Commercial Agents (Council Directive) Regulations 1993, SI 1993/3053.
[17] Note, however, that H. Kötz, A. Flessner, *European Contract Law* (Oxford, 1997) has no general treatment of good faith. H. McGregor, "The Codification of Contracts in England and Scotland (Equity and Good Faith)" in A.M. Rabello (ed.), *Aequitas and Equity: Equity in Civil Law and Mixed Jurisdictions* (Jerusalem, 1997), argues that the Contract Code which he drafted as a basis for unifying Scots and English law in the 1960s (published as *Contract Code drawn up on behalf of the English Law Commission* (Milan, 1993)) accepts the concept of good faith in general, but is explicit only in respect of performance, and even then expresses the matter in terms of "fair dealing". See s. 201. Note also, Kötz, "Towards a European Civil Code: The Duty of Good Faith" in P.Cane, J. Stapleton (eds.), *The Law of Obligations: Essays in Celebration of John Fleming* (Oxford, 1998), 243.
[18] For recent comment see P. Schlechtriem, *Good Faith in German Law and in International Uniform Laws*, Centro di Studi e Richerche di Diritto Comparato e Straniero, Saggi, Conferenze e Seminari 10, (Rome, 1997).

The question for the common lawyers is, therefore, whether to develop an indigenous principle of good faith from the existing specific rules appearing to be based upon it, or to await the harmonisation process as and when it comes, or to resist within that harmonisation process the establishment of a general good faith concept.[19] The forces lined up against explicit recognition of a principle of good faith have an impressive roll-call. They include Professor Roy Goode,[20] Lord Steyn,[21] Professor Hugh Collins,[22] and, most passionately, Professor Michael Bridge.[23] A common concern is the uncertainty which would result from the introduction of a standard of uncertain content with strong moral overtones, and the damage which would be done to the commercial contracting practices which have provided the bedrock of English contract law. Traditionally its approach has been founded on the perceived bases of a market economy, emphasising the right of each party to pursue its own interests, whether in the creation or the exercise of contractual entitlements, and to leave the other to do likewise: not at all consistent with a positive requirement of good faith, with its stress upon the need to take account of the other party's position and the regulation of abuse of right.

Most recently, Bridge has focused upon the problem of termination of contract, and has argued strongly that the heterogeneity of commercial activity means that the law cannot make use of broad general standards like good faith as a guide to whether or not termination should be allowed. In his view:

> [W]hat is needed is an informed treatment of different areas of commercial contract and market activity. A general standard of good faith would deflect

---

[19] For discussion, see H. Collins, "Good Faith in European Contract Law" (1994) 14 *Oxford Journal of Legal Studies* 229; G. Teubner, "Legal Irritants: Good Faith in British [*sic*] Law or How Unifying Law Ends up in New Divergences" (1998) 61 *Modern Law Review* 11.

[20] *Commercial Law in the Next Millennium* (London, 1998), 19–20; *The Concept of "Good Faith" in English Law*, Centro di Studi e Richerche di Diritto Comparato e Straniero, Saggi, Conferenze e Seminari 2, (Rome, 1992).

[21] "The Role of Good Faith and Fair Dealing in Contract Law: A Hair-Shirt Philosophy?" [1991] *Denning Law Journal* 131; "Contract Law: Fulfilling the Reasonable Expectations of Honest Men" (1997) 113 *Law Quarterly Review* 433.

[22] *The Law of Contract* (London, 3rd edn, 1997) chs 10 and 15. Collins prefers to speak of the duty to negotiate with care, and of implied terms about co-operation.

[23] "Does Anglo-Canadian Contract Law Need a Doctrine of Good Faith?" (1984) 9 *Canadian Business Law Journal* 385; "Good Faith in Commercial Contracts" in Brownsword *et al*, n. 14 above, 139.

attention from the need to deal with problem areas . . . in a critical and detailed way.[24]

Equally, however, there are eloquent voices in England calling for recognition of a principle of good faith,[25] who can pray in aid not only supporters from Canada[26] and Australia,[27] but also the adoption of the principle in the law of the greatest market economy in the world, the United States of America. Thus section 1–203 of the Uniform Commercial Code provides that "every contract or duty within this Act imposes an obligation of good faith and fair dealing in its performance or enforcement." Good faith itself is defined in section 1–201(19) as "honesty in fact in the conduct or transaction concerned" and in section 2–103(1)(b) as "the observance of reasonable standards of fair dealing in the trade." This has been reinforced by a provision in the Restatement (2nd) of Contracts 1981 that "every contract imposes upon each party a duty of good faith and fair dealing in its performance and its enforcement" (section 205).[28]

A distinguished protagonist for recognition of a good faith principle is the Australian judge, Paul Finn. While accepting that contracts are about the pursuit of self-interest, he argues that the law also requires a

---

[24] Bridge, n. 23 above, in Brownsword et al, 139, 147.

[25] An early proponent was R. Powell, "Good Faith in Contracts" (1956) 9 *Current Legal Problems* 16. More recently, see O'Connor, n. 14 above, ch. 3; J.N. Adams, R. Brownsword, *Key Issues in Contract* (London, 1995), 198–254. Brownsword has taken his arguments further in "'Good Faith in Contracts' Revisited" (1996) 49 (2) *Current Legal Problems* 111, and "Contract Law, Co-operation and Good Faith: The Movement from Static to Dynamic Market-Individualism" in S. Deakin, J. Michie (eds), *Contracts, Co-operation and* Competition (Oxford, 1997), 255.

[26] B.J. Reiter, "Good Faith in Contracts" (1983) 17 *Valparaiso University Law Review* 705. More cautious is S.M. Waddams, "Good faith, Unconscionability and Reasonable Expectations" (1995) 9 *Journal of Contract Law* 55.

[27] See H.N. Lücke, "Good Faith and Contractual Performance" in P.D. Finn (ed.), *Essays in Contract* (Sydney, 1987); P.D. Finn, "Commerce, the Common Law and Morality" (1989) 17 *Melbourne University Law Review* 87; "Australian Developments in Common and Commercial Law" (1990) *Journal of Business Law* 265. Priestly JA of the New South Wales Court of Appeal has argued in favour of a good faith standard judicially and extra-judicially: "A Guide to a Comparison of Australian and United States Contract Law" (1989) 4 *University of New South Wales Law Journal* 4; *Renard Construction* v. *Minister of Public* Works (1992) 26 NSWLR 234.

[28] The limitations to "performance and enforcement", however, make this significantly narrower than the good faith of Continental Europe. See H.O. Hunter, "The Duty of Good Faith and Security of Performance" (1995) 8 *Journal of Contract Law* 19. On the debate about good faith in US contract law, see the surveys of E.A. Farnsworth, *The Concept of Good Faith in American Law*, Centro di Studi e Richerche di Diritto Comparato e Straniero, Saggi, Conferenze e Seminari 10, (Rome, 1993), and in Beatson and Friedmann (eds), n. 14 above, 153–70.

contracting party to take the other party's interests into account in varying degrees. In this, good faith occupies the middle ground between the
principle of unconscionability and fiduciary obligations:

> "Unconscionability" accepts that one party is entitled as of course to act self-
> interestedly in his actions towards the other. Yet in deference to that other's
> interests, it then proscribes excessively self-interested or exploitative conduct.
> "Good faith", while permitting a party to act self-interestedly, nonetheless
> qualifies this by positively requiring that party, in his decision and action, to
> have regard to the legitimate interests therein of the other. The "fiduciary"
> standard for its part enjoins one party to act in the interests of the other—to
> act selflessly and with undivided loyalty. There is, in other words, a pro-
> gression from the first to the third: from selfish behaviour to selfless behav-
> iour.[29]

Finn is thus able to see good faith as operative in the commercial context, since it does not deny, but only confines, the legitimacy of the pursuit of self-interest. Nevertheless it is probably fair to say that many
other proponents of a good faith principle have seen it as an instrument
of social welfare in contract law as against the market and commercial
orientation of its critics.[30] It is striking that in the United Kingdom
good faith has emerged most strongly in the interventionist and pater-
nalist contexts of consumer protection and (in the guise of the obligations of "mutual trust and confidence" between employer and employee)
labour law.[31]

Scots Law

What then of Scots law? Whatever may have been the position before
the middle of the nineteenth century (a question into which I have

[29] P.D. Finn, "The Fiduciary Principle" in T.G. Youdan (ed.), *Equity, Fiduciaries and Trusts* (Toronto, Calgary, Vancouver, 1989) 1, 4.

[30] See in particular R. Brownsword, G. Howells, T. Wilhelmsson, *Welfarism in Contract Law* (Aldershot, 1994); C. Willett (ed.), *Aspects of Fairness in Contracts* (London, 1997).

[31] The Unfair Terms Directive is plainly a measure of consumer protection. The Commercial Agents Directive protects the self-employed commercial agent. For labour law generally, see J.D. Brodie, "The Heart of the Matter: Mutual Trust and Confidence" (1996) 25 *Industrial Law Journal* 121; "Beyond Exchange: the New Contract of Employment", (1998) 27 *Industrial Law Journal* 79. The leading case on mutual trust and confidence is now *Malik* v. *Bank of Credit and Commerce International SA* [1998] AC 20. For explicit recognition in Scotland of mutual trust and confidence as good faith, see e.g., *Taylor* v. *Confederation Management Ltd*, Perth Sheriff Court, 2 December 1997; *Hill* v. *General Accident Fire and Life Assurance Corporation plc* 1998 GWD 31–1622 (Lord Hamilton).

deliberately conducted no substantial research for this essay),[32] there can be no doubt that, if there is a general principle of good faith in Scots contract law, it has been mostly latent and inarticulate until now. Indeed, as Professor Thomson's contribution to this volume shows, there are judicial dicta against such a principle, at least insofar as it might connote a duty to take another's interests into account, or a power to strike down a bargain as unfair.[33] Interestingly, more or less the same can be said of the world's principal other uncodified mixed jurisdiction, South Africa.[34] It would seem that in both systems the way in which the principle has been expressed is through particular rules, and that the influence of the Common Law Approach has here greatly outweighed anything that might have come from Roman or Civilian roots.

Nonetheless, and even setting aside the recent Directives which apply as much in Scotland as in England and Ireland,[35] rules and cases from Scots contract law which could be said to stem from or relate to good faith can be identified without too much difficulty. In our forthcoming

[32] It does, however, appear to me that the only "institutional" writer to deal with the subject in anything like the way we are now discussing it is Kames, *Principles of Equity* (Edinburgh, 3rd edn, 1778), pp. 194–338: see in particular his reference to "contracts *bonae fidei*, that is, contracts in which equity may interpose to correct inequalities and to adjust all matters according to the plain intention of the parties" (pp. 199–200). Under this rubric he discusses the following nine topics: (1) where will is imperfectly expressed in the writing; (2) implied will; (3) whether an omission in a deed or covenant can be supplied; (4) a deed or covenant that tends not to bring about the end for which it was made; (5) equity with respect to a deed providing for an event that now can never happen; (6) errors in deeds and covenants; (7) relief in relation to deeds or covenants void at common law as *ultra vires*; (8) failure in performance; and (9) indirect means employed to evade performance.
None of Stair, Erskine or Hume discuss *bona fides* in their accounts of conventional obligations. Bankton does have the following, slightly ambiguous, passage: "Contracts, among the Romans, and the actions thereon, were either *bonae fidei*, or *stricti juris*; the first are these in which the judge had a liberty, upon the mutual obligations of parties, from the nature of the contract, according to their presumed will, as in Sale, Mandate, Location and others enumerated by the Emperor: the other, were these wherein the judge was tied down to the express covenant or words of the parties, as in Stipulation, and Loan of Money. We have little use for this distinction; only Loan and Promises are strictly interpreted". (*An Institute of the Law of Scotland* (Edinburgh, 1751–3), I.11.65). Cf. Stair, *Institutions of the Law of Scotland* (1681), I.11.6, D.M. Walker (ed.), (Edinburgh, 1983). Bell, *Principles of the Law of Scotland* (Edinburgh, 10th edn., 1899) para 474, talks of insurance as a "contract of good faith".
[33] J.M. Thomson, ch. 4.
[34] See R. Zimmermann, "Good Faith and Equity" in R. Zimmermann, D. Visser (eds), *Southern Cross: Civil Law and Common Law in South Africa* (Cape Town, 1996), 217–60, especially at 239–55.
[35] For further comment on the Unfair Terms Directive and good faith in Scotland, see I. MacNeil, "Good Faith and the Control of Contract Terms: the EC Directive on Unfair Terms in Consumer Contracts" 1995 *Juridical Review* 147.

text on contract law, Professor Thomson and I will argue that much of our law can be characterised by the high value which it places upon compelling performance. This can readily be seen as reflecting the requirements of good faith. As Professor MacCormick has commented:

> Conventional obligations can themselves be considered as exigible simply on grounds of the requirements of good faith. Each party to a contract necessarily engages the trust of the other, hence no action by each other which defeats the expectations in good faith formed by the other is a fair or reasonable action.[36]

This is not just a matter of the availability of the remedy of specific implement as of right,[37] but can also be seen in the importance of the Scottish version of the *exceptio non adimpleti contractus*, the principle of mutuality and the right of retention, as a means of pressuring a contract-breaker into proper performance.[38] Even when damages are awarded for breach of contract rather than an order for implement, the amount is commonly based on the expectation or, as it is perhaps better expressed, the performance interest.[39]

The argument that good faith underpins the requirement that contracts be performed may seem startling at first sight: surely at this point the principle is being used to explain too much to be useful? The answer to this, however, lies in the history of the law rather than in current application. Whereas in the modern law agreements giving rise to reasonable expectations of performance will generally be contracts, it has not always been so. The rise of the consensual (or formless) contract to become the typical contract, so that "every paction produceth action", was one of the achievements of the principle of good faith as identified and elaborated by the canon lawyers of the middle ages.[40] Scots law has

[36] *Stair Memorial Encyclopaedia*, vol. 11, para 1129.
[37] See W.W. McBryde, "Remedies for Breach of Contract" (1996) 1 *Edinburgh Law Review* 43, 48–54. Note also, *Retail Parks Investments Ltd* v. *Bank of Scotland (No.2)* 1996 SC 227.
[38] See McBryde, n. 37 above, 64–9; H.L. MacQueen, "Remedies for Breach of Contract: the Future Development of Scots Law in its European and International context" (1997) 1 *Edinburgh Law Review* 200, 207–9. Note also, *Bank of East Asia* v. *Scottish Enterprise* 1997 SLT 1213 (HL): commented on by W.W. McBryde, "Mutuality Retained" (1996) 1 *Edinburgh Law Review* 135.
[39] L.J. Macgregor, "The Expectation, Reliance and Restitution Interests in Contract Damages" 1996 *Juridical Review* 227.
[40] See, for example, F. Wieacker, *A History of Private Law in Europe* (Oxford, 1995), T. Weir (trans.), 52; H.J. Berman, *Law and Revolution: the Formation of the Western Legal Tradition* (Cambridge, Mass., 1983), 245–50; O.F. Robinson, T.D. Fergus, W.M. Gordon, *European Legal History* (London, 2nd edn, 1994), 88–9. The quotation, from Stair (*Institutions*, I.10.7) is the institutist's version of the canonist *pacta servanda sunt*.

gone even further, in upholding not just bilateral agreements but also unilateral promises.[41] The rules by which the few contracts requiring formal writing in Scots law may nonetheless come into existence as a result of informal agreement plus conduct by the parties also seem to hold them to expectations and reliance engendered in good faith.[42]

If we now group some other rules of Scottish contract law under the headings of the three major functions of good faith in contract identified by Martijn Hesselink—interpretation, supplementation and correction[43]—the extent to which these rules are imbued, or at least are consistent, with the requirements of good faith becomes even more apparent.

(1) *Interpretation*

The fundamental doctrine of contract interpretation, namely, the objective approach of determining, not the actual intentions of the parties, but rather, what each was reasonably entitled to conclude from the attitude of the other, reflects the requirements of good faith inasmuch as contracting parties are thereby protected from unfair surprise. Until a statutory remedy of rectification was introduced in 1985,[44] these principles also allowed the court to correct obvious errors of expression in contractual documents.[45] If the proposals of the Scottish Law Commission about contractual interpretation are implemented, however, the law will move a little further along the good faith route, because the courts will then be able to give effect to the particular sense in which one party used an expression if the other party knew or could not have been unaware of that intention.[46]

(2) *Supplementation*

Although there is no general duty of disclosure in the Scots law of contract, there are at least some cases where a party who knows of and takes

[41] W.W. McBryde, "Promises in Scots Law" (1993) 42 *International and Comparative Law Quarterly* 48.

[42] For the current rule see the Requirements of Writing (Scotland) Act 1995 s. 1(3). For the previous law, see McBryde, n. 4 above, 647–54.

[43] See n. 11 above and accompanying text.

[44] Law Reform (Miscellaneous Provisions) (Scotland) Act 1985 ss. 8 and 9.

[45] For the previous common law position, see McBryde, n. 4 above, 434–5.

[46] *Report on Interpretation in Private Law*, Scot. Law Com. No. 160 (1997).

advantage of another party's error in forming a contract with that party
has not been allowed to enforce the contract even when there has been
no misrepresentation.[47]

The doctrine of terms implied in law includes some which may be
implied in contracts generally and which look very like expressions of
good faith:[48] thus parties may be compelled to co-operate to ensure that
the contract is carried out,[49] to perform within a reasonable time,[50] to
exercise discretionary powers under the contract reasonably,[51] and not
to prevent another party from performing or to do anything else to dero-
gate from the contract.[52]

(3) *Correction*

The nineteenth-century development of doctrines such as undue influence and facility and circumvention alongside the classical grounds of
invalidity (error, fraud and force) can also be seen as essentially based
on good faith.[53] But, despite a hint once thrown out by Lord President
Cooper,[54] modern Scots contract law has never developed a general
doctrine permitting the challenge of "leonine", extortionate, or unfair
bargains as such:[55] statutory intervention has been required to achieve
that, at least in part.[56] At common law, however, penalty clauses and

---

[47] *Steuart's Trs* v. *Hart* (1875) 3 R 192; *Angus* v. *Bryden* 1992 SLT 884; *Security Pacific Finance Ltd* v. *T & I Filshie's* Tr 1994 SCLR 1100; 1995 SCLR 1171; *Stair Memorial Encyclopaedia*, vol. 15, para 694.

[48] The difference may be that as implied terms these obligations can be excluded by express provision, whereas the legal obligation of good faith will usually override the contract.

[49] *Mackay* v. *Dick & Stevenson* (1881) 8 R (HL) 37, at 40 per Lord Blackburn.

[50] McBryde, n. 4 above, 93–4.

[51] *Stair Memorial Encyclopaedia*, vol. 15, para 861 fn. 2; cf. Gloag, n. 4 above, 302–8. The decision of the First Division in *Glasgow West Housing Association Ltd* v. *Siddique* 1998 SLT 1081 that an absolute discretion conferred contractually could not be qualified by an implied term of reasonableness was not based upon a review of any relevant author-ity, and it is anyway stated that an action might have been brought if the holder of a dis-cretion failed to exercise it or acted in a wholly unreasonable way. See further, *Bradford & Bingley Building Society* v. *Thorntons plc* 1998 GWD 40–2071.

[52] *Barr* v. *Lions Ltd* 1956 SC 59.

[53] On these doctrines see McBryde, n. 4 above, chs 9–12; *Stair Memorial Encyclopaedia*, vol. 11, paras 701–42; vol. 15, paras 670–94.

[54] *McKay* v. *Scottish Airways* 1948 SC 254, at 263.

[55] McBryde, n. 4 above, 255–8; *Stair Memorial Encyclopaedia*, vol. 15, para 677.

[56] For example, Consumer Credit Act 1974, s. 137; Unfair Contract Terms Act 1977, Part II; Unfair Terms in Consumer Contracts Regulations 1994, n. 15 above.

the oppressive use of irritancies in leases are subject to judicial control.[57]

Remedies are also subject to controls which may be seen as brakes upon the abuse of rights. Thus specific implement, although a right, is nonetheless subject to the discretion of the court, which has been shaped to some extent into a set of rules as to when the remedy will not be granted.[58] Again, in the absence of specific contractual provision, termination is only available on *material* breach; that is to say, the response must be commensurate with the wrong.[59] The recent suggestions that in at least some circumstances a party should give a contract-breaker a second chance to perform before terminating might also be consistent with an approach based fundamentally on good faith.[60] In the law of damages, the rule that the claimant should act to mitigate or minimise loss looks very much like a good faith requirement, as might any rules which may exist on contributory negligence.[61]

The Utility of Recognising a Good Faith Principle

It is, however, relatively easy to proceed through a system of rules like Scots contract law, as I have just done, and to pick out those parts of it which seem to reflect the requirements and values of good faith as it has been understood in Europe in modern times. It would be surprising to find rules which encouraged or allowed bad faith; but not so for rules embodying requirements of good faith. The real question is, what difference does it make to the system to declare now that there is a general principle of good faith holding it all together? Given that the rules

---

[57] The rules on irritancies were so little used, however, that statutory intervention was deemed necessary. See the Law Reform (Miscellaneous Provisions) (Scotland) Act 1985 ss. 4 and 5. The law on both penalties and irritancies is under review once more: see *Report on Penalty Clauses*, Scot. Law Com. No. 171 (1999).

[58] McBryde, n. 4 above, 511–13.

[59] McBryde, n. 37 above, 58–64.

[60] *Lindley Catering Investments Ltd* v. *Hibernian Football Club Ltd* 1975 SLT (Notes) 56; *Strathclyde Regional Council* v. *Border Engineering Contractors Ltd* 1998 SLT 175; McBryde, n. 4 above, 329. For discussion of the utility of this approach in the context of software contracts, see H.L. MacQueen, M. Hogg, P. Hood, "Muddling Through? Legal Responses to E-commerce from the Perspective of a Mixed System" *Molengrafica: Europees Privaatrecht 1998* 199–200, 208, 220–1.

[61] *Stair Memorial Encyclopaedia*, vol. 15, paras 925–9. See also on contributory negligence, *Concrete Products (Kirkcaldy) Ltd* v. *Menzies and Anderson* 1996 SLT 587.

are expressions of good faith, why do they need to be reinforced by a
generalisation? What function that is not currently performed by the
system would such a generalisation bring about?

The answer would seem to be that the articulation of the general principle enables the identification and solution of problems which the existing rules do not, or seem unable to reach. The history of the good faith
doctrine in Germany illustrates this very well. The celebrated Article
242 of the BGB enabled the German courts to develop doctrines of *culpa
in contrahendo*, change in circumstances, contracts with protective effects
vis-à-vis third parties, positive breach of contract, abuse of contractual
rights and termination of long-term contracts, without any other support from the code. Problems arose for which no direct codal provision
appeared to exist, or which existed as the result of what the code said;
Article 242 enabled the court to overcome these obstacles without incurring the reproach of pure judicial law-making.[62]

Smith v. *Bank of Scotland* may be a domestic example of the same
phenomenon. The general principle of good faith enabled the House of
Lords to deal with a problem for which there was thought to be no satisfactory answer in the existing specific rules of Scots law. An apparent
gap was filled, and a new rule came into being.[63] It is exactly the same
as recognising a general duty of care in negligence,[64] or a principle
against unjustified enrichment;[65] the law can move on, and new rules
develop. As a result, the principle may remain relatively latent, or continue to be stated in extremely general terms, without doing too much
damage to the important values of certainty and predictability in the law,
since it is constantly in the process of being refined by the formulation
of more concrete rules in particular cases.[66] The principle also provides

[62] See W.F. Ebke, B.M. Steinhauer, "The Doctrine of Good Faith in German Contract
Law" in Beatson and Friedmann (eds), n. 14 above, 171; B.S. Markesinis, W. Lorenz, G.
Dannemann, *The German Law of Obligations Volume I: The Law of Contracts and
Restitution: A Comparative Introduction* (Oxford, 1997), ch. 7.

[63] Commentators are at one in seeing *Smith* as judicial innovation: G.L. Gretton,
"Sexually Transmitted Debt" 1997 *Scots Law Times* (News) 195; J.M. Thomson,
"Misplaced Concern?" (1997) 65 *Scottish Law Gazette* 124; R. Dunlop, "Spouses, Caution
and the Banks" (1997) 42 *Journal of the Law Society of Scotland* 446; L.J. Macgregor, "The
House of Lords Applies *O'Brien* North of the Border" (1998) 2 *Edinburgh Law Review* 90;
S.F. Dickson, "Good Faith in Contract: Spousal Guarantees and *Smith* v. *Bank of
Scotland*" 1998 SLT (News) 39.

[64] As in *Donoghue* v. *Stevenson* 1932 SC (HL) 31.

[65] As may have happened in *Shilliday* v. *Smith* 1998 SC 725 and *Dollar Land
(Cumbernauld) Ltd* v. *CIN Properties Ltd* 1998 SC(HL) 90.

[66] See also Hesselink's (n. 11 above, 309) conclusion that "if the role of the judge as a
creator of rules is fully recognised, there is no need for a general good faith clause in a

a basis upon which existing rules inconsistent with it can be criticised and reformed, whether judicially or by legislation.[67]

The following sections of this essay seek to elucidate another area of Scots law in which the recognition of the underlying principle of good faith might assist in the development from a rather incoherent and difficult body of cases of a set of rules dealing with a hitherto unrecognised problem, namely the legal effect of pre-contractual negotiations not involving any of the traditional bases of invalidity and liability such as misrepresentation, fraud or force. In other words, can Scots law, like German law before it, use the doctrine of good faith to develop rules on *culpa in contrahendo*?

That there is a problem in this field needing to be addressed is suggested by stories in the Scottish press concerned with failed negotiations in the domestic housing market. Under Scots law, contracts for the sale of heritable property must be in formal writing: a requirement which in normal practice is met by the prospective purchaser submitting a written offer and receiving the seller's written acceptance. Usually the seller has several offers from which to choose. The seller's formal acceptance of the preferred bid is often preceded by a verbal intimation of success to the selected bidder. However, this may be followed by a game of "missives tennis" in which the buyer's offer is formally met with a qualified, not a full, acceptance, thereby initiating what can be a protracted exchange of counter-offers between the parties, during which there is no concluded contract unless one or other side gives an unqualified acceptance of an offer open for the purpose.[68] In the recently reported stories, a seller who had made a verbal intimation of acceptance to one buyer then received another, higher offer from a third party, with whom a formal contract was subsequently concluded. The general understanding was that in these circumstances the disappointed offeror had no legal remedy, since no contract had been concluded by the purely verbal statement of the seller. However, the Law Society of Scotland declared that the seller's advisers had acted unprofessionally in

---

code or restatement of European private law. It may even do harm because it gives the courts an excuse for not formulating the rule that they apply. If however there is still some doubt as to the power of the courts, a good faith clause could be useful in order to assure that the judge may create new rules."

[67] An example here might be *White and Carter (Councils) Ltd* v. *McGregor* 1962 SC (HL) 1; [1962] AC 413.

[68] See, for example, *Rutterford Ltd* v. *Allied Breweries* 1990 SLT 249; *Findlater* v. *Maan* 1990 SC 150.

countenancing his behaviour, and adverse comment was also made in the media.[69]

Is it really the case that Scots law tolerates conduct of this kind in the name of freedom to negotiate and freedom to withdraw from negotiations which have not yet reached the stage of contract? Can an obligation to negotiate in good faith provide a solution to the problem?

Culpa in Contrahendo

In the English House of Lords decision *Walford* v. *Miles*,[70] Lord Ackner remarked:

> The concept of a duty to carry on negotiations in good faith is inherently repugnant to the adversarial position of the parties when involved in negotiations. Each party to the negotiations is entitled to pursue his (or her) own interest, so long as he avoids making misrepresentations. To advance that interest he must be entitled, if he thinks it appropriate, to threaten to withdraw from further negotiations or to withdraw in fact in the hope that the opposite party may seek to reopen the negotiations by offering him improved terms. ... [H]ow is a vendor ever to know that he is entitled to withdraw from further negotiations? How is the court to police such an "agreement"? A duty to negotiate in good faith is as unworkable in practice as it is inherently inconsistent with the position of a negotiating party. . . . In my judgment, while negotiations are in existence either party is entitled to withdraw from these negotiations, at any time and for any reason. There can be thus no obligation to continue to negotiate until there is a "proper reason" to withdraw.[71]

These remarks were greeted with horror on the Continent, as a classic example of how irreconcilably different English law is from the codified systems.[72] Continental lawyers, especially those in the Germanic tradition, regard the obligation to negotiate in good faith as a fundamental instance of the general principle of good faith.[73] In Germany the

[69] *The Scotsman*, 27 August 1998 ("Couple Threaten to Sue over Gazumping").

[70] [1992] 2 AC 128.

[71] At 138.

[72] See in particular the comparative commentaries in (1994) 2 *European Review of Private Law* 267–327.

[73] See generally, F.Kessler, E. Fine, "Culpa In Contrahendo, Bargaining in Good Faith, and Freedom of Contract: a Comparative Study" (1964) 77 *Harvard Law Review* 401; E.H. Hondius (ed.), *Precontractual Liability: Reports to the XIIIth Congress International Academy of Comparative Law* (Deventer, Boston, 1991); N. Cohen, "Precontractual Duties: Two Freedoms and the Contract to Negotiate" in Beatson and Friedmann (eds), n. 14 above, 25–56; Kötz, n. 17 above, 34–41; S. Van Erp, "The Precontractual Stage" in Hartkamp et al, n. 11 above, 201–18.

concept of *culpa in contrahendo*, first developed by Rudolf von Ihering
in the nineteenth century,[74] is now said to mean that:

> a party who negligently nourishes in the other party the hope that a contract
> will come about, although this is unfounded from an objective viewpoint,
> must make compensation for any outlay which the opposite party could have
> regarded as necessary under the circumstances.[75]

The liability thus protects the "negative interest"—broadly what in this
country would be known as the "reliance interest"—of the injured party.
In French law, following the development of Ihering's theory by the
jurist Raymond Saleilles,[76] withholding crucial information and breaking off pre-contractual negotiations in an "arbitrary" or "brutal and unilateral" way has been held by the courts to lead to delictual liability for
the expenditure of the party which was wasted in consequence.[77] The
Dutch Hoge Raad has gone further, distinguishing three stages in negotiations, namely: (1) initial, where there is freedom to withdraw; (2)
intermediate, where withdrawal involves payment of the other side's
reliance losses; and (3) ultimate, determined by gauging the extent of the
non-withdrawing party's reliance on ultimate success, when the other's
withdrawal leads to payment of expectation (i.e., the profit that would
have been made had the contract been concluded) rather than reliance
losses.[78] In all three countries this pre-contractual liability developed on
the basis of the codal principle of good faith. But in the Greek, Italian
and Yugoslavian codifications of this century there are specific rules on
the subject.[79]

It is thus not surprising to find the following in the forthcoming text
of the Principles of European Contract Law:[80]

[74] In a famous article entitled "Culpa in contrahendo oder Schadensersatz bei nichti-
gen oder nicht zu Perfektionen gelangten Verträgen" *Jahrbücher für die Dogmatik des heuti-
gen römischen und deutschen Privatrechts* iv (1861), 1–113. So far as I know this article has
never been translated into English.

[75] Markesinis *et al*, n. 62 above, 69.

[76] Saleilles, "De la responsabilité précontractuelle" (1907) 6 *Revue Trimestrielle de Droit
Civil* 697.

[77] B. Nicholas, *The French Law of Contract* (Oxford, 2nd edn, 1992), 69–71.

[78] J.M. van Dunné, "Netherlands" in Hondius (ed.), n. 73 above, 230–4; Van Erp, n.
73 above, 212.

[79] *Codice civile*, arts 1337, 1338; Greek Civil Code, art. 197; Yugoslavian Law of
Contract 1978, art. 30. Section 12 of the Israeli General Contracts Law 1973 provides that
"in negotiating a contract, a person shall act in customary manner and in good faith";
breach gives rise to an obligation "to pay compensation to the other party for the damage
caused to him in consequence of the negotiations."

[80] The wording here is virtually identical to that of the UNIDROIT *Principles of
International Commercial Contracts* (1994), art. 2.15.

Article 2.301: Negotiations Contrary to Good Faith

(1) A party is free to negotiate and is not liable for failure to reach an agreement.

(2) However, a party who has negotiated or broken off negotiations contrary to good faith is liable for the losses caused to the other party.

(3) It is contrary to good faith, in particular, for a party to enter into or continue negotiations with no real intention of reaching an agreement with the other party.

This represents a significant departure from the Common Law tradition embodied in *Walford* v. *Miles*. While in England, the USA and other common law jurisdictions a negotiating party may be liable for making contractual promises, or misrepresentations, or to make restitution of benefits received in the course of unsuccessful negotiations, it seems clear that there is no residual category of *culpa in contrahendo*.[81]

Scots Law on Pre-contractual Liability

A Scots law student asked about liability for pre-contractual negotiations would most likely agree with Lord Ackner and say that, some basic points apart, there is none.[82] The general rules are that parties negotiating a contract are at arms' length in the sense that each has to look after its own interests, and there are no obligations to the other party short of not telling lies (misrepresentation), practising deception (fraud), coercing the other party into entering the contract (force and fear), or exploiting a special relationship one has with the other party quite separately from the contract under negotiation (undue influence). If any of these factors is present in negotiations which lead to an apparent contract, then that contract may be either void or voidable, with obligations of unjustified enrichment or restitution arising in respect of any performance which may have been rendered prior to the discovery of the flaw

---

[81] See G.Jones, "Claims Arising Out of Anticipated Contracts Which Do Not Materialize" (1980) 18 *University of Western Ontario Law Review* 447; E.A. Farnsworth, "Precontractual Liability and Preliminary Agreements: Fair Dealing and Failed Negotiations" (1987) 87 *Columbia Law Review* 217; reports on Australia, Canada, England, New Zealand and USA in Hondius (ed), n. 73 above, E. McKendrick, "Work Done in Anticipation of a Contract Which Does Not Materialise" in W.R. Cornish, R. Nolan, J. O'Sullivan, G. Virgo (eds), *Restitution Past, Present and Future* (Oxford, 1998) 163.

[82] Note, however, T.B. Smith's undeveloped suggestion, n. 3 above, 863, that although "this doctrine of *culpa in contrahendo* . . . has yet to be considered fully by the Scottish courts . . . there are, however, straws to be clutched at".

in the lead-up to the contract.[83] Insofar as the perpetration of the flaw in the negotiations may also have been a civil wrong, there can be delictual liability, of which the most important examples in practice are negligent misrepresentation under section 10 of the Law Reform (Miscellaneous Provisions) (Scotland) Act 1985 and fraud at common law.[84] Again, where negotiations break down, but there has been some preceding transfer of value between the parties, then an obligation to restore any benefits received may arise under the rules of unjustified enrichment.

Although these rules may seem quite a substantial qualification on the general statement that there is no liability for pre-contractual negotiations, closer examination suggests that they are in fact quite limited. First of all, the issue of liability tends to arise only if a contract apparently results from the negotiations. For example, if there is no apparent contract, then usually there is no relevant loss upon which to base a delictual claim for any misrepresentation, fraud or force which may have been used.[85] It seems of the essence of the whole idea of contract that prior to the moment of formation and legal commitment to a set of obligations parties are free, and that freedom includes the right to withdraw from negotiations, the freedom not to contract. Thus, for example, if I invite tenders for the construction of a building on my land, I am not liable to the unsuccessful tenderers for the often quite substantial expenditure which they may have incurred in preparing their tenders, while the successful tenderer must look to the contract to recoup whatever he may have spent in order to obtain it.

Secondly, for most of the vitiating factors a positive action is required—a misstatement, innocent, negligent or fraudulent; an act of force; or giving advice or acting in a way which takes advantage of the trust and confidence reposed in one by another person. It is much harder to persuade a court to strike down an apparent contract or grant a delictual remedy in damages for inaction. Thus, the authorities, while by no means uniform, are on the whole against the idea of liability arising if I know that the other party is labouring under some misapprehension of which I take advantage although without misrepresentation, the classic example being my purchase of a painting which through

[83] See McBryde, n. 4 above, chs 9–12; *Stair Memorial Encyclopaedia*, vol. 15, paras 670–94.
[84] See *Stair Memorial Encyclopaedia*, vol. 11, paras 701–89.
[85] See *Clelland* v. *Morton Fraser Milligan WS* 1997 SLT (Sh Ct) 57, where a claim under the 1985 Act made against a third party in respect of a representation which had induced a contract between two others was held irrelevant.

superior information I know is much more valuable than the price the seller is putting upon it.[86] There is no general duty in Scots contract law to disclose material information to the other party, although there are specific instances in insurance, caution and fiduciary relationships such as trustee/beneficiary, principal/agent and company/director.[87]

Thirdly, claims on the basis of these rules are rare, and successful claims even rarer, suggesting that the courts are suspicious of attempts to undermine contracts by attaching significance to the preceding negotiations.

These basic rules, and the way in which they operate in practice, seem consistent with the ideals and values of a market economy in which each participant looks after the advancement of its own interests and does not have to be concerned with the position and interests of the other party. Yet what I have found over the years is that these basic rules are not necessarily consistent with how the players in the market place actually conduct the game of negotiating and concluding contracts.

To take a simple example: I teach a course on contracts in the construction industry, in which I give the course members a problem in which a tenderer omits to price for one of the items of work to be done on the job. The question is concerned with what happens if that tender is accepted, and the answer in my opinion is that the price for that item is nil. The discussion of the problem invariably reveals, however, that in practice the employer receiving such a tender would before accepting it go back to the tenderer to check whether there had been a mistake. Almost equally invariably the tenderer would answer that there had been no mistake (even if there had been), because the employer's inquiry shows that the tender is in with a chance of success. But the employer will always inquire, because with a clear answer ground for potentially costly later dispute is removed. Often too the employer deals constantly with the tenderers, and the overall relationship will be soured if one party seeks to take advantage of the other's mistakes. It may indeed be in the overall best interests of each side to have some awareness of the interests of the other and to take them into account: self-interest can include the interests of others on whom one depends in some way.

What is also clear, both from my personal experience and also the reported cases, is that the real world does not quite fit into a legal model in which negotiations take place, a contract is formed, and then and only

[86] Gloag, n. 4 above, 438; *Spook Erection (Northern) Ltd* v. *Kaye* 1990 SLT 676; but cf. n. 47 above.
[87] McBryde, n. 4 above, 215–17.

then do the parties commence the performance which the contract requires. In many commercial situations time does not allow for such dalliance: negotiations and performance go together, perhaps with an expectation that the formal contract to be concluded in due course will have retrospective effect. It may even be that the parties never make use of formal written contracts and pursue an entirely informal relationship in which negotiations, performance and contract are almost indistinguishable. Cases of these kinds have often come before the Scottish courts and, in at least some, the outcome has not been consistent with the legal model so far discussed of parties at arms' length, entitled to look after their own interests only and to ignore those of the other party without incurring liability as a result. In some the court has found that a contract has come into existence despite the continuation of negotiations.[88] Equally, where there has been a transfer of value between the parties but there is no contract, the party suffering loss in the transfer— for example, through payment or performance ahead of conclusion of the contract—may well have a claim in unjustified enrichment.[89]

But some other cases, involving successful claims for wasted pre-contractual expenditure without either delictual wrong by or enrichment of the other party, have caused great difficulties of analysis for commentators, since they do not fit easily into the traditional categories of the law of obligations.[90] However, an analysis of these difficult cases as

[88] A recent example is *Avintair Ltd* v. *Ryder Airline Services Ltd* 1994 SC 270. See H.L. MacQueen, "Contract, Unjustified Enrichment and Concurrent Liability" 1997 *Acta Juridica* 176, 188–9.

[89] For two modern examples of (unsuccessful) enrichment claims in respect of pre-contractual activity, see *Microwave Systems (Scotland) Ltd* v. *Electro-Physiological Instruments Ltd* 1971 SC 140; *Site Preparations Ltd* v. *Secretary of State for Scotland* 1975 SLT (Notes) 41.

[90] See Gloag, n. 4 above, 19–20, 176–7 (favouring a basically contractual explanation); D.I. Ashton-Cross, "The Scots Law Regarding Actions of Reparation Based on False Statements" 1951 *Juridical Review* 199 (favouring a reparation explanation); and W.J. Stewart, *The Law of Restitution in Scotland* (Edinburgh, 1992), paras 10.1–10.9 (Melville Monument liability: "doubtfully restitutionary but sufficiently 'quasi-contractual' to appear in any examination of restitutionary obligations" [para 10.1].) Stewart also suggests (para 10.8) that these cases may be examples of restitution for wrongs. With respect, it is difficult in many of them to see either restitution or wrongs. I have discussed the cases as a possible application of a concept of "unjust sacrifice" or "unjustified impoverishment" in an unpublished section of a paper on unjustified enrichment and contract delivered at a seminar mounted jointly by the Scottish Law Commission and the Universities of Edinburgh and Strathclyde on 23 October 1993. For "unjust sacrifice" see S.J. Stoljar, "Unjust Enrichment and Unjust Sacrifice" (1987) 50 *Modern Law Review* 603; G. Muir, "Unjust Sacrifice and the Officious Intervener" in P. Finn (ed.), *Essays in Restitution* (Sydney, 1990). For criticism see P. Birks, *Restitution: The Future* (Sydney, 1992), 100–5; A. Burrows, *The Law of Restitution* (London, 1993), 4–6, 299.

the application of the concept of good faith to pre-contractual negotiations yields interesting results. The foundation authority is the Melville Monument case, *Walker* v. *Milne*.[91] Walker owned the estate of Coates and he and his father developed the New Town in the West End of Edinburgh in the area which now embraces St Mary's Cathedral, Coates Crescent, Walker Street and Melville Street (the last two having a particularly striking intersection designed by Gillespie Graham). In this intersection (I suspect) there was to be located a monument to Viscount Melville, paid for by subscribers led by Milne. With Walker's permission, the subscribers entered the lands of Coates, broke it up and carried out operations which disrupted Walker's feuing plans on his estate. The subscribers then took their monument off to St Andrews Square, where it stands to this day. Walker sued for breach of contract. Milne defended on the basis that, as the alleged agreement related to heritage and was not in writing, he enjoyed *locus poenitentiae* and could not be liable. The Lord Ordinary upheld this argument. But the Inner House, although they agreed with the judge that no effectual contract had been concluded, held, *inter alia*, that the pursuer was entitled to be indemnified for any loss and damage he might have sustained and for the expenses incurred in consequence of the alteration of the site of the monument.

The court plainly did not see this as either a contractual or an enrichment case; but it is also not clear that it was one of reparation for wrongdoing. It seems rather to fit quite nicely into the concept of *culpa in contrahendo*, inasmuch as the subscribers took their decision unilaterally rather than as a result of disagreement about terms; the bargain being substantially settled, their abandonment of Coates in favour of St Andrews Square was contrary to good faith. Moreover, the court's award of damages was based upon what in Continental systems is known as the "negative interest", that is to say, what the pursuer had expended upon the faith of the bargain, rather than upon his "positive interest", namely the position he would have been in had the arrangement been carried through to contractual completion.

There is, of course, a link with contract in *Walker*, inasmuch as the reason why the contract "failed to materialise" was a result of the rules about writing in contracts relating to land, rather than because the parties were not agreed in substance. These rules have played an important part in the development of the Scots law relating to anticipated but non-

91 (1823) 2 S 379.

materialising contracts, because, as will be seen below, in many of the cases where recovery has been allowed, all that has stood between the facts and the conclusion that a contract exists is the requirement of writing. The key point in *Walker*, thinking about when it is contrary to good faith to break off a pre-contractual relationship, is that negotiations were essentially complete, making it reasonable to assume that the formalities would be carried through.[92]

Walker v. *Milne* was used in a number of subsequent cases in the nineteenth century. In *Bell* v. *Bell*[93] a son erected a house on his father's land on the faith of the latter's verbal and therefore unenforceable promise to convey the land to him. The father broke the promise and conveyed to his daughter. The son recovered his expenditure, two judges apparently finding for him on the basis of fraud, and a third on the basis of *Walker* v. *Milne*. In *Heddle* v. *Baikie*[94] the pursuer, Heddle, possessed the defender's, Baikie's, farm for six years without any formal lease (although it was understood that one was to be executed) and made improvements. He was then ejected. A claim for loss and expenditure was allowed.[95] In *Dobie* v. *Lauder's Trs*[96] the pursuer undertook the care of certain children in return for an annual payment from the Trustees. Because it was envisaged that this arrangement would last some years, she entered a seven-year lease of a house in Frederick Street, Edinburgh, and incurred other expenses. After a dispute about the amount of the annual payment, the children were withdrawn from her charge. She claimed successfully against the trustees for reimbursement of her expenses. The Second Division was clear that there was no contract in this case but only a family arrangement.[97] But, said Lord Justice-Clerk Moncreiff, "the arrangement necessarily included the condition that if the arrangement was terminated it should not be to the loss of one party".[98] Lord Neaves took a slightly different view:

> I think that the legal principle applicable to the case is this: that when parties are engaged mutually in promoting an object of common interest, and the

---

[92] See further on *Walker* the contribution of J.W.G. Blackie to this volume.
[93] (1841) 3 D 1201.
[94] (1846) 8 D 376. See the comments on this case in *Allan* v. *Gilchrist* (1875) 2 R 587, at 590 per Lord Deas.
[95] In both cases there might have been an enrichment claim in respect of the improvements, but recovery under such claims would probably have been less than the amount expended. For similar cases in which claims were refused, see *Gowans' Trs* v. *Carstairs* (1862) 24 D 1382 and *Fowlie* v. *McLean* (1868) 6 M 254.
[96] (1873) 11 M 749.
[97] There is perhaps here some idea of there being no intention to create legal relations.
[98] See n. 96 above, at 755.

expenses entailed in furthering that object are thrown on one of the parties, then when that expenditure fails of obtaining the end aimed at the party-disburser must be recompensed, as being the disburser for a common object.[99]

This reference to recompense makes it possible to see *Dobie* as an enrichment case. While it is thought that in Scots law services of the type being offered by Dobie in this case are capable of giving rise to enrichment of the recipient, determining its extent for the purposes of recovery can be problematic. The losing party's expenditure is one convenient, although perhaps not precise, way of measuring the enrichment. But the approach of Lord Justice-Clerk Moncreiff is much more redolent of good faith, and that approach avoids the inherent inconsistency and difficulties of measuring one party's enrichment through another's loss. The protection of the "negative" or "reliance" interest stands in its own right, quite independently of any benefit to the defender.

The last case in which recovery was allowed is *Hamilton* v. *Lochrane*[100] where a party made alterations to his villa in reliance on a verbal agreement for its sale. When the buyer withdrew, the selling party made a claim for reimbursement of his expenses. He was allowed a proof. Here it could not be said on any view that the defender had been enriched; the claim was purely one of reimbursement for the pursuer's reliance expenditure. Again, we have unilateral withdrawal from an arrangement the terms of which were substantially settled.

To summarise the principles to be drawn from these cases is far from easy. In most of them it could be said that the parties had reached (or at least averred) an agreement, which was not contractual only because some other legal rule about the constitution and proof of contracts stood in the way.[101] At one level, then, these cases are not about anticipated contracts so much as about agreements which are only non-contractual for technical reasons. Further, the cases are not about the recovery of enrichment (although in some there was undoubtedly an enrichment element). Instead the pursuer is reimbursed or indemnified against expenditure incurred on the faith of the non-contractual agreement, although in none of the cases had this expenditure been made to the defender. In some of them—*Walker* v. *Milne* is the prime example—a claim for other loss is also allowed. The injustice of the situation of the

[99] See n. 96 above, at 755.
[100] (1899) 1 F 478.
[101] See also Gloag, n. 4 above, 19.

pursuer seems to arise from the other side's unilateral withdrawal from arrangements which could reasonably have been regarded as settled.

Restriction of the scope of *Walker* v. *Milne* began in 1875, with the decision of *Allan* v. *Gilchrist*[102] in which the court declared that it did not give rise to a principle of general application. Lord Deas held that a claim for reimbursement only arose if "substantial loss [was] occasioned to the one party by the representations and inducements *recklessly and unwarrantably* held out to him by the other party".[103] As already indicated, the cases are more about agreements than representations, and this case marks the first appearance of misrepresentation as well as of recklessness and unwarrantability as substantive requirements of the claim.[104] In *Hamilton* v. *Lochrane*, although the claim was successful, it was again said that *Walker* did not give rise to a principle of general application.[105]

The idea of misrepresentation as the basis of the action was also important in *Gilchrist* v. *Whyte*,[106] a case which arose following the breakdown of negotiations for a contract of loan. The lender had sought to impose a condition about the fulfilment of which the borrower's agent (wrongly, as it turned out) anticipated no difficulty. It was held that this was only a statement of opinion, not a representation. The lender's claim was to damages or, alternatively, to recompense for his loss and expense incurred in reliance on the borrower's representations, relying on *Walker* v. *Milne*. Lord Ardwall commented that there could be damages only for wrongdoing, and recompense only where one was enriched at another's expense. Neither was present in this case of abortive contract negotiations.

Gloag regarded *Gilchrist* v. *Whyte* as the leading case on the whole subject, and commented that it had disapproved earlier decisions, as well as noting that "it is not easy to see any legal principle on which liability can be imposed when nothing is averred beyond an expression of intention".[107] He explained *Bell* v. *Bell* on the ground of fraud and recompense.[108] He accepted that starting with *Walker* v. *Milne*:

---

[102] See n. 94 above.

[103] *Ibid.*, at 590.

[104] Admittedly Lord Shand talked about representations and an "unwarrantable" refusal to go with the arrangement in *Dobie*: n. 96 above, at 753.

[105] At 483 per Lord Moncreiff.

[106] 1907 SC 984.

[107] See n. 4 above, 19.

[108] *Ibid.*, 176–7.

[T]here is a good deal of authority for the contention that [where A, in circumstances where it is impossible to suggest fraud, has resiled from a verbal agreement after B has been led to incur expenditure, but expenditure in no wise beneficial to A], A is bound to meet the expenditure B has incurred.[109]

Gloag went on to note, however, that this was not a general principle. The latest cases confirm the narrow approach to *Walker* v. *Milne*. In *Dawson International plc* v. *Coats Paton plc*[110] two companies were negotiating a merger whereby Dawson would purchase Coats Paton's shares. This also included a "lock-out" arrangement under which Coats Paton would not encourage third party bids.[111] Dawson incurred expense in preparing offer documentation. A third party bid materialised, with which Coats Paton co-operated, and which was ultimately successful. Dawson claimed unwarrantable and reckless misrepresentations by Coats and sought reimbursement of their expenditure. The claim failed. In an impressive opinion later approved by the First Division, Lord Cullen gave detailed consideration to all the authorities from *Walker* v. *Milne* onward.[112] He held that this was an exceptional branch of the law and that any tendency to expand its scope should be discouraged. It was equitable in nature and not dependent upon contract, recompense or delict for its concepts. He continued:

> Having reviewed the cases in this field to which I was referred I am not satisfied that they provide authority for reimbursement of expenditure by one party occasioned by the representations of another beyond *the case where the former acted in reliance on the implied assurance by the latter that there was a binding contract between them when in fact there was no more than an agreement which fell short of being a binding contract* . . . I should add that I consider that there are sound reasons for not extending the remedy to the case where the parties did not reach an agreement. It is clear that *the law does not favour the recovery of expenditure made merely in the hope or expectation of agreement being entered into or of a stated intention being fulfilled.*[113]

A key concept here is that of the "implied assurance" of the binding contract when there was no more than an agreement falling short of being a contract. In other words, claims did not depend upon misrepresentation, at least in the conventional sense of a positive statement.

[109] See n. 4 above, 177.

[110] 1988 SLT 854. Lord Cullen's opinion was affirmed in the Inner House: see 1989 SLT 655. At a later stage it was held by Lord Prosser that the negotiations had not given rise to a contract between the parties (1993 SLT 80).

[111] Cf. *Walford* v. *Miles*, n. 70 above.

[112] See 862K ff.

[113] See n. 110, at 866: emphasis added.

Lord Cullen's analysis was applied in *Bank of Scotland* v. *3i PLC*.[114] The bank made a loan to a company which subsequently went into receivership. The bank sued 3i in respect of a representation that it had provided financial accommodation to the company. The claims were for (1) damages for negligent misrepresentation and (2) reimbursement of expenditure. Both claims failed. Lord Cameron of Lochbroom said of the reimbursement claim:

> There is no suggestion that the pursuers acted in reliance on an implied assurance by the defenders that there was a binding contract between them when, in fact, there was no more than an agreement which fell short of being a binding agreement . . . In addition, there is a second and, in my opinion, equally conclusive answer to the pursuers' case on this head. The remedy given by the court is an equitable one and is only available in limited circumstances . . . I agree with Lord Cullen where he says (1988 SLT at p. 865K–L), "I should also add that in the present state of the law I see no need for a court to resort to an equitable remedy to deal with a case in which one party has by means of a representation which is in *mala fides* or fraudulent misled another into incurring expenditure or suffering other loss. The law of delict provides a remedy for fraudulent misrepresentation. It also covers negligent misrepresentation, including where the latter has given rise to the making of a contract. See s 10 of the Law Reform (Miscellaneous Provisions) (Scotland) Act 1985".[115]

The claim for reimbursement proceeding upon exactly the same facts as that for delictual misrepresentation, it should be rejected.

With the opinions of both Lord Cullen and Lord Cameron of Lochbroom, therefore, quite clear limits are drawn upon the remedy of reimbursement in Scots law, including the notion that it is excluded by facts (i.e., fraudulent or negligent misrepresentation) giving rise to the alternative of a delictual remedy. However, while each opinion is in the negative for the *application* of the remedy in the particular circumstances, neither denies its *existence*, and the analysis by Lord Cullen in particular clearly shows its separation from the established concepts of contract, delict and enrichment. The idea of an expenditure-based liability arising from an "implied assurance" that an agreement was a binding contract seems perfectly consistent with an overall basis in good faith, while at the same time manifesting the tendency of Scots law to concretise that concept in carefully defined rules. In this connection, however, the emphasis on the "equitable" nature of the liability carries

[114] 1990 SC 215.
[115] *Ibid.*, at 225.

with it the risk of a perception, perhaps not wholly avoided in Lord Cameron's opinion, that it can be used only when there is no other remedy "at law": i.e., instead of understanding that the principles of the law are suffused with, and based upon, equity; the position, it is submitted, of Stair and of Scots law in general.[116]

These authorities nevertheless support an argument that, in the type of case which provided our point of departure for a discussion of *culpa in contrahendo* in Scots law, the seller of heritable property who verbally accepts a formal offer and then withdraws from the arrangement could at least be liable for the wasted expenditure of the disappointed offeror. There is an agreement which, however, falls short of a binding contract, and an assurance that there is a contract can surely be readily implied in the circumstances, given most people's ignorance of the law's requirements for contracts for the sale of land. The only question is how much of the offeror's wasted expenditure might be recoverable? Would it extend to the surveyor's fees, for example? Or would it cover only expenditure incurred after the conclusion of the informal agreement? Would there be an element for foregone opportunities to purchase another property?

On the basis stated by Lord Cullen, however, a Scottish court would probably have reached the same result as Rattee J in the recent English case, *Regalian Properties plc* v. *London Dockland Development Corporation*.[117] An agreement to build a residential development in London Docklands was "subject to contract" while the parties negotiated about details for over two years between 1986 and 1988. Regalian, who were the contractors, spent three million pounds on the project, although none of this went directly to LDDC. By the end of the period the housing market had collapsed and LDDC, realising that the original arrangement had ceased to be commercially viable, withdrew after attempts to renegotiate. Rattee J held that parties making arrangements "subject to contract" took the risk that if no contract was ultimately concluded any losses would lie where they fell. Regalian had undertaken the expenditure for their own benefit and LDDC had not been enriched thereby.

---

[116] I find attractive and helpful the recent analysis of this subject in E. Örücü, "Equity in the Scottish Legal System" in Rabello (ed.), n. 17 above, 383–94. For other recent views, see J.M. Thomson, "The Role of Equity in Scots law" in S. Goldstein (ed.), *Equity and Contemporary Legal Development* (Jerusalem, 1992); *Stair Memorial Encyclopaedia*, vol. 22 (1987), paras 394–432.

[117] [1995] 1 All ER 1005 (Rattee J). The result but not the reasoning is approved by E. McKendrick, "Negotiations Subject to Contract and the Law of Restitution" [1995] 3 *Restitution Law Review* 100.

The failure of the negotiations was due to genuine disagreement about price. Now the phrase "subject to contract" has no special magic in Scots law, unlike English law, but where, as here, its use manifests an intention of the parties that their agreement should not have contractual force, the Scottish courts will give effect to that intention.[118] Thus there is no question on *Regalian*-type facts of any implied assurance that the agreement was a binding contract, and so no possibility that the expenditure of the contractors could be recouped by way of *Walker* v. *Milne*.[119]

Conclusion

This essay has argued that good faith does play a substantial role in the Scottish law of contract, but that on the whole this has been expressed by way of particular rules rather than through broad general statements of the principle. As a result its role in the law has been submerged, or subterranean, and the effects have not been so far-reaching as in the Continental systems. The overall result is rather typical of the mixed system that is Scots law. A particularly good example is provided by the authorities on pre-contractual liability discussed in the final section of this essay. These authorities do recognise a form of such liability which appears to go beyond anything established in the Anglo-American common law but which is not nearly as extensive as that recognised in Germany, France or the Netherlands.

The comparison of Scots law with the *Principles of European Contract Law* is also of interest. The *Principles* begin with the proposition that parties are free to negotiate and are, in general, not liable for failure to conclude a contract. This is the Scottish position too. For over a hundred years, courts and text writers have said that *Walker* v. *Milne* does not give rise to a general principle, but is rather an equitable exception to the general rule; by implication, that general rule is one of no pre-contractual liability. This is perhaps most explicit in Lord Cullen's observation in *Dawson International plc* v. *Coats Paton plc*, that "the law does not favour the recovery of expenditure made merely in the hope or expectation of agreement being entered into or of a stated intention

---

[118] *Erskine* v. *Glendinning* (1871) 9 M 656; *Stobo Ltd* v. *Morrisons* (*Gowns*) *Ltd* 1949 SC 184.

[119] A similar conclusion would probably arise in *Walford* v. *Miles*, n. 70 above, where the agreement to sell the business was likewise "subject to contract".

being fulfilled".[120] Such a starting point seems entirely consistent with
the values and policies which underlie a market economy: each person
must look after its own interests and if risks are taken on the basis of
hopes or expectations not resting upon a contractual base, then the loss
must lie where it falls in the absence of wrongdoing by the other party.

Having freedom to negotiate and to break off negotiations unless there
is some special factor explains why, for example, a party inviting bids
or tenders from a number of other parties is not liable for the expenses
of the unsuccessful tenderers or bidders. Unless the invitor's conduct
has reasonably induced other expectations, the competing offerors
assume the risk of failure and there is no breach of good faith in leaving the losses where they fall. It is important to remember Finn's point
that good faith does not involve the complete protection of the other
party's interests at the expense of one's own, and that in this it is to be
distinguished from a fiduciary obligation.

However, Article 2:301 of the European Principles states the exception to the general rule of freedom to give up negotiations in much
wider terms than have so far emerged in Scots law. The exception rests
squarely on the principle of good faith and is exemplified (although not
exhausted) by entry into or continuation of negotiations without any real
intention of concluding a contract thereby. In contrast, Lord Cullen's
theory of pre-contractual liability depends upon there being an "implied
assurance" that an *agreement* already reached is a binding contract. If we
recognise, as it is submitted we must, that this rests upon the principle
of good faith in contracting, is it possible to take that principle as a basis
for further extensions of Scots law in this field?

We may begin with the specific example of bad faith given in Article
2:301 of the European Principles, the problem of negotiations which
amount to no more than "stringing along"; that is, unknown to one of
the negotiating parties, A, the other, B, has no intention of ever forming
a contract. B's reason for appearing to enter into negotiations is an effort
to force a third party, C, with whom B does intend to contract to make
a better offer than C would otherwise have been prepared to do. When
an acceptable offer is made to B by C, negotiations with A are dropped.
In a number of jurisdictions, A will have a claim against B in such circumstances by which at least reliance losses will be recoverable;[121] but in

[120] 1988 SLT at 866D–E.

[121] For example, see the French decision of 1972 discussed in Nicholas, n. 77 above,
70–1; *Hoffmann* v. *Red Owl Stores* (1965) 133 NW (2d) 267 (USA); *Walton Stores
(Interstate) Ltd* v. *Maher* (1988) 164 CLR 387 (Australia).

Scotland, under the current understanding of *Walker* v. *Milne*, A would have no recovery, since there is no implied assurance that there is a binding agreement.

A variety of cases from around the world raise further questions about the limitations which have so far been placed upon the Scots law of pre-contractual liability. The denial of recovery in the *Regalian* case may be contrasted with the Australian decision, *Sabemo Pty Ltd* v. *North Sydney Municipal Council*.[122] Sabemo tendered to carry out a commercial development of land owned by the Council. The parties negotiated for three years and Sabemo spent large sums on preparatory works before the Council finally decided to abandon the development. The Supreme Court of New South Wales held that Sabemo could recover their wasted expenditure, on the basis that the termination was a unilateral decision of the Council rather than the result of an inability to agree upon terms, and that the Council's decision took account only of its own interests, not those of Sabemo. The court spoke of "fault" in relation to the Council's behaviour, and certainly there is much in the judgment to conjure up thoughts of *culpa in contrahendo*. However, the case was both distinguished and doubted by Rattee J in *Regalian*. The distinction lay first in the use of the "subject to contract" formula in *Regalian*, and in the fact that there was also genuine dissensus about price in that case: the doubt concerned the existence in English law of any principle that unilateral termination of negotiations without taking into account the interests of the other party inferred liability for that other's consequently wasted expenditure. What of Scots law? Do the facts of *Sabemo* suggest that there was an agreement between the parties and that there was also an implied assurance that this agreement was a binding contract? If not, is this another case where there nevertheless ought to be liability?

There are other cases where it is reasonably clear that there was no agreement and no implied assurance that there was a contract, yet there was enough to suggest that there would be a contractual agreement in the reasonably near future after some further negotiation. The best example is the "letter of intent" by which a party will signal to one of a group of tenderers or bidders for a contract that he now intends to enter a contract with that party although the tender/bid is not to be accepted without further negotiation. The purpose of the letter of intent is to allow the chosen party to commence preparation for the

[122] [1977] NSWLR 880, NSW SC.

contract, and it is not unusual for preparation to pass on to performance before the contract is concluded. Typically the letter of intent will provide that such work will be paid for at the contract price once agreed.[123] But suppose the contract is never concluded because the negotiations are unsuccessful. What, if any, claims may be made by the recipient of the letter of intent? Now where the performance involves a transfer of value to the party who has issued the letter of intent, the solution may well lie in unjustified enrichment.[124] If, however, there is no transfer of value but only reliance expenditure by the recipient of the letter, enrichment solutions may not be available or appropriate to cover the loss. As I have argued elsewhere, Scots law could here call upon its doctrine of unilateral promise, giving the letter obligatory effect and implying some sort of reasonable payment for the recipient's wasted work.[125] But given that letters of intent are often expressly not intended to have obligatory effect, the promise analysis may be rather forced. An approach based on good faith, allowing recovery of justified reliance or the "negative interest", is perhaps more attractive and avoids the need for strained construction and the implication of terms based, however artificially, upon the intention of the party issuing the letter of intent.

Another interesting situation can be illustrated from the English case of *Blackpool & Fylde Aero Club Ltd* v. *Blackpool Borough Council*.[126] The Council invited tenders for a contract in a document which set out the procedure which it would follow in considering the tenders received. The Court of Appeal held that the Council was liable in damages to an unsuccessful tenderer for having failed to follow this procedure, but left unclear whether this was a matter of tort or of contract. The decision seems unquestionably right, but the judgments reveal the relative conceptual limits of the English law of obligations. A Scots lawyer might approach this case, not through a contractual or delictual, but rather

---

[123] On letters of intent and the legal difficulties to which they give rise see S.N. Ball, "Work Carried Out in Pursuance of Letters of Intent—Contract or Restitution?" (1983) 99 *Law Quarterly Review* 572; M.P. Furmston, J. Poole, T. Norisada, *Contract Formation and Letters of Intent* (Chichester, 1998).

[124] As in *British Steel Corporation* v. *Cleveland Bridge and Engineering Co Ltd* [1984] 1 All ER 504. See further E. McKendrick, "The Battle of the Forms and the Law of Restitution" (1988) 8 *Oxford Journal of Legal Studies* 197.

[125] H.L. MacQueen, "Constitution and Proof of Gratuitous Obligations" 1986 SLT (News) 1, 3–4

[126] [1990] 1 WLR 1995. The case has recently been followed by Finn J of the Federal Court of Australia in *Hughes Aircraft Systems International* v. *Air Services Australia* (1997) 146 ALR 1: noted by M.P. Furmston, (1998) 114 *Law Quarterly Review* 362.

through a promissory route.[127] But if this is thought artificial or to involve strained construction of the invitation to tender, then a wider concept of good faith might provide a better solution. This would undoubtedly go further than anything found in Lord Cullen's opinion in *Dawson International plc* v. *Coats Paton plc*. Again there is no real question of agreements and implied assurances that a binding contract exists. The contract, if it is going to come into existence at all, is not assured to any particular party.[128]

In the final analysis, therefore, Scots law appears to have a number of specific tools or concepts with which to address liability issues in pre-contractual negotiations—that is, not just contract, misrepresentation and enrichment, but also promise and *Walker* v. *Milne* reimbursement of expenditure. While these tools can be turned to a good number of different jobs, not all the potential issues of pre-contractual liability have yet been addressed or could be handled with them alone. Good faith appears to permeate the existing law in this area. If this principle is allowed the role suggested for it earlier in this essay—that is, the identification and solution through the creation of new rules of problems which the existing rules do not, or seem unable to reach—Scots law can still respond creatively, yet consistently with what has already been decided, when these as yet unanswered questions arise for decision in the future. If so, equity, in its proper Scottish sense as the basis of the whole law, will not after all turn out to be past the age of child-bearing.

---

[127] The concept of promise might also be the way in which Scots law would solve such famous "difficult" cases as *Hoffman* v. *Red Owl Stores* and *Walton Stores (Interstate) Ltd* v. *Maher*.

[128] Note that it is common for invitations to tender of the kind under consideration here to provide that the invitor is not bound to accept the highest or lowest (as the case may be) or indeed any offer that may be made.

–

3

Good Faith: A Matter of Principle?

Ewan McKendrick*

Introduction

Imagine the scene. The instructing solicitor is a civilian lawyer. He instructs an English barrister in relation to a transaction which is governed by English law. The transaction is a joint venture which has gone wrong. The dispute is now the subject of an international commercial arbitration and the arbitrators are drawn from three different jurisdictions. The essence of the dispute is that the claimant maintains that the client (that is to say, the party whom the barrister has been instructed to represent) has broken its duty to act in good faith and that it has broken various fiduciary duties owed to the claimant, in particular the duty to avoid a conflict of interest and the duty not to make a secret profit. The barrister informs the solicitor that he intends to argue that the client neither owed to the claimant a duty of good faith nor any fiduciary duty. The solicitor expresses his disbelief at this proposition. The idea that his client should deny that he was required to act in good faith is one that shocks him; after all, everyone is subject to a duty to act in good faith and any argument which seeks to deny that elementary proposition is unlikely to appeal to an arbitrator. The solicitor states that his clients were certainly not trustees but, as joint venturers, they were surely subject to some fiduciary duties. Yet it is the fact that an English court might apply *Phipps* v. *Boardman*[1] in all its rigour which is one of the factors which persuades the barrister that the safest course is to deny the existence of a fiduciary duty rather than seek to modify the content of that duty.

* Professor of English Law, University College London. I am grateful to the participants at the Aberdeen Symposium on good faith for helpful comments on an earlier draft of this essay.
[1] [1967] 2 AC 46.

The apparent readiness of the English lawyer to deny the existence of fiduciary duties or duties of good faith and fair dealing in commercial transactions marks him or her out from his or her counterparts in other jurisdictions. This denial is not, on first hearing, an appealing one. But appearances can deceive. In the context of the joint venture agreement, the argument of the barrister is, essentially, that the relationship between the parties is governed by the terms, both express and implied, of their contract and that the claimant cannot have resort to notions of good faith or to fiduciary duties in order to impose on the client a more onerous obligation than that contained in the contract. This view is not in fact inconsistent with the recognition of a doctrine of good faith as long as good faith is defined in terms of honouring the promises which one makes; on this view the essence of good faith is that promises should be honoured. As we shall see, English law offers little by way of comfort to those who act in bad faith or who do not honour the promises which they make, but it does hesitate to impose more positive obligations than those assumed by the terms of the contract.

Good Faith in Other Jurisdictions

The proposition that English law stands out because of its refusal to recognise a general principle of good faith and fair dealing can easily be demonstrated by reference to the experience of other jurisdictions. In the United States of America the Uniform Commercial Code states in section 1–203 that "every contract or duty within this Act imposes an obligation of good faith in its performance or enforcement" and, for this purpose, section 1–201 defines good faith as "honesty in fact in the conduct or transaction concerned".[2] The recognition of a duty of good faith and fair dealing in the performance and enforcement of contracts in section 205 of the Restatement (Second) of Contracts has been hailed as a reflection of "one of the truly major advances in American contract law during the past fifty years".[3] Article 242 of the German *BGB* states that "the debtor is bound to effect performance according to the requirements of good faith, giving consideration to common usage". Article 1134 al. 3 of the French Civil Code provides that contracts must be executed or performed in good faith. Article 7(1) of the 1980 UN

---

[2] See also the definition of good faith in UCC s. 2–103.
[3] R. Summers "The General Duty of Good Faith—Its Recognition and Conceptualization" (1982) 67 *Cornell Law Review* 810.

Convention on Contracts for the International Sale of Goods states that in the interpretation of the Convention regard is to be had, *inter alia*, to the "observance of good faith in international trade". Article 1.7 of the 1994 UNIDROIT *Principles of International Commercial Contracts* provides that "each party must act in accordance with good faith and fair dealing in international trade" and further that "the parties may not exclude or limit this duty".[4] The comment to the article states that "good faith and fair dealing may be considered to be one of the fundamental ideas underlying the Principles". Article 1.106(1) of the *Principles of European Contract Law* states that "in exercising his rights and performing his duties each party must act in accordance with good faith and fair dealing" and it is further provided in Article 1.106(2) that the parties may not exclude or limit this duty.

Is English law really so different?

Given this evident willingness of other jurisdictions to embrace a doctrine of good faith and fair dealing, why does English law remain so aloof and suspicious? One possible answer is that the outcome, in terms of substantive law, of the recognition of a doctrine of good faith and fair dealing would be undesirable. This view is difficult to accept largely because the difference between English law and other jurisdictions is not so stark as it might appear at first sight.[5] Many, if not most rules of English contract law, conform with the requirements of good faith and cases which are dealt with in other systems under the rubric of good faith and fair dealing are analysed and resolved in a different way by the English courts, but the outcome is very often the same. The view that there is no yawning chasm between English law and other systems can be illustrated in two ways.

In the first place, while English law does not presently recognise a duty of good faith, it can be very firm (possibly even harsh) in its

---

[4] The EC Directive on Unfair Terms in Consumer Contracts (Council Directive 93/13/EEC of 5 April 1993, OJ L95/29) also makes explicit reference to "the requirement of good faith" and the Directive has been implemented into domestic law by what is now the Unfair Terms in Consumer Contracts Regulations 1999 (SI 1999/2083) which contain a reference to good faith: notwithstanding the fact that there is no such doctrine in English law.

[5] A study carried out by Professor Reinhard Zimmermann and Dr. Simon Whittaker, *Good Faith in European Contract Law* (Cambridge, 2000), has found that English law was out of line with the other jurisdictions in only one of the thirty case studies which they conducted.

treatment of those who act in bad faith. Specific examples of bad faith, such as telling lies, using illegitimate pressure,[6] exploiting the weakness of others and abusing positions of confidence[7] all constitute grounds upon which a contract can be set aside. Take the case of the defendant who induces the plaintiff to enter into a contract by telling him a piece of information which, unknown to the defendant, is false. The plaintiff is, in principle, entitled to set aside the contract, notwithstanding the fact that the defendant was entirely unaware of the mistake he had made.[8] Those who tell lies will find little to cheer them in English law. It is when one turns from the negative (not telling lies) to the positive (requiring disclosure of the whole truth[9]) that English law may be found wanting.[10]

Secondly, other legal systems may use the doctrine of good faith to deal with issues which English law manages in other ways. In some cases the refusal of English law to resort to good faith can be portrayed as a strength (in that the relevant rules of law can be explained in clearer, more precise terms) but in other cases it can be argued that it is a weakness. An example where it is suggested that the refusal of English law to invoke good faith is a strength is the way in which the law responds to events which occur after the formation of the contract which have the effect of rendering performance of the contract impossible, illegal or impracticable. It has developed a distinct doctrine of frustration to deal with these issues, albeit that the doctrine operates within rather narrow limits.[11] German law, on the other hand, has had to resort to the doctrine of good faith to regulate these matters.[12] It is not clear what

[6] The recognition of the doctrine of economic duress in recent years has done a great deal to enable the courts to regulate the exercise of economic pressure in the negotiation and, more particularly, the renegotiation of contracts.

[7] A number of doctrines, some of which may overlap, compete to regulate what might loosely be called exploitative behaviour. Recent examples of the invocation of such doctrines can be found in *Barclays Bank plc* v. *O'Brien* [1994] 1 AC 180, *CIBC Mortgages plc* v. *Pitt* [1994] 1 AC 200, *Boustany* v. *Pigott* (1995) 69 P & CR 298 and *Credit Lyonnais Bank Nederland NV* v. *Burch* [1997] 1 All ER 144. The basis of these doctrines has been the subject of vigorous debate: see P. Birks, Chin Nyuk Yin, "On the Nature of Undue Influence" in J. Beatson, D. Friedmann (eds), *Good Faith and Fault in Contract Law* (Oxford, 1995), 57 and R. Bigwood, "Undue Influence: 'Impaired Consent' or 'Wicked Exploitation' " (1996) 16 *Oxford Journal of Legal Studies* 503.

[8] See, for example, *Redgrave* v. *Hurd* (1881) 20 Ch D 1, a case which strikes many readers as being particularly harsh on the innocent misrepresentor.

[9] Although it must be said that examples can be found in English law of the recognition of a duty of disclosure.

[10] Thus the one case in the study of Zimmermann and Whittaker see n. 5 above where English law was found to diverge from all other jurisdictions involved the existence of a duty of disclosure in the context of the sale of a painting at a considerable undervalue.

[11] For example, see, *Davis Contractors Ltd* v. *Fareham UDC* [1956] AC 696 and *J. Lauritzen AS* v. *Wijsmuller BV* (*The "Super Servant Two"*) [1990] 1 Lloyd's Rep 1.

English law stands to gain from abandoning a clearly focused doctrine such as frustration in favour of the more amorphous, multi-purpose notion of good faith. Of course, it could be argued that it might encourage English courts to develop a broader, more flexible doctrine of frustration but such a development would not necessarily be desirable[13] and, in any event, that development can occur within the existing doctrine of frustration and does not need to wait for the creation of a doctrine of good faith.[14] Alternatively, it could be argued that good faith is in fact the basis of the doctrine of frustration so that an analogy can indeed be drawn here between English law and German law. While it is true that English lawyers have never been able to identify the basis[15] of the doctrine of frustration with any precision,[16] it would not seem to be much of an advance to conclude that the foundation of the doctrine is, in fact, good faith because such a conclusion would only serve to open up the debate as to what we mean by good faith. Further, it is not clear what practical consequences, if any, would follow from the conclusion that good faith was the basis of the doctrine of frustration.[17]

In other areas, however, the unwillingness of English courts to resort to good faith and fair dealing can be portrayed as a weakness. A good example is perhaps the law relating to the incorporation of onerous terms into a contract. The more unreasonable or unusual the contract term, the greater the steps which must be taken to draw the existence of that term to the attention of the other party before it can be incorporated into the contract.[18] This rule is open to criticism in that it fails

[12] For example, see B.S. Markesinis *The German Law of Obligations Volume I: The Law of Contracts and Restitution: A Comparative Introduction* (Oxford, 1997), 516–42: W.F. Ebke, B.M. Steinhauer, "The Doctrine of Good Faith in German Contract Law" in Beatson and Friedmann (eds), n. 7 above, 171, especially 180–8.

[13] The objections to the development of a broader doctrine of frustration are set out in E. McKendrick "The Regulation of Long-Term Contracts in English Law" in Beatson and Friedmann (eds), n. 7 above, 305, 321–32.

[14] Lord Denning did not require the creation of a doctrine of good faith to advance the case for the development of a broader doctrine of frustration, see *British Movietone News Ltd* v. *London and District Cinemas Ltd* [1951] 1 KB 190. His innovative approach did not, however, meet with the approval of the House of Lords. See [1952] AC 166.

[15] While the basis of the doctrine has never been clear, the rules of law are well-established and there is a substantial amount of agreement about the scope of the doctrine and the circumstances in which it can be invoked.

[16] The competing theories are set out in *Chitty on Contracts* (London, 28th Edn 1999), paras 43–007– 24–017.

[17] It has been said that the debate about the basis of the doctrine of frustration is devoid of practical consequences: *ibid.*, para 24-018.

[18] *J. Spurling Ltd* v. *Bradshaw* [1956] 1 WLR 461; *Interfoto Picture Library Ltd* v. *Stiletto Visual Programmes Ltd* [1989] QB 433; *AEG (UK) Ltd* v. *Logic Resource Ltd* [1996] CLC 265.

to explain why it is that certain terms are more difficult to incorporate into a contract than others.[19] A doctrine of good faith and fair dealing might more readily provide a foundation for the hostility which the courts have expressed towards onerous or unusual contract terms.[20] But even if it is accepted that good faith provides a more secure conceptual foundation for the rule,[21] it is not an argument in favour of a change in the present substantive law. Rather, it is an argument which relates to the way in which we organise or classify the existing rules.

To conclude from this sketch that the recognition of a doctrine of good faith and fair dealing would have no impact on English substantive law is to press the argument too far. It would have an impact, at least at an organisational level, although the extent of that impact is difficult to assess.[22] The point of the argument is that the principal reason for the refusal of English law to recognise the doctrine is not to be found in its likely substantive effects. It has more to do with the approach which English law adopts to the recognition of general principles than to the content of the general principle itself.

An Aversion to General Principles?

In some ways, the task of creating a general principle of good faith and fair dealing could be undertaken without enormous difficulty. Much academic ink has been spilt on the subject (though, admittedly, not all of it supports the creation of a doctrine of good faith and fair dealing)[23]

---

[19] See in particular the vigorous dissenting judgment of Hobhouse LJ in *AEG (UK) Ltd* v. *Logic Resource Ltd*, n. 18 above, especially at 276–7.

[20] A point which was acknowledged by Bingham LJ in *Interfoto Picture Library Ltd* v. *Stiletto Visual Programmes Ltd*, n. 18 above, at 439, when he said that many legal systems, particularly civil law systems, would deal with this issue via a doctrine of good faith and fair dealing. The inability of the courts to regulate broadly-drafted exclusion clauses is discussed in more detail by J.M. Thomson at chapter 4 in this volume.

[21] A proposition which would not be universally accepted.

[22] Good faith, once recognised, might be used in such a way as to challenge some of the present rules and so may actually result in changes to substantive law.

[23] See, for example, R. Powell, "Good Faith in Contracts" [1956] *Current Legal Problems* 6; M. Bridge, "Does Anglo-Canadian Contract Law Need a Doctrine of Good Faith?" (1984) 9 *Canadian Business Law Journal* 385; Lord Steyn, "The Role of Good Faith and Fair Dealing in Contract Law: A Hair-Shirt Philosophy?" [1991] *Denning Law Journal* 131; M. Clarke "The Common Law of Contract in 1993: Is There a General Doctrine of Good Faith?" (1993) 23 *Hong Kong Law Journal* 318; R. Brownsword, "Two Concepts of Good Faith" (1994) 7 *Journal of Contract Law* 197; R. Brownsword, " 'Good Faith in Contracts' Revisited" [1996] *Current Legal Problems* 111.

and many if not most of the rules of contract law presently conform with notions of good faith. The individual bricks which could be used to create a general principle of good faith and fair dealing can already be identified. The clearest example of the express recognition of a role for good faith is in relation to insurance contracts which are generally known as contracts *uberrimae fidei*.[24] Other examples can be found of rules which could be rationalised in terms of good faith: e.g., the rule which prevents a party snapping up a bargain which he knew was not intended by the other contracting party;[25] the limited duty of disclosure which English law recognises;[26] the operation of the doctrines of promissory estoppel[27] and estoppel by convention;[28] the law applicable to fiduciaries; the rules which the courts apply when seeking to interpret contracts;[29] and the willingness of the courts to imply terms into contracts in particular situations.[30] As Dr. Clarke has acknowledged, the "foundations of a general rule of good faith can be discerned in the common law dust"[31] and the question which must now be answered is whether "the particular rules already in place may be used as the piles for the building of a principle of good faith"?[32]

In my view, the fact that English law has not yet used these piles to build a general principle of good faith can be attributed to the attitude of English lawyers to general principles rather than to their reaction to good faith itself. The proposition that English law is not concerned with

---

[24] *Carter* v. *Boehm* (1766) 3 Burr 1905: on which see Forte's chapter 5 in this volume. Lord Mansfield's judgment might have formed the basis for the development of a general principle of good faith and fair dealing, but the opportunity was not taken by judges in subsequent cases.

[25] *Hartog* v. *Colin & Shields* [1939] 3 All ER 566.

[26] For example, see *Nottingham Patent Brick and Tile Co* v. *Butler* (1886) 16 QBD 778; *With* v. *O'Flanagan* [1936] Ch 575; *Gordon* v. *Selico* (1986) 11 HLR 219.

[27] See, in particular, *Central London Property Trust Ltd* v. *High Trees House Ltd* [1947] KB 130. Although the wider doctrine espoused by Winn LJ in *Panchaud Frères SA* v. *Etablissements General Grain Co* [1970] 1 Lloyd's Rep 53, 59, has recently been disapproved by the Court of Appeal in *Glencore Grain Rotterdam BV* v. *Lebanese Organisation for International Commerce* [1997] 4 All ER 514, 529.

[28] For example, see *Amalgamated Investment and Property Co Ltd* v. *Texas Commerce International Bank Ltd* [1982] QB 84.

[29] See in particular the restatement of the principles of interpretation by Lord Hoffmann in his speech in *Investors Compensation Scheme Ltd* v. *West Bromwich Building Society* [1998] 1 WLR 896, especially 912–13.

[30] For example, see *Scally* v. *Southern Health and Social Services Board* [1992] 1 AC 294. The implication of an appropriate term into the contract is a convenient technique which can be used by an English court to arrive at a solution which would be reached by a civilian court on the basis of good faith.

[31] Clarke, n. 23 above, 319.

[32] *Ibid.*

matters of good faith and fair dealing is demonstrably untrue. A judge will think long and hard before reaching a conclusion which is not consonant with generally accepted notions of good faith and fair dealing.[33] It is the elevation of good faith and fair dealing to the status of a general principle which is the real stumbling block.

It would, I think, be true to say that English lawyers generally, and English contract lawyers in particular, have a deep-seated distrust of general principles. When confronted with a broad general principle their instinct is to object that it is too vague, too uncertain or, otherwise, unworkable. Perhaps it is not too much of an exaggeration to conclude that one of the reasons why all English law students know about *Donoghue* v. *Stevenson*[34] is because it is atypical: it is a rare example of a judge seeking to deduce a general principle from what had hitherto been a wilderness of single instances. English tort law has, of course, long since distanced itself from the attempt to formulate a broad general principle which is capable of application to all negligence cases, preferring to focus instead on the facts of the individual case and to reason "incrementally" and by analogy with existing authorities.[35]

Elsewhere in the law of contract, attempts to formulate new general principles have not met with much judicial support. The best-known example is, perhaps, the attempt made by Lord Denning to introduce into English law a doctrine of inequality of bargaining power.[36] His innovation did not meet with the approval of the House of Lords in *National Westminster Bank plc* v. *Morgan*.[37] Broadly speaking, two reasons can be discerned for the rejection of the doctrine of inequality of bargaining power. The first is that it was thought by the House of Lords to be unnecessary, given that Parliament has undertaken the task of "enacting such restrictions on freedom of contract as are necessary"[38] to enable a court to grant relief against the consequences of the exercise of inequality of bargaining power. The second reason is that their Lordships were of the view that the focus of the courts should be on the facts and not on some broad general principle. Referring to the court's equitable jurisdiction to relieve against undue influence, Lord

---

[33] *First Energy (UK) Ltd* v. *Hungarian International Bank Ltd* [1993] 2 Lloyd's Rep 194, at 196 per Steyn LJ.

[34] [1932] AC 562; 1932 SC (HL) 31.

[35] See, in particular, the speech of Lord Bridge in *Caparo Industries plc* v. *Dickman* [1990] 2 AC 605, at 617–18.

[36] *Lloyd's Bank Ltd* v. *Bundy* [1975] QB 326, 339.

[37] [1985] AC 686.

[38] *Ibid.*, 708.

Scarman stated:

> [A] court in the exercise of this jurisdiction is a court of conscience. Definition is a poor instrument when used to determine whether a transaction is or is not unconscionable; this is a question which depends on the particular facts of the case.[39]

It can of course be pointed out that English jurists were not always so averse to the creation and recognition of general principles.[40] At the end of the last century the most influential contract scholars were Sir Frederick Pollock and Sir William Anson. Both authored textbooks in the latter part of the nineteenth century which sought to rationalise the existing case law in terms of general principles of contract law. The doctrines of consideration and privity were elevated to the status of central doctrines which were declared to be of general application. Of consideration, Anson stated: "there must be some universal test of actionability, and this test was supplied by the doctrine of consideration".[41] And privity similarly was perceived to be an "integral part of our conception of contract".[42] One hundred years later many would rue these statements of general principle on the basis that both consideration and privity have been the subject of harsh criticism in recent years. But, notably, neither Anson nor Pollock sought to articulate a general principle of good faith and fair dealing.[43]

In the absence of academic support at a critical stage in the development of English contract law, it was, perhaps, rather optimistic to expect the creation of such a principle to emanate from the judges. Judges were and are generally much too concerned with the resolution of individual cases to be concerned with the formulation of new general principles. And, once a legal system concludes, for one reason or another, that there is no general principle or doctrine of good faith, it is not easy for it then

---

[39] *Ibid.*, 709.

[40] See further E. McKendrick, "English Contract Law: A Rich Past, An Uncertain Future?" in M. Freeman (ed.) *Law and Opinion at the End of the Twentieth Century* (Oxford, 1997) 25, especially 47–8.

[41] W. Anson, *Law of Contract* (Oxford, 7th edn, 1899), 52.

[42] *Ibid.*, 230.

[43] Neither the index to the first edition of Anson nor the index to the first edition of Pollock make any reference to good faith. Anson discusses contracts *uberrimae fidei* at 139–141 and duress and undue influence at 154 *et seq.* But, while he deals with the broad notion of fraud in equity, he does not attempt to articulate any general principle of good faith and fair dealing. A similar approach is adopted by Pollock. The absence of any mention of good faith may be thought to be all the more surprising given Pollock's declared aim of incorporating the rules of equity into his book (where one might have expected to discover some role for good faith) and his willingness to draw on the experience of civilian jurisdictions.

to change course and recognise the existence of such a general principle. A judge, faced with a hard case which cries out for the recognition of an obligation to act in good faith, is likely, given that English law does recognise the existence of good-faith type obligations in certain exceptional cases, to extend the scope of the exceptions to fit the facts of the case. He or she will not throw out years of learning and embrace a new general principle which is of uncertain ambit and distinctly dubious pedigree.

There is, therefore, a real practical obstacle in the way of the recognition of a doctrine of good faith and fair dealing in English contract law.[44] Parliament is unlikely to find the time, even if it had the inclination, to enact such a general principle and the judges, for the reasons just given, are unlikely to attempt to create such a general principle unless it is absolutely clear that its recognition would have substantial beneficial effects. Would its recognition have such beneficial effects?

There are, it is suggested, three principal effects which may follow from the recognition of a doctrine of good faith and fair dealing.

Contracting for Good Faith

It is one thing for a legal system to refuse to imply into a contract an obligation of good faith and fair dealing. It is quite another for a legal system to refuse to give effect to an obligation to act in good faith and fair dealing which has been expressly assumed by the parties. Yet this is precisely what English law does, at least according to the decision of the House of Lords in the controversial case of *Walford* v. *Miles*.[45] The case concerned the validity of lock-in and lock-out agreements,[46] both of which were held to be unenforceable on the facts. The lock-out agreement was held to be unenforceable because it was not of a fixed dura-

---

[44] A rather more optimistic view is taken by R. Harrison, *Good Faith in Sales* (London, 1997), especially chs 1, 2 and 18. Her claim (at 2) that the traditional view that English law does not have a principle of good faith is "quite wrong" seems to confuse cases which might be explained on the basis of good faith and the existence of such a principle. There is no doubt that English law has cases which could be explained on the basis of good faith but we do not yet have a general principle of good faith and fair dealing.

[45] [1992] 2 AC 128: on which see P. Neill, "A Key to Lock-Out Agreements" (1992) 108 *Law Quarterly Review* 405. It has, however, been argued that the actual result in the case was correct: see *Chitty on Contracts*, n. 16 above, para 2–126.

[46] The former is an agreement which obliges the defendant to negotiate exclusively with the plaintiff, while the latter is an agreement under which the defendant agrees not to continue negotiations with third parties but assumes no positive obligation to negotiate with the plaintiff.

tion; a defect which can be cured by more careful drafting.[47] But the lock-in agreement was held to be inherently unenforceable. This was not a matter of drafting deficiencies. It was a question of law and the law did not recognise the existence of an obligation to negotiate in good faith.[48] This was so for reasons of certainty (such an obligation being "too uncertain to have any binding force")[49] and of policy. The policy reasons were clearly spelt out by Lord Ackner when he stated:

> The concept of a duty to carry on negotiations in good faith is inherently repugnant to the adversarial position of the parties involved in negotiations. Each party to the negotiations is entitled to pursue his (or her) own interest, so long as he avoids making misrepresentations.[50]

He therefore concluded:

> A duty to negotiate in good faith is as unworkable in practice as it is inherently inconsistent with the position of a negotiating party.[51]

Notwithstanding the clarity and force of these statements, the hope has recently been expressed extra-judicially by Lord Steyn that, if the issue in *Walford* were to arise again, "the concept of good faith would not be rejected out of hand".[52] Why do these reservations about the correctness of *Walford* persist in the minds of some English lawyers? It is suggested that there are three reasons for these doubts.

The first is that the rejection of an obligation to negotiate in good faith sits uneasily with their Lordships apparent willingness to give effect to an obligation to use "best endeavours"[53] and the express

---

[47] An example of a lock-out agreement which was held to be enforceable is provided by *Pitt* v. *PHH Asset Management Ltd* [1993] 4 All ER 961.

[48] *Courtney and Fairbairn Ltd* v. *Tolaini Brothers (Hotels) Ltd* [1975] 1 WLR 297: approved in *Walford* v. *Miles*, n. 45 above.

[49] *Courtney and Fairbairn Ltd* v. *Tolaini Brothers (Hotels) Ltd*, n. 48 above, 301.

[50] *Walford* v. *Miles*, n. 45 above, 138. Contrast the approach taken by the New South Wales Court of Appeal in *Coal Cliff Collieries Pty Ltd* v. *Sijehama Pty Ltd* (1991) 24 NSWLR 1, 25–6.

[51] *Walford* v. *Miles*, n. 45 above 138.

[52] Steyn LJ, "Contract Law: Fulfilling the Reasonable Expectations of Honest Men" (1997) 113 *Law Quarterly Review* 433, 439. The scope of *Walford* has also been narrowed somewhat by judicial decision. In *Re Debtors (Nos 4449 and 4450 of 1998)* [1999] 1 All ER (Comm) 149, Carnwath J held that the fact that the defendants, Lloyds, were performing functions in the public interest within a statutory framework meant that there was "some limitation on their freedom of action, analogous to *Wednesbury* principles". He was not convinced that Lloyds were in an identical position to an ordinary party negotiating a private contract. This being the case, the argument that Lloyds were subject to an implied obligation to negotiate in good faith could not be dismissed as unsustainable.

[53] See n. 45 above, 138.

recognition by the Privy Council of the validity of an obligation to use
"reasonable endeavours".[54] The difference as a matter of principle
between an obligation to use reasonable endeavours and an obligation to
negotiate in "good faith" is not at all clear.[55] The second point, made
by Lord Steyn, is that Lord Ackner failed to give sufficient attention to
the case of the party who "negotiates in bad faith not intending to reach
agreement with the other party".[56] Should such a party, especially a
party who has expressly assumed an obligation to negotiate in good faith,
be allowed to walk away from the negotiations without incurring any
liability for doing so? At the very least, should he not be liable for the
reliance loss incurred by the other party in entering into the abortive
negotiations? The third problem with *Walford* is that it takes away the
parties' freedom of contract in that it denies to them the ability to
assume voluntarily an obligation to negotiate in good faith. Why should
the courts refuse to give effect to such an agreement? The policy argument invoked by Lord Ackner cannot apply where the parties abandon
their adversarial stance and employ co-operative language. The argument from uncertainty still looms large, but is it really so persuasive?
Good faith could be given a meaning by the courts which the parties are
presumed to have adopted, unless the terms of their contract suggest
otherwise. An objective definition of good faith in terms of "the observance of reasonable commercial standards of fair dealing in the trade"[57]
would not seem to be so uncertain as to be unworkable.

Also to be weighed against the uncertainties which would accompany
the recognition of an express obligation to negotiate in good faith, are
the advantages which would accrue to the parties from such a recognition. A lock-in agreement can perform a useful commercial purpose in
that it buys the parties time in which to reach an agreement and for one

[54] *Queensland Electricity Generating Board* v. *New Hope Collieries Pty Ltd* [1989] 1
Lloyd's Rep 205. See also *Lambert* v. *HTV Cymru (Wales) Ltd*, *The Times*, March 13 1998.
The requirements which an obligation to use "reasonable endeavours" impose on a contracting party may not be great. While each case must ultimately turn on a construction
of the phrase in the context of the contract as a whole, it was held in *Phillips Petroleum
Co. UK Ltd* v. *Enron Europe Ltd*, Court of Appeal, 10 October 1996 (unreported) that it
did not require a party to disregard his own financial position when deciding how to dis-
charge his obligation to use reasonable endeavours to agree.
[55] Although it is suggested in *Chitty on Contracts*, n. 16 above, para 2–127 that a possible distinction between them is that an agreement to use best endeavours could be interpreted as referring to the *machinery* of negotiation, while one to negotiate in good faith is
more plausibly interpreted as referring to its *substance*.
[56] Steyn, n. 52 above, 439.
[57] UCC s. 2–103 (1) (b).

party to put together a package which is likely to be attractive to the other party. Why should the parties be denied the ability to create such an agreement? Many commercial contracts concluded today are long-term contracts where the parties, as a result of their inability to predict the future course of events, are sometimes compelled to express their obligations in rather vague, aspirational terms. Provision must be made for disputes which may arise over the life-time of the contract. For example, a clause which is not infrequently found in a joint venture agreement is one which states that the "parties shall endeavour by good faith efforts to resolve by mutual agreement any dispute arising in connection with this Agreement". Is such a clause enforceable after *Walford*? And what about the following clause?

> Both Buyer and Seller recognise a long-term relationship requires mutual collaboration and assistance should either Buyer or Seller suffer hardship or unfairness. Both Buyer and Seller agree that they will make their best efforts to solve any problem due to any such circumstances in the spirit of mutual understanding and collaboration.[58]

Where such a provision is supported by a comprehensive arbitration clause[59] or a third party intervener clause[60] the clause should be enforceable. But considerable doubt surrounds the enforceability of a bare clause of the type set out above.[61] The existence of this doubt is unfortunate and the reasoning which has created that doubt cannot be supported. Had their Lordships in *Walford* v. *Miles* been fully aware of the need to preserve a degree of flexibility and co-operation in long-term contracts, they might have been rather more ready to embrace the concept of an enforceable obligation to negotiate in good faith. Where the parties expressly assume an obligation to negotiate in good faith, the argument that such an obligation is too uncertain to be enforced does not trump the argument from freedom of contract and the commercial advantages which would follow from allowing parties to express their

---

[58] Quoted by Daintith, "The Design and Performance of Long-Term Contracts" in T.C. Daintith, G. Teubner (eds), *Contract and Organisation: Legal Analysis in the Light of Economic and Social Theory* (Berlin, New York 1986) 164, 182.

[59] As in *Queensland Electricity Generating Board* v. *New Hope Collieries Pty Ltd*, n. 54 above.

[60] Where a third party is empowered to resolve the issue should the parties themselves fail to reach an acceptable solution.

[61] Although it could be argued that *Walford* does not apply where the obligation to negotiate in good faith relates to an issue which is not "essential" to the agreement: see *Chitty on Contracts*, n. 16 above, para 2–127. The difficulty with this view relates to the problems involved in distinguishing between essential and non-essential issues.

agreements in co-operative language.[62] It follows that the broad dicta in *Walford* cannot be supported and English law should recognise an obligation to negotiate in good faith where it has been expressly assumed by the parties.[63]

The Global Economy

Should English law go further and *impose* on contracting parties a duty of good faith and fair dealing? One argument in support of such a move is that other jurisdictions recognise such an obligation, albeit the scope of the obligation varies as between different jurisdictions,[64] and it is also to be found in the UNIDROIT *Principles*, the *Principles of European Contract Law* and the UN *Convention on Contracts for the International Sale of Goods* 1980.[65] The argument that just because other people do something, we should do it also, is generally not a convincing one. However, before the argument is dismissed out of hand, account must be taken of the contribution which English contract law makes to the English economy. A glance at the law reports is enough to demonstrate that many parties who have no other connection with England choose English law as the law governing their contract and they arbitrate or litigate (or, if they are particularly unfortunate, they may have to do both) in London. Why do they do this? The answer is not entirely clear.

It may be because of tradition. London is a well-established commercial centre and many commercial parties may choose English law as the applicable law for no other reason than their predecessors have done so and have found the result to be, at the least, reasonably satisfactory. Alternatively, they may choose English law because they believe that

[62] See further J.M. Paterson, "The Contract to Negotiate in Good Faith: Recognition and Enforcement" (1996) 10 *Journal of Contract Law* 120.

[63] The same result should also follow where the parties have impliedly assumed an obligation to negotiate in good faith. The difficulty here of course is in deciding whether or not the parties did impliedly intend to assume such an obligation. In long-term contracts such an implication might be made rather readily. On the other hand, in the case of commodity contracts, such an implication is unlikely to be made in many instances. A willingness to recognise such an implied obligation might take the law in the direction of the recognition of what Brownsword has called "a good faith requirement": see Brownsword, n. 23 above, 111, 118–32.

[64] It can apply pre-contractually, to the performance of the contract and to the enforcement of the contract. It need not embrace all three aspects.

[65] Although in the case of the *Convention on Contracts for the International Sale of Goods* the role of good faith is confined to the interpretation of the provisions of the Convention.

English law is particularly well-suited to the regulation of commercial relationships. Or they may choose English law because English trained lawyers are particularly good at handling commercial disputes in a fair and efficient manner. There is, to my knowledge, no empirical evidence which would enable us to answer this question with any confidence. Identification of the correct answer is, however, of considerable importance to the debate over good faith. If parties choose English law because of the quality of its substantive law, then that points in the direction of the maintenance of the status quo: commercial parties may choose English law precisely because it does not give extensive discretionary powers to courts or arbitrators[66] in the name of good faith. On the other hand, if commercial parties choose English law because of tradition or for reasons of procedure, then the recognition of a doctrine of good faith will not have any substantial impact on the willingness of contracting parties to choose English law as the applicable law.

This argument should not be over-stated. It is not being said that the future of the English economy turns on the decision whether or not to recognise a doctrine of good faith and fair dealing. But, as has been pointed out, good faith is an almost universal feature of any document relating to what might be called "transnational" contract law. And, to the extent that the existence of a good faith doctrine within these documents prevents or hinders England from ratifying or otherwise giving effect to them, damage may be being done to the economy as a whole.

At the end of the day this is largely an economic argument, the merits of which it is not presently possible to assess. But our attitude to good faith may, in many ways, be the litmus test of our attitude towards the creation of an international or a European law of contract. Resistance to good faith and to the creation of an international or European contract law are likely to march hand in hand. But our ability to resist the incursion of good faith into English law is likely to be limited as a result of our membership of the European Union. The Unfair Terms in Consumer Contracts Regulations 1994[67] and the Commercial Agents (Council Directive) Regulations 1993,[68] both of which were enacted in

---

[66] Although the Arbitration Act 1996 now recognises the validity of clauses which give arbitrators the power to decide *ex aequo et bono* or to act as an *amiable compositeur* (see ss 1(1)(b), 33(1), and 46(1)(b)).

[67] SI 1999/2083. See, in particular, reg. 5(1) and (5) together with Sched. 2.

[68] SI 1993/3053. See, in particular, regs 3(1) and 4(1). In *Moore* v. *Piretta PTA Ltd* [1999] 1 All ER 174 John Mittings QC, sitting as a Deputy Judge of the High Court, had regard to German law and French law when interpreting reg. 17. It will be interesting to see whether the courts also have regard to French and German law when called upon to

implementation of a European Directive, make express reference to good faith and sooner or later English courts will be required to give meaning to these phrases. As European law intrudes to an ever greater extent into the traditional heartland of domestic private law references to good faith are likely to multiply. And, once admitted into the language of the courts, it is likely to be difficult to ring-fence these. Judges may well not wish to appear out of step with their Continental counterparts and begin to employ the language of good faith to a greater extent.[69] In this context, it is perhaps no surprise to note that the Court of Appeal has adopted a more sympathetic stance to good faith on three occasions recently.[70]

The present momentum towards the creation of an international or a European law of contract should not be underestimated. The next stage is likely to take place in international arbitrations as arbitrators are asked to apply the UNIDROIT *Principles* and *the Principles of European Contract Law*. A European Code of Contract law is probably some way off yet and may indeed never materialise, but one of the stated objectives of the *Principles of European Contract Law* is "to serve as a basis for any future European Code of Contracts".[71] In a global economy the pressure for an international or a European contract law is likely to increase and, in such a context, the traditional resistance of English law to the doctrine of good faith is unlikely to be able to withstand this onslaught. Sooner or later domestic objections are likely to have to give way to these international, largely economic, pressures.

Challenging Rules which do not Presently Conform with Good Faith

The third consequence of the recognition of a doctrine of good faith and fair dealing in English contract law may be that it will act as a sterner

decide the meaning of "good faith". The role of good faith in the Regulations is discussed by S. Santier (1998) 19 *Company Lawyer* 248.

[69] A good recent example of this phenomenon is provided by the judgment of Brooke LJ in *Laceys Footwear (Wholesale) Ltd* v. *Bowler International Freight Ltd* [1997] 2 Lloyd's Rep 369, 384–5.

[70] *Timeload Ltd* v. *British Telecommunications plc* [1995] EMLR 459; *Philips Electronique Grand Publique SA* v. *British Sky Broadcasting Ltd* [1995] EMLR 472; *Balfour Beatty Civil Engineering Ltd* v. *Docklands Light Railway Ltd* (1996) 78 BLR 42, 67–8.

[71] O. Lando, H. Beale (eds), *The Principles of European Contract Law Part I: Performance, Non-performance and Remedies* (Dordrecht, Boston, London, 1995) xvii.

challenge to rules which presently do not conform with good faith and fair dealing. At present, English law is *influenced* or *shaped* by notions of good faith but does not recognise the existence of a *doctrine* of good faith. The point was well-made by Steyn LJ (as he then was) in *First Energy (UK) Ltd* v. *Hungarian International Bank Ltd*, when he said:

> A theme that runs through our law of contract is that the reasonable expectations of honest men must be protected. It is not a rule or a principle of law. It is the objective which has been and still is the principal moulding force of our law of contract. It affords no licence to a judge to depart from binding precedent. On the other hand, if the prima facie solution to a problem runs counter to the reasonable expectations of honest men, this criterion sometimes requires a rigorous re-examination of the problem to ascertain whether the law does indeed compel demonstrable unfairness.[72]

In this way, notions of good faith may be said to inform our law of contract, one of the aims of which is to produce fair and workable rules which conform to the standards of fair and reasonable people. To the extent that a rule appears to encourage bad faith, it will be the subject of "rigorous re-examination" by the courts. But those who advocate the introduction of a doctrine of good faith argue that this is not sufficient because, as Steyn LJ acknowledged, it does not enable judges to depart from "binding precedent". Thus good faith presently cannot be used to overrule a case such as *Arcos* v. *Ronaasen*,[73] nor to give effect to the agreement of the parties in *Walford* v. *Miles*. It can therefore be argued that the influence of good faith is presently rather muted and that judges require stronger weapons to combat bad faith, and that this can only be done by elevating good faith to the status of a legal doctrine or a principle of law. At this point we encounter what might be called the "subtext". To what extent would it be true to say that supporters of the doctrine of good faith hope to use it as a vehicle to challenge the existing rules of contract law and replace them with new ones? Is the point made earlier in this paper, that English lawyers do not object to good faith on the basis of the impact which it would have on the content of the rules of law, unduly naïve?

There is no doubt that some supporters of good faith do think that it will have an effect, possibly a profound effect, on substantive law. Thus Friedmann has argued that:

---

[72] See n. 33 above, 194, 196.
[73] [1933] AC 470.

> good faith may provide a unifying concept for a number of distinct rules dealt
> [with] under different headings, and contribute to a greater consistency in the
> law by exerting pressure upon rules which are incompatible with the idea of
> good faith.[74]

The first part of this quotation makes an organisational point, but the
latter part goes well beyond re-organisation and takes on a reforming
mission. The potential of good faith to bring about change and reform
can also be illustrated by the experience of German law where it has
been said that the "doctrine of good faith has been used by the courts
to create new causes of action where no cause of action existed in statutory law".[75] So what impact might the doctrine of good faith have on
the present rules of English contract law? By way of illustration I want
to take the relatively recent decision of the Privy Council in *Union Eagle
Ltd* v. *Golden Achievement Ltd*.[76] Would this case be decided the same
way if English law recognised a doctrine of good faith?

The facts of the case are straightforward. The plaintiff purchaser
agreed to buy a flat in Hong Kong and paid ten per cent of the purchase price (HK $420,000) as a deposit. The agreement specified the
date, time and place of completion, and time was stated to be in every
respect of the essence of the agreement. Completion was to take place
on or before 30 September 1991 and before 5 p.m. on that day. Clause
12 of the agreement stated that, if the purchaser failed to comply with
any of the terms and conditions of the agreement, the vendor had the
right to rescind the contract and forfeit the deposit. The plaintiff failed
to complete by the stipulated time and tendered the purchase price ten
minutes after the time for completion had passed. The vendors refused
to accept late payment, rescinded the contract and forfeited the deposit.
The plaintiff refused to accept the defendants' decision to rescind the
contract and brought an action seeking to have the contract specifically
enforced. His attempt was unsuccessful.

Lord Hoffmann stated that the "chief question" in the case was
"whether the court has, and should have exercised, an equitable power

---

[74] "Good Faith and Remedies for Breach of Contract" in Beatson and Friedmann (eds),
n. 7 above, 399–400.

[75] Ebke and Steinhauer, n. 12 above, 171. The point could be made that there is greater
need for a doctrine such as good faith in a codified system because a code tends to be
rather rigid and good faith is a flexible tool which can be adapted to fit the needs of society. Where, however, the legal system is based largely on case-law, the law is much more
fluid and can be adapted without recourse to a doctrine such as good faith.

[76] [1997] AC 514, noted by J.D. Heydon (1997) 113 *Law Quarterly Review* 385 and
R. Stevens (1998) 61 *Modern Law Review* 255.

to absolve the purchaser from the contractual consequences of having been late and to decree specific performance".[77] The plaintiff argued that the court did have such an absolving power and that equity would intervene to restrain the enforcement of legal rights when it would be unconscionable to insist upon them. The plaintiff maintained that the element of unconscionability was present on the facts of this case: the breach was a slight one, but the consequences were, to say the least, drastic.

Lord Hoffmann rejected the plaintiff's argument and answered the chief question in the negative. He maintained that the principle invoked by the plaintiff was both contrary to the authorities and to the needs of the business world. In his view the parties should be able to know with certainty that the terms of the contract will be enforced. A jurisdiction to intervene in cases of "unconscionability" would not produce such certainty. Indeed, the mere existence of a discretion to grant relief would be used as a negotiating tool by a defaulting purchaser. While equity will intervene to grant relief in cases of late payment of money due under a mortgage or rent due under a lease,[78] this jurisdiction did not extend to the case of a contract for the sale of land. In a volatile market a vendor will want to know whether or not he can terminate the contract and deal with someone else. The law should, as far as possible, enable the vendor to know whether or not he is entitled to terminate.

The need for certainty was therefore paramount, and the existence of a jurisdiction to grant relief in cases where it would be unconscionable for the vendor to exercise his right to rescind was rejected on the ground that it would detract from the need for a certain rule. This is an issue on which reasonable people will disagree and, indeed, other jurisdictions take a broader view of the equitable jurisdiction to grant relief.[79] A case can be made out that greater emphasis should have been placed upon the motive of the vendor in deciding to terminate and forfeit the deposit. Surely he behaved unreasonably in refusing to accept a ten minute delay in receiving the purchase money? Should a vendor be entitled to act capriciously and terminate because, for example, he does not like the purchaser or because the market has moved in his favour and it has become economically advantageous for him to find a way out of the

---

[77] See n. 76 above, at 517.

[78] *G and C Kreglinger* v. *New Patagonia Meat and Cold Storage Co. Ltd* [1914] AC 25, 35; *Shiloh Spinners Ltd* v. *Harding* [1973] AC 691, 722.

[79] For example, see Australia *in Legione* v. *Hateley* (1983) 152 CLR 406 and *Stern* v. *McArthur* (1988) 165 CLR 489. See also Friedmann, n. 74 above, at 417–21

contract which he has concluded? The argument is not without its merits.[80] My purpose here is not, however, to debate these rival merits. It
is, rather, to point out that the law cannot accept the validity of both
arguments. It has to choose and English law has chosen to come down
on the side of certainty. That decision should not be open to challenge
simply because English law incorporates a doctrine of good faith and fair
dealing.

It could be said that good faith and fair dealing is in fact implicit in
the decision of the Privy Council in *Union Eagle* v. *Golden Achievement
Ltd* because Lord Hoffmann left open the possibility that the purchaser
may be able to obtain relief in extreme cases. In so far as the sum
retained by the vendor exceeds a genuine pre-estimate of the loss or a
reasonable deposit[81] the court has "a discretion to order repayment of
all or part of the retained money".[82] And where the vendor has been
unjustly enriched by improvements made at the purchaser's expense,
the purchaser may have a personal restitutionary claim to recover any
unjust enrichment which the vendor has obtained as a result of the work
done prior to the termination. But there is no need to resort to good
faith or fair dealing to explain these remedies. They are personal restitutionary claims and we do not need good faith to explain their existence. Nor do such remedies undermine the promotion of certainty.
While the vendor should be able to know whether or not he is free to
terminate the contract with the purchaser and deal with the land, it does
not follow that the vendor should know with the same certainty whether
or not he is entitled to retain any prepayment made by the purchaser.
In other words, while the vendor should have restored to him the "freedom to deal with his land as he pleases",[83] he should not have the same
freedom in relation to the financial consequences of termination. This
accommodation of the conflicting interests of the vendor and purchaser
seems to be a reasonable one and it should not be disturbed by the creation of a doctrine of good faith and fair dealing.

---

[80] For a critical analysis of *Union Eagle* along similar lines see Stevens n. 76 above.
Some support for a restriction upon the right to terminate might be derived from the
recently enacted section 15A of the Sale of Goods Act 1979.

[81] On which see *Workers Trust Merchant Bank Ltd* v. *Dojap Investments Ltd* [1993] AC
573.

[82] See n. 76 above, 514, 520.

[83] *Ibid.*

The Need for Clarity

In practical terms it is likely that, sooner or later, English contract law will come to accept the existence of a doctrine of good faith and fair dealing. In a global economy England will not want to be seen to be standing almost alone. So it will have to climb on board. At that point debates about the desirability or otherwise of the recognition of a doctrine of good faith and fair dealing will become practically redundant. Instead the vital questions will become: (1) what does the doctrine mean?; (2) what impact will it have on the existing rules of contract law, such as the rule laid down in the *Union Eagle* case?; and (3) what is the scope of the doctrine—does it apply to pre-contractual dealings, performance and enforcement of the contract, or only to some of these? The incorporation of a doctrine of good faith is unlikely to be a painless one; it may act as an "irritant".[84]

In seeking to give a meaning to good faith it is important to keep principles of law and morality firmly in view and not to get lost in the facts of the case and distracted by vague, unarticulated feelings of sympathy for one or other party. For example, in so far as good faith incorporates the principle that the expectations engendered by a binding promise must be honoured, few problems are likely to arise. Similarly, in so far as good faith is used to explain why wrongs, whether legal or equitable, must be remedied or why unjust enrichments must be reversed, few practical problems are likely to arise. But the point to be made here is surely that good faith is redundant in these contexts. These principles can stand in their own right and the invocation of good faith is more likely to distract than illuminate.

Where good faith comes into its own is when it goes beyond these principles and it is at this point that I begin to have difficulty. Two examples will illustrate the difficulties. The first arises where good faith is used in an attempt to impose on a contracting party a more onerous obligation than that contained in the contract. The second arises where good faith is used to limit the ability of a negotiating party to withdraw from contractual negotiations without incurring any liability for doing so. My difficulties can, I think, be set out briefly.

The first arises where good faith is used to add to the terms of the contract. The same point can, in fact, be made about the use of

---

[84] G. Teubner, "Legal Irritants: Good Faith in British Law or How Unifying Law Ends Up in New Divergences" (1998) 61 *Modern Law Review* 11.

fiduciary duties. They have been readily embraced in Canada[85] but the English courts have remained sceptical[86]—rightly so in my view. The courts must be careful not to be too ready to find the existence of a fiduciary relationship or to give too free a rein to good faith, because the effect of finding the existence of such a relationship or such a duty might be to change in a significant respect the nature of the bargain which the parties have concluded. As Hoyano has remarked in the context of fiduciary duties:

> [T]he defendant is generally entitled by the law of tort and contract to be *primarily* self-interested, provided that he or she is honest and respects the legal entitlements of others, but equity demands that the fiduciary be utterly selfless and dedicated to acting solely for the benefit of another.[87]

Such a duty should not be lightly imposed in a commercial context. The parties have chosen to enter into a contract and have made to each other binding promises. What justification is there for imposing on the parties a greater obligation than the obligations they themselves have voluntarily assumed? The broad invocation of good faith should not suffice to trump a legally binding, but limited promise.

The same point can be made about the invocation of good faith to explain the erosion of the ability of a party to withdraw from negotiations without incurring any liability for doing so.[88] What principle has led to this erosion? In some cases it is that the parties have gone beyond the negotiation stage and have, in fact, concluded a contract. Such a conclusion is acceptable in principle but it is open to criticism in that it involves the court in adopting what might appear to be a rather strained con-

---

[85] For example, see *Frame* v. *Wilson* (1987) 42 DLR (4th) 81; *Norberg* v. *Wynrib* (1992) 92 DLR (4th) 449; *KM* v. *WM* (1992) 96 DLR (4th) 289; *Hodgkinson* v. *Simms* (1994) 117 DLR (4th) 161. Many of the cases are, admittedly, not commercial ones and the use of the fiduciary label has been largely instrumental, as a means to a desired end. But cases can be found in which fiduciary duties have been allowed to stray into the commercial sphere, particularly in joint venture cases: see, for example, *Erehwon Exploration Ltd* v. *Nothstar Energy Corp.* 52 CPR 3d 170 (1993).

[86] For example, see *Henderson* v. *Merrett Syndicates Ltd* [1995] 2 AC 145, 205–6; *Re Goldcorp Exchange Ltd* [1995] 1 AC 74, 98; *Bristol and West Building Society* v *Mothew* [1998] Ch 1, 18.

[87] Hoyano, "The Flight to the Fiduciary Haven" in P. Birks (ed.), *Privacy and Loyalty* (Oxford, 1997), 172.

[88] The cases dealing with this issue are discussed in more detail by MacQueen at Chapter 2 in this volume.

[89] See, for example, *Blackpool and Fylde Aero Club Ltd* v. *Blackpool Borough Council* [1990] 1 WLR 1195 and *Hughes Aircraft Systems International* v. *Air Services Australia* (1997) 146 ALR 1, especially 25–32.

struction of the facts.[89] In other cases the basis upon which liability has been imposed is that the defendant was unjustly enriched as a result of the work done by the plaintiff.[90] Once again this is acceptable in principle provided that the ingredients of a restitutionary claim have been made out on the facts.[91] But in the absence of a breach of contract by the defendant or the receipt by the defendant of an unjust enrichment, the case for imposing liability on a party who has withdrawn from negotiations is not secure. And it cannot be made secure by the simple expedient of the appeal to good faith. Where the defendant has induced the plaintiff to act to his detriment by telling the plaintiff lies, the plaintiff may have a claim based on the wrong of telling lies. But, in the absence of a lie, why impose liability? It has been argued that the law should explicitly recognise the existence of a "duty to ensure the reliability of induced assumptions"[92] which would encompass the case where the defendant unilaterally withdraws from negotiations for a reason which has nothing to do with the plaintiff.[93] The difficulty with the duty to ensure the reliability of induced assumptions lies, however, in locating its precise basis in principle and morality. To adapt the words of Professor Fried,[94] why should the defendant's liberty be constrained by the harm which the plaintiff will suffer from the disappointment of the expectations which the plaintiff chooses to entertain about the defendant's choices? The broad mix of factors which have been used to support the existence of a duty to ensure the reliability of induced assumptions do not reveal any obvious basis in either principle or morality.

It is at this point that the need for clarity of thought becomes paramount. There is a risk, and in my view it is a real one, that good faith will become an excuse for engaging in "well-meaning sloppiness of

---

[90] *British Steel Corporation* v. *Cleveland Bridge and Engineering Co Ltd* [1984] 1 All ER 504. But where the negotiations have been entered into on a "subject to contract" basis this will generally shut out the restitutionary claim: see *Regalian Properties plc* v. *London Dockland Development Corp.* [1995] 1 All ER 1005.

[91] On which see E. McKendrick, "Work Done in Anticipation of a Contract which does not Materialise" in W.R. Cornish, *et al*, *Restitution Past Present and Future* (Oxford, 1998), 163.

[92] M. Spence, "Australian Estoppel and the Protection of Reliance" (1997) 11 *Journal of Contract Law* 203.

[93] Cases which would fall within this category include *Walton Stores (Interstate) Ltd* v. *Maher* (1988) 164 CLR 387 and, possibly, *Hoffman* v. *Red Owl Stores* (1965) 133 NW (2d) 267. English courts have not yet gone as far as these cases because estoppel cannot create a cause of action, although there are signs that they might yet do so: see, for example, *Salvation Army Trustee Co. Ltd* v. *West Yorkshire Metropolitan County Council* (1980) 41 P & CR 179.

[94] Fried, *Contract as Promise* (Cambridge, Massachusetts, 1981), 10.

thought".[95] This must not be allowed to happen. We must always endeavour to work out the basis on which liability is imposed in an individual case. While good faith has something to offer us in terms of enabling us to free ourselves from the restraint imposed on the freedom of the parties in *Walford* v. *Miles*, and in terms of bringing us into line with the majority of legal systems in the world, it also brings with it considerable problems of definition. These difficulties must be addressed so that good faith can go forward on a sound basis in legal principle and morality.

---

[95] To use the words of Scrutton LJ in *Baylis* v. *Bishop of London* [1913] 1 Ch 127, 140.

4

Good Faith in Contracting: A Sceptical View

Joseph M. Thomson*

Introduction

In this essay I ask myself a simple question: why am I sceptical of the introduction into Scots law of a general principle of contracting in good faith? I believe that I am a decent man who attempts to live a moral life: though whether I have succeeded in doing so is less a matter for this world than the next. However, I admit to two failings. First, I like to get a bargain. I enjoy booking a cruise at the last minute and obtaining a cabin at half the price paid by my fellow travellers; though, of course, I have sufficient courtesy not to discuss my bargain with them over cocktails before the captain's dinner. On the other hand, I may delay too long so that no cabin is available; in which case I do not get a holiday. Second, I like to make a profit. In this respect, I resemble my late father who was a fish curer. He used to buy herring at two (old) pence a basket, smoke them and sell them as kippers at two (old) pence a pair! Of course, he had to fillet the fish, cure them and pay the expenses of running his kilns and fish shop: nevertheless, the profit per kipper was not inconsiderable.

I am no economist and cannot explore the operation of perfect markets. I do know, however, that our markets are imperfect and allow us to make good bargains and high profits. But A's good bargain can *sometimes* be B's bad bargain, and A's profit can *sometimes* be B's loss. But that is what a free market is about. I believe that we should have the opportunity to make good bargains if we are clever enough. I believe that we should have the opportunity to make profits by utilising our talents. In grasping these opportunities we also take the risk of making a

* Regius Professor of Law, University of Glasgow.

bad bargain, or incurring a loss. The freedom to contract in the market seems to me to be a fundamental tenet of western democracies. Any interference with this freedom has therefore to be justified, either to protect a particularly vulnerable group in society or to prevent distortion of the market as a result of monopolies. But the insistence that A should act in good faith when contracting with B, that A must put B's interests on a par with his own (and vice versa), undermines the whole rationale of contractual freedom.

Let me give some specific examples. A owns a company. B makes a publicised bid. C is also interested and makes a higher bid. If B loses interest, in current Scots law, A is not obliged to inform C. Indeed, it would be gross negligence on the part of A's financial and legal advisers to do so. While A must not positively misrepresent that B is still a potential purchaser, A can continue negotiations with C, even although it is clear to A that C believes that B is still a rival bidder. If C then raises the purchase price, A can exploit the informational imbalance between them and accept the higher price. As Lord Curriehill observed in *Gillespie* v. *Russel and Son*, in many bargains made in business life there is

> a certain degree of cunning, craft, and even deceit, against which, although they may be transgressions of the strict rules of morality, the law does not protect the contracting parties, but leaves them to protect themselves.[1]

In his view concealment of information did not amount to fraud, since the object of entering into business bargains is to gain and there is no duty to disclose to the other party the basis of the calculation of the gain. If, however, the principle of good faith in contracting involves an obligation to redress informational imbalance by creating a duty to disclose information in the circumstances just described, then the opportunities to make a good bargain will be seriously diminished.

It could be argued that the principle of good faith should be concerned not so much with the formation of a contract but rather with contractual performance. A typical example is where A and B have negotiated a contract which contains an express term that entitles A to withdraw from performance of the contract if B breaches a term in the contract. B then breaches the term with minimal economic consequences for A. Is A entitled to withdraw? Provided it is expressly stipulated that *any* breach of the term by B, however trivial, is sufficient to trigger A's right to withdraw, current Scots law allows A to do so. As

[1] (1856) 18 D 677, at 686.

Law President Normand opined in *Bell Brothers (HP)Ltd* v. *Aitken*: "Parties can always agree in a contract to treat any breach as justifying rescission".[2] A's motive in exercising his contractually stipulated right of rescission (i.e., his right to withdraw from further performance of the contract) is irrelevant. Yet, if parties to a contract have to exercise their rights in accordance with good faith, it could be argued that A has no right to rescind the contract as a result of a trivial breach by B, particularly if his motive for doing so was to enter a more profitable contract with C. I find it difficult to defend such a conclusion given that the parties have, *ex hypothesi*, expressly stipulated that *any* breach by B gives A the right to rescind. In theory at least, B should not have agreed to the term unless B was satisfied that the other terms of the contract constituted a good bargain from B's point of view.

Let us consider one last example. A enters into a contract with B for the purchase of machinery. During the pre-contractual negotiations, B tells A that the machinery has been tested by an engineer. After the machinery has been delivered, A discovers that it has not been tested. Under current Scots law A is entitled to reduce the contract and recover the price, since A was induced to enter the contract as a result of B's fraudulent misrepresentation. It does not matter that the machinery is working properly and that A has not suffered any loss. Moreover, A's motive for electing to reduce the contract is irrelevant. Thus A could rely on the technicality and reduce the contract when A's reason for doing so is that A can obtain similar machinery from C at a much lower price. If there was a general doctrine of contracting in good faith, A could be denied the remedy if A had not suffered any loss as a consequence of B's misrepresentation. Again, such a conclusion seems to me to be difficult to defend since, *ex hypothesi*, B has been guilty of fraud.

These examples are illustrative of the fundamental changes which would be required, not only to the substantive rules of Scots contract law, but, more importantly, perhaps, to the business environment in which the rules currently operate, were we to incorporate a general principle of good faith into the law. But what would we actually be incorporating into the law? It is to this question that I now turn.

---

[2] 1939 SC 577, at 558.

What is Good Faith?

In 1996, I became involved in the Common Core of European Law project. My first task was to act as the Scottish rapporteur on good faith in contracting, under the general editorship of Simon Whittaker and Reinhard Zimmermann. The national reports with Whittaker and Zimmermann's introduction and conclusion are shortly to be published. In their conclusion Whittaker and Zimmermann identify five meanings of good faith:

(1) *Dishonesty constitutes bad faith*

This can be characterised as an emanation of a general principle of contracting in good faith. However, in Scots law, we already adhere to the principle by recognising that a dishonest misrepresentation not only relieves the innocent party from performance of the contract, but also forms the basis of a restitutionary claim or damages in delict. Indeed, Scots law goes further and provides relief where the misrepresentation is not dishonest, but merely negligent or, even, innocent. As the learned authors point out, the difficulty is to determine what circumstances constitute dishonesty. As we have seen, Scots law does not demand disclosure in order to remedy informational imbalance. But of course, Scots law has traditionally provided relief when there has been fraud or when a party's consent has been vitiated as a result of force and fear or facility and circumvention. Moreover, error can be a ground of reduction. This is important because in at least some analyses, misrepresentation is perceived as a development of the law on error. When, for example, a contract is reduced on the grounds of innocent misrepresentation *both* parties are acting under error and arguably the right to be relieved from the performance of the contract stems from the error under which they have been acting.

(2) *A person should keep to his or her word*

Here the idea that a promisor is bound by his promise is said to derive from the principle of good faith. However, provided the requisite formal requirements have taken place, Scots law has always recognised the enforceability of unilateral (including gratuitous unilateral) obligations. The theoretical basis lies in the acceptance by Scots law of the will theory of voluntary obligations: i.e., that a person is obliged on the declaration of his intention to be obliged. There is, therefore, no need to establish reliance on the part of promisee. But when the formal requirements have not been met, the promisor can still be held to the promise, if there has been reliance on the part of the promisee. At common law this was done through the doctrines of *rei interventus* and homologation, which have now been replaced by sections 1(3) and (4) of the Requirements of Writing (Scotland) Act 1995. However, it is important to note that outwith the scope of the 1995 Act the general principle of personal bar continues. The point to be made is that there is no need in Scots law to rely on a general principle of good faith in order to seek a rationale for these doctrines.

(3) *One party should not make the other's position worse as a result of his behaviour*

Where this aspect of good faith is important is in those legal systems which provide relief in pre-contractual situations through some doctrine of *culpa in contrahendo*. Scots law does not recognise such a doctrine and prima facie, therefore, does not provide a remedy where, for example, a party breaks off pre-contractual negotiations. But relief can often be achieved either through the concept of enforceable unilateral obligations or the law of unjustified enrichment, in particular, an action for recompense. Given the increasing recognition of liability for pure economic loss, a remedy might also be possible by an imaginative use of the law of delict.

(4) *Parties must be relieved from absurd consequences which appear to follow from their agreement*

The traditional way that Scots law attempted to protect parties in this context was either by the implication of terms or by judicious construction of the terms of their contract. For example, in *Wilkie* v. *Bethune*,[3] a master agreed to give his servant nine bolls of potatoes over

---

[3] (1848) 11D 132.

and above his wages. When the potato crop failed, the master could only fulfil his obligation by purchasing potatoes at treble their usual price. In an action by the servant for damages based on the highest market price of the potatoes, the court held on an "equitable" construction of the contract that he was only entitled to a sum which would enable him to purchase an equivalent amount of other food. The servant's claim was "too onerous for equity to support".[4] It was well recognised that the courts could not alter the meaning of express stipulations in a contract, however unfair. Extremely robust dicta can be found in the cases, particularly in nineteenth century appeals to the House of Lords. A *locus classicus* is the approach taken by Lord Bramwell in *Auld* v. *The Glasgow Working-Men's Provident Investment Building Society*:[5]

> It seems to me so utterly wrong, when people have entered into a defined bargain, that it should be set aside upon some more or less fanciful notion of equity or right, that I will not discuss it . . . I think it particularly mischievous that any notion of that sort should be countenanced nowadays when there is such disposition, and such a foolish, stupid, disposition, on the part of people to think they can make better arrangements for those who have made their own, and that it is right to set aside a particular and distinct bargain that has been entered into.[6]

Even when the courts recognised a contract as *bona fide*, their aim was to give effect to the intentions of the parties, not to subject the contents of the contract to a test of substantive fairness. As Lord Curriehall observed in *Wright* v. *Earl of Hopetoun*,[7] while the court is not allowed to alter express terms of the contract:

> [Y]et it is a principle of our law that certain contracts are to be regarded as contracts *in bona fide*, and are to be construed so as to give effect to the probable intention of the parties.[8]

Another technique to save parties from absurd consequences of their contract was, of course, the development of the doctrine of frustration. Once again, however, recourse was not made to the concept of good faith but, initially at least, to the implication of terms.

---

[4] But note how this "equitable" construction of the contract resulted in a decision favourable to the master. Nineteenth century Scottish courts did not like pursuers who dared to sue their betters: see, for example, *Countess of Dunmore* v. *Alexander* (1830) 9 S 190.
[5] (1887) 14R (HL) 27.
[6] At 31–2.
[7] (1858) 20D 955.
[8] At 958.

In short, while Scots law sometimes recognised the need to relieve the parties in these situations, the techniques used did not have the concept of good faith as their rationale. Moreover, the courts consistently refused directly to "police" the substantive fairness of a bargain. This is, of course, consistent with the function of contract in a capitalist economy. It is a trend which continues today. As Lord President Hope observed in *EFT Commercial Ltd* v. *Security Change Ltd and Another*:[9]

> [I]t is the function of the court to enforce contracts according to the bargain which the parties have made for themselves. It is not for the court to interfere in order to modify a bargain which one of the parties later considers to be unfair.[10]

(5) *Deliberate breach of contract*

Again, it is argued to be contrary to a general principle of good faith, deliberately to breach a contract. In Scots law, a breach of contract is a breach of contract whether it be deliberate or not. However, while still controversial in some quarters, Scots law does recognise the doctrine of anticipatory breach of contract. One important consequence of this is that the innocent party can elect not to treat the anticipatory breach as a material breach and can perform the contract and recover the price without having to mitigate his or her loss.[11] It could be argued that such an election (i.e., providing unwanted goods or services in return for the contractually agreed consideration) goes against the concept of performing a contract in good faith. Nevertheless, in the context of the law on commercial leases, we have seen how a tenant can be compelled to continue occupying premises even although the tenant wanted to throw up the lease and pay damages.[12]

We have been exploring the meanings of good faith considered by Whittaker and Zimmermann in the conclusion to their comparative study of the operation of the doctrine in modern Western European legal systems. It should be no surprise that Scots law often protects the same interests as the principle of good faith, but by developing specific doctrines and techniques which, during their evolution, did not expressly recognise the principle. Moreover, when there was tension

---

[9] 1992 SC 414.
[10] At 424.
[11] *White and Carter (Councils) Ltd* v. *McGregor* 1962 SC (HL) 1.
[12] *Retail Parks Investments Ltd* v. *Royal Bank of Scotland plc (No. 2)* 1996 SC 227.

between freedom of contract and the unfairness of the bargain, the courts have consistently held in favour of the former. This is consonant with the approach to contracting outlined in the introduction to this paper. In the present writer's view, it continues to make much social and economic sense.

Good Faith and Consumers

Before I am dismissed as a reactionary, neo-conservative, an important point must be made. The system of contracting outlined above presupposes equality of bargaining power between the contracting parties. There is no doubt that for many years Scots law could justifiably be criticised for its failure to protect the economically (and socially) vulnerable from grossly unfair terms which, in effect, were imposed upon them by economically dominant enterprises.

One of the many ironies which must be faced by those who believe in the civilian tradition of Scots law, is that little, if any, attempt was made by the courts to regulate substantively unfair terms in consumer contracts. By the end of the eighteenth century, it was settled that the substantive unfairness of the contract was not in itself sufficient to have it modified or set aside. Nor would it appear that there was any presumption of fraud or deceit to be drawn from a substantively unfair bargain, unless in the very exceptional circumstances where the contract *ex facie* demonstrated oppression. As Lord Gillies maintained in *McKirdy* v. *Anstruther*:[13] "A sale is never set aside on the mere ground that the price has been inadequate . . . Lesion, of itself, affords no ground for reduction".[14] And in *Latta* v. *Park & Co.*,[15] Lord Cowan confirmed that every price the parties had agreed in their contract is "in the judgment of the law of Scotland, just, if they have not been drawn into the contract by fraud or deceit".[16]

One reason often articulated in the cases to justify this policy of non-intervention was that the court could not alter the terms of the contract. In *Cadzow* v. *Lockhart*,[17] for example, Lord Ardmillan explains:

[13] (1839) 1 D 855.
[14] At 863.
[15] (1865) 3 M 508.
[16] At 512.
[17] (1876) 3 R 666.

This court cannot make for the parties a contract different from that which they have made for themselves, and cannot exclude or ignore a clearly expressed stipulation if it be not illegal or immoral.[18]

It would appear that Stair accepted, in the context of partnership, that if one partner has all the loss and the other all the profit, then, the agreement could be unenforceable as a *societas Leonina*.[19] There are also occasional later dicta suggesting that this doctrine is part of Scots law. In *Andrew* v. *Henderson and Dimmack*,[20] Lord Neaves observed:

It is difficult to say that parties cannot bargain what they like, but there is some difficulty. I let you a house, but I am entitled to take it away whenever I please, and you are still to pay me £100 a year as rent for nineteen years. That is like the old leonine contract, so called from the old fable of the lion who carried off everything. It is very doubtful if the Court would consider such to be a good contract. But this at all events is clear, that they will not do so unless compelled by the clearest words. They will not only use astuteness, but the very greatest astuteness, to avoid giving effect to it.[21]

In the twentieth century, while accepting that a leonine bargain might not be enforced, the courts continued to uphold the validity of the (often extremely unfair) contract under consideration in the particular case.[22] The most famous example is that of the Lord President Cooper in *McKay* v. *Scottish Airways Ltd*.[23] The case concerned the validity of an exemption clause excluding the airline's liability to pay damages for the death or injury of a passenger during carriage. In the course of his judgment, Lord Cooper said:

[T]he remarkable feature of these conditions is their amazing width, and the effort which has evidently been made to create a leonine bargain under which the aeroplane passenger takes all the risks and the company accepts no obligations, not even to carry the passenger or his baggage nor even to admit him to the aeroplane. It was not argued that the conditions were contrary to public policy, nor that they were so extreme as to deprive the contract of all meaning and effect as a contract of carriage; and I reserve my opinion upon these questions.[24]

The court, of course, upheld the validity of the clause!

[18] At 674
[19] Stair, *Institutions of the Law of Scotland* (1681), I.16, D.M. Walker (ed.), (Edinburgh, 1983).
[20] (1871) 9 M 554.
[21] At 570.
[22] For example, see *Roberts & Cooper Ltd.* v. *Christian Salvesen & Co.* (1918) 2 SLT 160; *B. Fraser & Co.* v. *Denny, Mott & Dickson* 1944 SLT 139; *Bell Brothers (HP) Ltd* v. *Reynolds* 1945 SLT 229.
[23] 1948 SC 254.
[24] At 263.

What is interesting is that there is no attempt to challenge such clauses as a breach of the parties' obligation to contract in good faith. Instead, the Scottish courts followed the approach of their English counterparts in protecting consumers from extortionate exemption clauses by resorting to various artificial devices, none of which involved the concept of good faith. First, it was argued that the clause had not been incorporated into the contract because insufficient notice of the clause had been given to the consumer at the time the contract was made.[25] Second, a clause would not be regarded as incorporated if it was to be found in a non-contractual document such as a receipt.[26] Third, if the clause had been incorporated, it was construed *contra proferentem*.[27]

In these cases, the tension between freedom of contract and the unfairness of the exemption clause is palpable, yet there is no resort to the principle of good faith. The courts were not prepared to grasp the nettle and strike down unfair exemption clauses. *Prima facie*, both parties must abide by the contract they make—even if an exemption clause has been incorporated. In *McCutcheon* v. *David MacBrayne Ltd*[28] Lord Devlin explains:

> What is sauce for the goose is sauce for the gander. It will remain unpalatable sauce for both animals until the Legislature, if the Courts cannot do it, intervenes to secure that when contracts are made in circumstances in which there is no scope for free negotiation of the terms, they are made upon terms that are clear, fair and reasonable and settled independently as such.[29]

The legislature did eventually intervene. The Unfair Contract Terms Act 1977 now provides a complex regime for the judicial control of exemption clauses. In relation to exemption clauses in consumer contracts, the preferred solution has been simply to declare that in the most common situations, the exemption clause is null. Where a clause is not automatically null under the Act, it is doubtful whether it would satisfy the requirement of reasonableness under the Act, given that the statutory criteria to be considered include the resources of the parties, the relative strength of their bargaining positions and the consumer's know-

[25] *Lyons.* v. *The Caledonian Railway Co.* 1909 SC 1185; *Hood* v. *Anchor Line Ltd* 1918 SC (HL) 143.
[26] *Taylor* v. *Glasgow Corporation* 1952 SC 440.
[27] *Hamilton* v. *Western Bank of Scotland* (1861) 23 D 1033; *W&S Pollock & Co.* v. *Macrae* 1922 SC (HL) 192.
[28] 1964 SC (HL) 28.
[29] At 43.

ledge of the term. In other words, the Act provides not inconsiderable protection for the consumer from unfair exemption clauses. It should be noted, however, that the criteria for assessing whether a clause satisfies the requirement of reasonableness are objective. There is no express reference to the principle of contracting in good faith. But, as we have seen, in so far as good faith involves fairness in contracting, the Unfair Contract Terms Act 1977 goes far to meet that objective, at least in the context of consumer contracts.

The 1977 Act is largely concerned with exemption clauses however. The Unfair Terms in Consumer Contracts Regulations 1994[30] provide protection to consumers in respect of a wider range of terms, though exemption clauses are also included. These could be, for example, disproportionately high compensation clauses, penalty clauses, clauses which allow unilateral variation of the contract by the non-consumer, accelerated price clauses etc. The provisions only apply to consumer contracts for the sale of goods (arguably also including land) and services, including insurance and financial services. They do not apply to contracts which have been individually negotiated.

The regulations purport to implement the EC Directive on Unfair Terms in Consumer Contracts.[31] The influence of the civil law is readily apparent both in the Directive and implementing Regulations. No more so can this be seen than in the definition of unfairness. This provides that a term is unfair if, contrary to the requirement of good faith, it causes a significant imbalance in the parties' rights and obligations arising under the contract, to the detriment of the consumer. For the first time in United Kingdom legislation about contracts there is an express reference to good faith. But it is problematic. It might be thought that before the courts' powers are triggered there has to be a breach of the requirement of good faith: that is to say, the breach of the requirement of good faith is independent of any imbalance to the detriment of the consumer. It is the present writer's view that where there is an imbalance to the detriment of the consumer that should be taken as indicative of a breach of the principle of good faith: in other words the two issues are interdependent. In assessing whether there has been a breach of the requirement of good faith, the courts are directed to criteria familiar to Scots and English lawyers from the Unfair Contract Terms Act 1977, *viz.*: (a) the strength of the parties' bargaining positions; (b) inducements to secure the consumer's consent; (c) whether

[30] SI 1994/3159.
[31] Council Directive 93/13/EEC of 5 April 1993, OJ L95/29.

goods or services were to the consumer's special order; and (d) the extent to which the seller or supplier has dealt fairly with the consumer. While we must await authoritative guidance, it would appear that the requirement of good faith in the Regulations is simply formulaic: what the courts are being asked to do is to determine whether a term is substantively unfair in that it creates an imbalance to the detriment of the consumer in the light of the criteria laid down in the regulations.

What is important to note is that the legislative controls do *not* apply to what we might call the "gist" of the contract. In particular, they do not apply to the adequacy of the price or remuneration as against the value of the goods or services sold or supplied. Thus even in consumer contracts, *caveat emptor* continues. As in traditional Scots law, lesion *per se* is not a ground to modify a bargain. To that extent, the free market continues to prevail.

There is no doubt that Scots private law was not effective to protect consumers from unfair contractual terms. Freedom of contract was preferred to consumer protection, though artificial devices were sometimes used to relieve a consumer from extortionate provisions. Legislation has now attempted to redress the worst excesses which derive from the unequal economic bargaining positions of the parties. The principle of good faith has played little part in these developments. The Unfair Terms in Consumer Contracts Regulations, while playing lip service to the concept, define the requirement of good faith in such a way that it is comprehensible to Scots lawyers familiar with the requirement of reasonableness in the Unfair Contract Terms Act 1977. Given these developments, even in consumer contracts, there is no need to resort to a general principle of good faith in contracting.

Conclusions

It has been argued that there is no general principle of good faith in contracting in Scots law. While there are various doctrines which achieve similar objectives as some of the meanings of good faith, Scots law allows a party to a contract a large degree of freedom to use economic power, knowledge and skill to conclude a bargain or make a profit. Where there is economic imbalance between the parties, particularly in consumer contracts, legislative regimes exist to protect consumers from unfair terms, but even here the substantive fairness of the actual exchange is not subject to scrutiny. Again, this seems to me to be consonant with the economic demands of a western capitalist society. In short, there is no need for the adoption of such an amorphous concept as good faith in contracting, the meanings and parameters of which are controversial, resulting in an enormous volume of doctrine and jurisprudence in those modern civilian legal systems which adopt it.

That said, there are stirrings afoot at the highest judicial levels that the concept of good faith in contracting not only should be but, indeed, is already part of Scots private law. I am, of course, referring to *Smith* v. *Bank of Scotland*.[32] There, in a blatant example of judicial legislation, the House of Lords held that a lender, who sought security from the debtor's wife, was obliged to ensure that she received independent advice before signing a standard security. While, in my view, the policy considerations advanced by the House of Lords display a misplaced concern for the social and economic position of wives in contemporary Scottish society, the ratio of the case, in so far as there is one, was clearly based on the "element of good faith which is required of a creditor on the constitution of a contract".[33] It is not surprising that authority for such a principle was scant, but his Lordship did refer to cases relating to cautionary obligations. As is well known, cautionary obligations, like contracts of insurance, form a particular (and peculiar) area of the law of contract. Moreover, the potential scope of *Smith* has been severely restricted by the decision of the Lord Ordinary (Hamilton) in *Braithwaite* v. *Bank of Scotland*.[34] There Lord Hamilton insisted that before the creditor's obligation arose to ensure that a wife obtained independent advice, it must be averred that she was in fact under the undue influence of her husband or had been a victim of a misrepresentation made by him as to the legal effects of the transaction he was asking her to enter. In these circumstances, it is unlikely that the concept of good faith relied upon by Lord Clyde in *Smith*, will percolate beyond the confines of inter spousal/cohabitant security transactions. No doubt this will be to the chagrin of those academic commentators who have treated Lord Clyde's speech as if it were a statute in order to find authority for a general principle of good faith in contracting in Scots law.

It will be clear that the debate on the value of a principle of good faith in contracting has not been won by either side: indeed, in Scots law, the debate has only begun. As this paper has argued, proponents of the doctrine can find little support for its existence in Scots law before *Smith*.

---

[32] 1997 SC (HL) 111.
[33] At 121 per Lord Clyde.
[34] 1999 SLT 25.

More importantly, perhaps, great care should be given to transplanting the doctrine into Scots law. It is amorphous, complex and at variance with the cultural values which have moulded the current law. In particular, the Scottish Parliament should be cautious before embarking on such a task—and so should the Scottish judiciary. In the present writer's view, it is *not* the function of a system of private law to compel persons to act in an altruistic manner nor, indeed, is it its function to ensure that they do not act in a morally reprehensible way. To do so, would be to remove the edge of competition and self interest which are also human values and which have created the wealth upon which our society currently depends.

5

Good Faith and Utmost Good Faith: Insurance and Cautionary Obligations in Scots Law

A.D.M. Forte*

Introduction

"Contracts", wrote Bankton in 1751,

> among the Romans . . . were either *bonae fidei, or stricti iuris*: the first are
> these in which the judge had a liberty to determine, upon the mutual oblig-
> ations of parties, from the nature of the contract, according to their presumed
> will, as in Sale, Mandate, Location and others . . . : the other were these
> wherein the judge was tied down to the express covenant or words of the
> parties, as in Stipulation, and Loan of Money. We have little use for this dis-
> tinction; only Loan and Promises are strictly interpreted.[1]

Bankton's meaning here may be thought somewhat opaque perhaps.
Was he simply referring to the position under Roman law? Or was he
saying (as I think he was) that Scots law, in relation to most commercial contracts, subscribed to the belief in a general principle of good faith
with some exceptions? It is clear, however, that Kames,[2] writing after
Bankton, accepted that some contracts were *bonae fidei*, and Bell's
position is consistent with the belief that all contracts in Scotland are
subject to a requirement of good faith.[3] The position of the other institutional writers cannot be stated with any precision.

---

* Professor of Commercial Law, University of Aberdeen.
[1] Bankton, *An Institute of the Law of Scotland* (Edinburgh, 1751–3), 1.11.65.
[2] Kames, *Principles of Equity* (Edinburgh, 3rd edn, 1778), 194 ff.
[3] Bell, *Commentaries on the Law of Scotland in relation to Mercantile and Maritime Law, Moveable and Heritable Rights and Bankruptcy* (Edinburgh, 7th edn, 1870), I, 263; *Principles of the Law of Scotland* (Edinburgh, 4th edn), para 13.

The modern literature has not really changed much. Gloag, in his treatment of the Scots law of contract, discussed the concepts of good faith and utmost (*sic*) good faith in a variety of contexts. But although he did not specifically state that Scots law subscribes to a general principle of good faith, his observation that contracts must be interpreted "on the assumption of honest dealing" would seem to assume a requirement to contract in good faith.[4] More recent works have simply ignored the issue of good faith as a principle underpinning commercial contracts.[5] However, those writers whose work has stressed the importance of maintaining the civilian tradition in Scotland have argued for the recognition of such a general principle. The late Professor T.B. Smith, for example, although he produced little evidence in support, asserted that *bona fides* was a general concept known in the Scots law of contract and that the concept of *uberrima fides*, or utmost good faith, was no more than a synonym for *bona fides*. Smith also suggested, correctly in this writer's view, that *uberrima fides* is not an indigenous concept but one imported from English law.[6] J.J. Gow, in an elaborate but fundamentally futile attempt to convince his audience that the Sale of Goods Act 1893 made little difference to the common law of sale, considered the role of good faith in more detail. Gow concluded that good faith was the "animating principle" of the contract of sale,[7] which manifested itself by imposing a duty on the seller to "disclose hidden imperfections known to him" only.[8] In other words, non-disclosure was tantamount to fraudulent concealment. Gow also took the view that contracts for the hire of moveables (*locatio conductio rei*) were *bonae fidei*[9] and, like Smith, he seems to regard insurance contracts as being of good faith rather than of utmost good faith.[10]

[4] W. M. Gloag, *The Law of Contract—A Treatise on the Principles of Contract in the Law of Scotland* (Edinburgh, 2nd edn, 1929), 400.

[5] For example, see W.W. McBryde, *The Law of Contract in Scotland* (Edinburgh, 1987); D.M. Walker, *The Law of Contracts and Related Obligations in Scotland* (Edinburgh, 3rd edn, 1995); "Voluntary Obligations" in *The Laws of Scotland. Stair Memorial Encyclopaedia* (Edinburgh, 1996), vol. 15. As one would expect, books on Scots commercial law make reference to good faith and utmost good faith in a variety of contexts, but none addresses the issue of good faith as a unifying concept, or the relationship between good faith and utmost good faith. See, for example, E. Marshall, *Scots Mercantile Law* (Edinburgh, 3rd edn, 1997); Forte (ed.), *Scots Commercial Law* (Edinburgh,1997).

[6] T.B. Smith, *A Short Commentary on the Law of Scotland* (Edinburgh, 1962), 297–8.

[7] J.J. Gow, *The Mercantile and Industrial Law of Scotland* (Edinburgh, 1964), 73.

[8] *Ibid.*, 161.

[9] *Ibid.*, 245.

[10] *Ibid.*, 386. Here, under reference to the Marine Insurance Act 1906, s. 17, which proclaims marine insurance contracts to be "based upon the utmost good faith", Gow pointedly describes these contracts as predicated upon good faith.

Despite his industry, however, it is far from clear that all of the cases cited by Gow,[11] particularly those based upon implied warrandice of priceworthiness in contracts for the sale of goods, were consciously perceived as applications of good faith: although terms as to quality and fitness are certainly explicable as reflective of a need for good faith.[12] But there is one, in which the court declared that the deliberate non-disclosure of a latent defect by the seller was "nothing short of fraud", which does, I think, carry that implication.[13] There are, however, other expressions of judicial support for the existence of a general principle of good faith which Gow omits to mention. In *Smith* v. *Bank of Scotland*,[14] for example, concerning a guarantee of the good conduct of a bank agent, Lord Pitmilly said:

> I found on a statement of Lord Mansfield as laying down the regulatory principle of all contracts, in the following words: "The governing principle is applicable to all contracts and dealings. Good faith prohibits either party, by concealing what he privately knows, to draw the other into a bargain, from his ignorance of that fact, and his believing the contrary." This opinion was given in an insurance case; but it was given as a doctrine applicable to all dealings.[15]

There is perhaps a certain irony here because a recent Scottish appeal to the House of Lords, *Smith* v. *Bank of Scotland*,[16] also suggests that good faith is a principle of general application in our law of contract. But it is only with the flurry of comments which followed in the wake of this case that we have managed to generate the same level of critical and evaluative debate so readily observable in England and throughout western Europe.[17] Most Scottish comments, however, have been largely

---

[11] *Hill* v. *Pringle* (1827) 6 S 229; *Gilmer* v. *Galloway* (1830) 8 S 420; *Deuchars* v. *Shaw* (1833) 11 S 612; *Brown* v. *Boreland* (1848) 10 D 1460; *Rough* v. *Moir and Son* (1875) 2 R 529.

[12] The seller of goods, sometimes explicitly, more usually implicitly, creates an expectation in the buyer that those goods will not be defective or shoddy. It is not unreasonable for the buyer to rely on that expectation and the seller does not act in good faith if he or she knows that the buyer's expectations are unjustified. If goods are consistent with the expectation generated, a buyer would not act in good faith if he or she were to reject these. See, generally, C. Willett, "Fairness in Sale of Goods Act Quality Obligations and Remedies" in C. Willett (ed.), *Aspects of Fairness in Contract* (London, 1996), 125.

[13] *Stewart* v. *Jamieson* (1863) 1 M 525, at 529 per Lord President Boyle.

[14] (1829) 7 S 244.

[15] At 253. The case referred to is *Carter* v. *Boehm* (1766) 3 Burr. 1905.

[16] 1997 S.C. (HL) 111.

[17] For example, J.F. O'Connor, *Good Faith in English Law* (Aldershot, 1990); J. Beatson, D. Friedman (eds), *Good Faith and Fault in Contract Law* (Oxford, 1995); Willett (ed.), n. 12 above; R. Brownsword, N.J. Hird, G. Howells (eds), *Good Faith in*

negative or downright hostile to the view that a general principle exists.[18] To some outside observers of Scots law, such as Ewoud Hondius, the absence of a general principle of good faith is puzzling.[19] Others, however, have been more positive; arguing that our law of contract is informed by a principle of good faith but that Scots lawyers have never attempted, or never achieved, a coherent account of this.[20] That is a view to which I would certainly subscribe.

In part, the objection to a general principle of good faith rests on the belief that it would destabilise the requirement of certainty in commercial dealings. But there is also, I think, a feeling that it is too amorphous, too difficult to define, too difficult to be explained in terms of unitary application. Many Scots lawyers would probably accept that good faith may play an interstitial role, but, equally probably, many would demur at the suggestion that it ought to be recognised as a general principle. Within the context of that debate, insurance and cautionary obligations make interesting subjects for examination. Both, so the evidence would seem to suggest, articulate a duty of disclosure, or, if not of disclosure in the narrow sense, at least a duty of warning or of advice which, *prima facie*, are grounded in good faith.[21] And if the enforceability of these contracts is predicated upon an underlying substratum of good faith, then this must have implications for commercial obligations generally,

Contract: Concept and Context (Aldershot, Brookfield USA, Singapore, Sydney, 1999). In the periodic literature there have been notable contributions by M.G. Bridge, "Does Anglo-Canadian Contract Law Need a Doctrine of Good Faith?" (1984) 9 *Canadian Business Law Journal* 385 and "Good Faith in Commercial Contracts" in Brownsword *et al*, 139; R. Goode, "The Concept of "Good Faith "in English Law" (1992) *Centro di Studi e Ricerche di Diritto Comparato e Straniero*; H. Collins, "Good Faith in European Contract Law" (1994) 14 *Oxford Journal of Legal Studies* 229; R. Brownsword, "Good Faith in Contract Revisited" (1996) 49 *Current Legal Problems* 111; G. Teubner, "Legal Irritants: Good Faith in British Law or How Unifying Law Ends Up in New Divergences" (1998) 61 *Modern Law Review* 11.

[18] G. Gretton, "Sexually Transmitted Debt" 1997 *Scots Law Times* (News) 195; J. Thomson, "Misplaced Concern" (1997) 65 *Scottish Law Gazette* 124; L. Macgregor, "The House of Lords Applies O'Brien North of the Border" (1998) 2 *Edinburgh Law Review* 90; R. Dunlop, "*Smith* v. *Bank of Scotland*: Spouses, Caution and the Banks" (1997) 42 *Journal of the Law Society of Scotland* 446; S. Dickson, "Good Faith in Contract: Spousal Guarantees and *Smith* v. *Bank of Scotland*" 1998 *Scots Law Times* (News) 39. Excepting the last, these views have tended to be negative.

[19] E. Hondius, "European Approaches to Fairness in Contract Law" in Willett (ed.), n. 12 above, 61, at 64.

[20] O. Lando, H. Beale (eds), *The Principles of European Contract Law Part I: Performance, Non-Performance and Remedies* (Dordrecht, Boston, London, 1995), 58.

[21] Such duties may be viewed as representing, at least in part, the content of good faith in relation to contract formation. See M. Hesselink, "Good Faith" in A. Hartkamp (ed.), *Towards a European Civil Code* (Nijmegen, 2nd edn, 1998).

and may offer an opportunity to consider at least some of the premises upon which a general principle may be thought to rest.

Insurance and the Concept of Utmost Good Faith

Despite its relatively late date (1873), the first occasion on which the term "*uberrima fides*" is found in Scotland is an insurance case where the issue was one of non-disclosure of allegedly material facts. In the course of his judgment Lord President Inglis said:

> Contracts of insurance are in this, among other particulars, exceptional, that they require on both sides *uberrima fides*. Hence without any fraudulent intent, and even in *bona fide*, the insured may fail in the duty of disclosure.[22]

The Lord President was alone however in resorting to the concept of utmost good faith. Lord Ardmillan considered insurance to raise an inference of *bona fides* and concluded that where, as in the instant case, the insured had acted throughout in good faith, then, non-disclosure was excusable "given the particular circumstances".[23] Lord Deas, who disposed of the non-disclosure on the basis of the absence of fraud or negligence on the part of the insured, also considered insurance to be "a contract of good faith on both sides".[24] It is, however, Lord President Inglis' view, unsupported it must be said by any reference to authority on the point, which has prevailed. A recent pronouncement, for example, declares:

> Because a contract of insurance is a contract *uberrima fides*, the utmost good faith is required from the parties. There is thus a duty on a party to disclose all relevant facts to enable the other party to make an accurate estimate of what he is undertaking.[25]

---

[22] *Life Association of Scotland* v. *Foster* (1873) 11 M 351, at 360 per Lord President Inglis.

[23] At 370. The circumstances were that the insured had failed to appreciate that a small swelling on her groin was indicative of a rupture and so answered a question asking if she suffered from rupture in the negative.

[24] At 364.

[25] *Hooper* v. *Royal London General Insurance Co Ltd* 1993 SC 242, at 245D-E per Lord Justice-Clerk Ross. Note also *H. Demetriades & Co.* v. *The Northern Assurance Co. Ltd* 1924 SC 182, at 196 per Lord Justice-Clerk Alness: "Now there can be no doubt that a contract of marine insurance is *uberrimae fidei*, and that every material circumstance which is known to the assured must be disclosed to the insurer before the risk is covered". Section 17 of the Marine Insurance Act 1906 states, of course, that marine contracts are of the "utmost good faith".

These dicta may not be entirely reconcilable however. The latter would appear to articulate two propositions. The first, is that a positive duty to disclose material facts arises because the contract is one of insurance. The second, is that this duty is the content of the concept of utmost good faith or, put otherwise, utmost good faith requires disclosure of all material facts. But it is arguable that Lord President Inglis' view that an insurance contract, unlike other types of commercial contracts, generates a positive duty of disclosure was predicated, not on the fact that the contract was one of insurance, but rather on the "exceptional" nature of this contract (a point to which I will later return). It is true that the Lord President appears to connect the existence of the duty of disclosure to the concept of utmost good faith, but it is likely that he intended nothing more by his use of the expression *uberrima fides* than to convey the message that there was a distinction to be drawn between contracts of insurance and other commercial obligations. And if he did not articulate a basis for that distinction, he did no less than the other judges who advanced no reasons for their view of insurance as requiring the observance of good faith.

There are perfectly sound reasons in logic as well as in law for disliking the notion of *utmost* good faith. As a South African Appellate Division judge trenchantly put it:

> In my opinion *uberrima fides* is an alien, vague, useless expression without any particular meaning in law. . . . Our law of insurance has no need for *uberrima fides* and the time has come to jettison it.[26]

But while Joubert JA's extensive use of the Roman-Dutch and other civilian sources[27] to justify his position may be thought to lend intellectual weight to his dismissal of the concept of utmost good faith, it does apply a very large sledgehammer to crack an exceedingly small nut. Miller JA, who clearly wished to dissociate himself from a too literal

---

[26] *Mutual and Federal Insurance Co. Ltd* v. *Oudtshoorn Municipality* 1985 (1) SA 419 (A), at 433E-F per Joubert JA. This view was shared by Cillié, JA, Viljoen, JA and Galgut AJA. In *Bank of Lisbon and South Africa Ltd* v. *De Ornelas* 1988 (3) SA 580 (A), Joubert JA deployed a similar technique to dispose of the *exceptio doli generalis*—a defence based on the exhibition of bad faith by a contracting party. On good faith generally in South Africa, see R. Zimmermann, "Good Faith and Equity" in R. Zimmermann, D. Visser (eds), *Southern Cross: Civil Law and Common Law in South Africa* (Oxford, 1996), 218; D. Hutchison, "Good Faith in the South African Law of Contract" in Brownsword *et al*, n. 17 above, 213.

[27] These are examined by R. Zimmermann, "Synthesis in South African Law: Civil Law, Common Law and *Usus Hodiernis Pandectarum*" (1986) 103 *South African Law Journal* 259.

approach to *uberrima fides*, took the view that the phrase was simply a brief and convenient way of expressing the idea that insurance contracts require positive disclosure by the parties to them.[28] Indeed, *MacGillivray and Parkington on Insurance Law* treats "*uberrima fides*" as being merely "a convenient though not always strictly accurate expression".[29] The phrase has also been judicially described as being no more than "short and convenient".

In *Mutual and Federal Insurance Co. Ltd* v. *Oudtshoorn Municipality* the court, although it stressed that insurance contracts were *bonae fidei*,[30] and did not disturb the substantive rule on disclosure, was nonetheless reluctant to link the requirement of disclosure to that of good faith. This position was reached by reasoning that if all contracts are based on good faith, but not all contracts require the observance of a duty of disclosure, then the latter cannot be predicated on the former. The court also rejected the idea that the duty might be based on an implied term of the contract.[31] Instead, the duty was said to arise *ex lege*,[32] or, as Miller JA put it, the duty "has long been recognised and accepted . . . as being part of our law".[33] I would argue that the duty of disclosure also arises

---

[28] At 443D: "The words '*uberrimae fidei*' must not . . . be taken too literally. One may be less than honest but one cannot be more honest than honest. After the very many years in which the term has been used in this context, it is not, I think, potentially misleading".

[29] (London, 8th edn, 1988), para 634. Note also A.K. Turner and R.J. Sutton (eds), Spencer Bower, *The Law Relating to Actionable Non-Disclosure* (London, 1915, 1990), para 1.02: "It has occasionally, though perhaps not very felicitously been said, whereas in all contracts . . . good faith is required, there is demanded in negotiation for [other] contracts . . . a higher degree of good faith extending always to a duty of disclosure. . . . It may be doubted whether such terms are judiciously chosen, and whether it is wise to introduce and encourage the idea of comparative degrees of honesty at all".

[30] At 432B–C per Joubert JA: "I have been unable to find any Roman-Dutch authority in support of the proposition that a contract of . . . insurance is a contract *uberrimae fidei*. On the contrary, it is indisputably a contract *bonae fidei*". In *Bank of Lisbon and South Africa Ltd* v. *De Ornelas*, n. 26 above, the very existence of a general principle of good faith seemed to be abrogated. However, in *Sasfin (Pty) Ltd* v. *Beukes* 1989 (1) SA 1 (A), the Appellate Division appears (at least to an outside observer) under the guise of "public policy" to have reintroduced a role for good faith.

[31] Although no explanation is offered, it may be argued that as the duty of disclosure is mainly a pre-contractual one it cannot therefore be grounded on an implied contract term. See A.J. Kerr, "The Duty of Disclosure in a Pre-Contractual Context—Good Faith and the Role of the Reasonable Man" (1985) *South African Law Journal* 611.

[32] At 433A–C per Joubert JA: "The duty of disclosure is imposed *ex lege*. It is not based upon an implied term of the contract of insurance, nor does it flow from the requirement of *bona fides*. . . . By our law all contracts are *bonae fidei* . . . Yet the duty of disclosure is not common to all types of contract. It is restricted to those contracts, such as contracts of insurance, where it is required *ex lege*".

[33] At 442G.

by force of law in Scotland.[34] But, with respect, this explanation does not justify the dismissal of good faith from the equation. In the first place, it does not explain the policy of the law in choosing to impose this duty in this particular contract. Secondly, it does not articulate in acceptable detail just why the legal principle informing that policy is not one of good faith. Thirdly, it ignores the possibility that disclosure is just one of several ways in which good faith may manifest itself, and that this particular duty, though appropriate to insurance contracts, may not be appropriate to other kinds.[35] Finally, if the duty of disclosure is not rooted in good faith in insurance contracts, the question still remains— why does the law insist on total disclosure?

In South Africa the approach taken to the first question has been to assert that there is no special significance to be attached to labels. Consequently, where there is a disclosure requirement this is not dependent on the argument that this is the type of contract where that requirement arises. It does not follow from the fact that some contracts are *uberrimae fidei*, and that insurance is (or rather was) such a contract, that a duty of disclosure exists in insurance contracts by virtue of the fact that these are insurance contracts.[36] Instead, the duty of disclosure should be thought of as arising in pre-contractual negotiations for any type of contract so long as those negotiations "are characterised by the involuntary reliance of one party [on the other] for information material to his decision [to contract]".[37] What this means is that a duty of disclosure does not follow from the fact that the contract is one of insurance, and that insurance contracts are contracts of the utmost good faith. Rather, the justification for the rule that there must be no con-

---

[34] A.D.M. Forte, "Insurance" in *The Laws of Scotland: Stair Memorial Encyclopaedia* (Edinburgh, 1992), vol. 12, para. 858, fn. 6.

[35] Remedies for extortion, misrepresentation and undue influence can all be said to be predicated on a principle of good faith. In South Africa the requirement that all contracts "should receive an equitable interpretation" has been said to be a manifestation of the observance of good faith. See *Rand Rietfontein Estates Ltd* v. *Cohn*, 1937 AD 317 at 330–1 per De Wet JA, quoting with approval J.W. Wessels, *The Law of Contract in South Africa* (Durban, 1951), para 1974. Note also, R.H. Christie, *The Law of Contract in South Africa* (Durban, 2nd edn, 1991), 253. This last may well become the law in Scotland if the proposals of the Scottish Law Commission on interpretation of contracts are enacted. See *Report on Interpretation in Private Law*, Scot. Law Com. No. 160 (1997).

[36] See *Iscor Pension Fund* v. *Marine and Trade Insurance Co. Ltd* 1961 (1) SA 178 (T), at 185B per Roberts JA: "In some contracts parties are required to place their cards on the table to a greater extent than in others, but the determination of the extent of the disclosure does not depend on the label we choose to stick on the contact".

[37] *Pretorius* v. *Natal South Sea Investment Trust Ltd* 1965 (3) SA 410 (W), at 418A–B per Vieyra JA, quoting with approval M.A. Millner, "Fraudulent Non-Disclosure" (1957) 74 *South African Law Journal* 177, at 189.

cealment of material circumstances rests upon the presence of "involuntary reliance" by one of the contracting parties on the other for information. In any contract the prevailing circumstances may be such as to create a state of involuntary reliance and, therefore, may require disclosure of facts which it might not otherwise have been necessary to disclose.[38]

If the circumstances surrounding pre-contractual negotiations create involuntary (and justifiable) reliance by A on B, then we have a situation in which A may conclude a contract not only in reliance on the truthfulness of what B has said, but also in the trust that B has not left unsaid anything which would have influenced A's decision on whether or not to make the contract. This, of course, is exactly the premise upon which the law originally saw fit to impose a positive duty of disclosure in insurance contracts in England and Scotland. In the eighteenth century, as litigation on the vacation of policies for non-disclosure steadily increased, both the English and Scottish courts tended to the view that, in the circumstances in which insurances (particularly marine contracts) were most commonly made, it was generally the insured who knew most about the nature of the risk to be covered.[39] The insurer, in taking a business judgment as to acceptance of the risk proposed or to the appropriate premium to be levied, was necessarily reliant upon the insured not withholding vital information from him.[40] Where the undisclosed

[38] R.H. Christie, n. 35 above, 336–7.

[39] Although observance of good faith is a bilateral requirement in insurance (see, e.g., Marine Insurance Act 1906, s. 17; *Life Association of Scotland* v. *Foster*, n. 22 above), non-disclosure is rarely an issue against the insurer: cf. *Banque Financière de la Citié SA* v. *Westgate Insurance Co. Ltd* [1991] 2 AC 249. However, proposal forms employed by members of the Association of British Insurers for use by non-business customers should contain: (a) a warning to the proposer of the consequences of failure to disclose all material facts; and (b) an injunction to disclose facts if the proposer is uncertain as to their materiality: *Statement of Long-Term Insurance Practice*, 1986, s. 1(a)(i) and (ii); *Statement of General Insurance Practice*, 1986, s. 1(c)(i) and (ii). There may be no legal duty to warn proposers, but the voluntary imposition of one smacks of good faith in the sense of the observance of industry standards of fair dealing.

[40] The *locus classicus* is, of course, *Carter* v. *Boehm* (1766) 3 Burr. 1905, at 1906 per Lord Mansfield: "Insurance is a contract upon speculation; the special facts upon which the contingent chance is to be computed, lie most commonly in the knowledge of the insured only. The underwriter trusts to his representation, and proceeds upon confidence, that he does not keep back any circumstances in his knowledge to mislead the underwriters into a belief that the circumstance does not exist, and to induce him to estimate the risque, as if it did not exist". The earliest writers in Scotland to deal fully with insurance also viewed the contract as one-sided: see G. Campbell H. Paton (ed.), *Baron Hume's Lectures 1786–1822* (Edinburgh, 1952), Stair Society, vol. 15, Appendix A, "Contract of Insurance" 310–402; John Millar (jnr), *Elements of the Law Relating to Insurances* (Edinburgh, 1787), *passim*.

facts were such that the insurer ought to have known about these (in other words where reliance upon the insured was unjustified), the contract would be enforced.[41] Otherwise, the position adopted in a line of decisions can be summarised as follows:

> [T]he case of the underwriters is, in all situations, to be viewed in a favourable light; that comparatively few of the circumstances which are known to the owner [of a ship] can be known to [the underwriter]; and, consequently, that in entering into this contract, while the insured can practise many frauds upon the underwriter, he can scarcely ever deceive the insured. . . . [I]f the owner should presume to be the judge of what is material to the risk, the underwriter would probably seldom have the real circumstances for estimating the risk explained to him.[42]

I would argue that by imposing a positive duty of disclosure in the case of insurance the law was, in this earlier period, stipulating that a valid contract was predicated upon a principle of good faith. That is certainly how Lord Mansfield saw it. And in the tenth edition of Bell's *Principles*, published in 1899, despite Lord President Inglis' description of insurance as requiring utmost good faith, the contract was stated to be simply one of "good faith, in which the insurer . . . greatly relies on the . . . insured" neither to misrepresent nor conceal material information.[43] Even innocent concealment transgresses the requirement for good faith here, because, regardless of the motive for the non-disclosure, the insurer can still only trust in the totality of the information which he has been asked to believe in and on the basis of which he will have to decide whether or not to contract. Our courts have, however, over the years manoeuvred themselves into the position of accepting an unsatisfactory rationale for the existence of the duty of disclosure in insurance contracts, namely the concept of utmost good faith. They have also adopted a labelling approach: insurance is a contract of utmost good faith, cautionary obligations are not *uberrimae fidei*; therefore in the former nothing material may be concealed, while in the latter it may be. However, recent development in the law of cautionary obligations has had the wholly beneficial consequence of compelling Scots lawyers to reconsider their attitude to good faith generally.

---

[41] *Thomson* v. *Buchanan* (1781) Mor 7085, affirmed on this point in (1782) 2 Pat 592 (HL). The current position is articulated by s. 18(3)(b), Marine Insurance Act 1906.

[42] *Allan and Others* v. *Young, Ross, Richardson and Co.* (1803) Mor 7092, at 7094. In this case the insured was a merchant located in St. Petersburg and the insurer was based in Edinburgh. Note *also Stewart* v. *Morrison* (1779) Mor 7080; *Thomson* v. *Buchanan*, n. 41 above ; *Keay* v. *Young* (1783) Mor 7088; *Scougal* v. *Young* (1798) Mor 7091.

[43] Bell, *Principles* (Edinburgh, 10th edn), para 474.

Cautionary Obligations and the Principle of Good Faith

Despite the fact that both insurance contracts and cautionary obliga-tions[44] are concerned with the allocation of risk, the latter have tended to be viewed as the very antithesis of insurance. If insurance contracts were conceived of as *uberrimae fidei*, in cautionary obligations there was:

> "no universal obligation on the creditor to make disclosure of the whole state of matters to the proposed cautioner; in other words, guarantee is not, like insurance, a contract *uberrimae fidei* where full disclosure is required on the part of one of the contracting parties".[45]

Leaving aside the unfortunate classification of some contracts as being of the utmost good faith, this statement is unobjectionable so long as it is understood to state the exception to a general rule and not the gen-eral rule itself. Indeed, the same text prefaces the above comment with the statement:

> In the constitution of guarantees, it is a general rule, applicable to all the spe-cial forms which the contract may take, that there must, at entering into the engagement, be perfect fairness of representation so far as the creditor is con-cerned; otherwise the cautioner is free.[46]

So in the case of a bank which seeks an undertaking from a third party in support of a request for some credit facility by a customer, the bank is under no duty to disclose to the proposed cautioner the financial standing of its customer as reflected in its accounts:

> There can be no ground of complaint because of concealment by the bank-agent, for nothing is better settled than this, that a bank-agent is entitled to assume that the cautioner has informed himself upon the various matters material to the obligation he is about to undertake. The agent is not bound to volunteer any information or statement as to the accounts, although if information be asked he is bound to give it, and give it truthfully.[47]

---

[44] *Anglice* "suretyship".

[45] W.M. Gloag, J.M. Irvine, *Law of Rights in Security Heritable and Moveable Including Cautionary Obligations* (Edinburgh, 1897), 706.

[46] *Ibid.* Note also Bell, *Principles*, para 251.

[47] *Young* v. *Clydesdale Bank Ltd* (1889) 17 R 231, at 244 per Lord Shand. To like effect were Lord Adam at 240 and Lord President Inglis at 247–8. Note also, *Royal Bank of Scotland* v. *Greenshields* 1914 SC 259, at 266–7 per Lord President Strathclyde: "The bank-agent is entitled to assume that an intending guarantor has made himself fully acquainted with the financial position of the customer whose debt he is about to

It is different, however, where it becomes clear to the banker that the proposed cautioner is obviously proceeding under some error regarding the state of the customer's accounts.[48] And should it become obvious to the bank that its customer has practised fraud in order to secure the cautioner's consent, then, once again, it must voice its concern to the latter.[49] Quite clearly the bank must not misrepresent such information as it does make available to the proposed cautioner, but nor can it snatch at a bad bargain either.[50] Consequently, the law has adopted a position which prohibits the exploitation of an unfair advantage possessed by the creditor. Where a bank possesses information regarding an increased and unexpected risk to the potential cautioner which the latter cannot reasonably be expected to discover for himself, then, if the bank does not reveal what it knows, the cautioner may be liberated from his obligation.[51] Suppose, for example, that in order to ensure repayment of a loan the creditor, in connivance with the principal debtor, disguises the loan figure as part of the price of goods sold to the debtor, repayment of the price of which is supported by a cautionary obligation.[52] It is one thing to say that the cautioner can expect to be held liable if the buyer defaults in payment for the goods, but it would be quite unreasonable to expect him to be liable to support the buyer's other debts to the seller.

Those situations in which a creditor is required to make disclosure to an intending cautioner are clearly rooted, as the general rule stated by Gloag and Irvine makes plain, in a requirement of "fairness" or, as I think one may legitimately designate it, "good faith". It may also be suggested that what appear, superficially, to be different reasons for requiring disclosure to be made by the creditor are not truly so. Where the creditor actively misrepresents the true situation to the cautioner, the latter's reliance thereon liberates him from the obligation. But this

guarantee. And the bank-agent is not bound to make any disclosure whatever regarding the customer's indebtedness to the bank".

[48] *Royal Bank of Scotland* v. *Greenshields*, n. 47 above, at 268, per Lord President Strathclyde: "The only circumstance in which I can conceive that a duty of disclosure would emerge and a failure to disclose would be fatal to the Bank's case, would be where a customer put a question or made an observation in the presence and hearing of the bank-agent which necessarily and inevitably would lead anyone to the conclusion that the intending guarantor was labouring under a misapprehension with regard to the customer's indebtedness".

[49] Gloag and Irvine, n. 45 above, 712–13, citing in support *Owen and Gutch* v. *Homan* (1853) 20 LJ Ch 323; 4 HLC 997.

[50] *Young* v. *Clydesdale Bank Ltd*, n. 47 above; Gloag and Irvine, n. 45 above, 708.

[51] Gloag and Irvine, n. 45 above, 709.

[52] The example is based on Gloag and Irvine, n. 45 above , 709.

should also be the case where the creditor is in possession of unexpected, material information because this creates a situation in which the cautioner is now involuntarily reliant on the creditor's probity. The undisclosed fact is not one which the cautioner can discover from any source other than the creditor or the principal debtor. Business may well be about the taking of calculated risks, and there is no duty to look after the interests of people who can (but do not choose to) do so for themselves. But in the situation under discussion, it runs counter to any notion of business morality to allow the creditor to exploit his advantage.[53] Consequently, while it has never I think been expressed in this way, I would suggest that when one looks at a situation in which the cautioner seeks liberation on the ground that the creditor ought to have disclosed certain information to him or her, then what makes the crucial difference between the application of the general rule of good faith to their dealings, or the exceptional rule that the creditor was under no duty to disclose that information and, in consequence, good faith is not infringed, is the presence or absence of involuntary and justifiable reliance on the creditor's non-disclosure. The justification for the exceptional rule, that the bank is not under a duty to disclose the state of its customers' accounts, is based on the duty of confidentiality owed by the banks to their clients.[54] In the course of its dealings with customers the bank will become privy to their personal financial details which they may not wish to enter the public domain. In some cases the bank will have no option but to disclose these details if asked to do so, but compulsion apart,[55] disclosure may only be made with the consent of the customer. If it were otherwise, there would be nothing to prevent disclosure to a business or trade rival (or any inquisitive person) who misrepresents that has been asked to act as cautioner by the customer to whose accounts access is sought.[56] The objective of concealment (or of confidentiality) here is benign, since it protects customers from the adverse

---

[53] On business morality see P.D. Finn, "Commerce, the Common Law and Morality" (1989) 17 *Melbourne University Law Review* 87.

[54] *Tournier* v. *National Provincial and Union Bank of England* [1924] 1 KB 461: *Parry-Jones* v. *Law Society* [1969] 1 Ch 1.

[55] For discussion of the circumstances in which a bank must make disclosure, see L.D. Crerar, *The Law of Banking in Scotland* (Edinburgh, 1997), 108–14.

[56] Neither *Young* v. *Clydesdale Bank Ltd* nor *Royal Bank of Scotland* v. *Greenshields*, n. 47 above, advances an adequate explanation for the rule against disclosure. However, this is dealt with quite fully in *Hamilton* v. *Watson* (1842) 5 D 280; affirmed in (1845) 4 Bell's App 67. Note in particular, Lord Medwyn at 290: "It is easy to see how easy it would be for anyone who would wish to obtain information as to the credit and dealings of a trader, to pretend that he was a cautioner for him, and the disclosure might be most prejudicial".

consequences of unwarranted disclosure while simultaneously protecting the bank against claims for such disclosure. Here the law and what
constitutes "good banking practice" have become congruent.[57] And
since all that the potential cautioner has to do in order to eliminate the
risk of guaranteeing a bad debt is to ask the debtor to authorise his bank
to provide him with the full details of his bank accounts, the latter cannot be adjudged to be in bad faith when it acts in compliance.
Cautioners cannot found on non-disclosure by banks where the latter are
under an obligation not to disclose. Reliance on disclosure by the bank
is unjustified where the cautioner has the means to discover the facts.
This is not, however, to argue that financial disclosure is the only manifestation of good faith in the particular context of personally secured
lending by Scottish banks. If good faith is an operational principle which
underpins the enforceability of cautionary obligations, it must then follow that its operation cannot necessarily be confined solely to the issue
of non-disclosure or concealment. Recent developments would seem to
confirm this.

In *Smith* v. *Bank of Scotland*,[58] reversing the decisions of both the
Outer and Inner Houses of the Court of Session,[59] the House of Lords
determined that there are circumstances in which a bank is under a duty
to advise a prospective cautioner to seek independent advice before
undertaking to guarantee repayment of any credit facility which the
bank might advance to its customer against that guarantee. Perhaps the
decision simply came at a bad time for Scots lawyers still smarting from
another decision of the House which has been seen as altering the law
(unwisely) on the passing of ownership of heritable property.[60] At any
rate, the decision has attracted largely adverse criticism.[61] To some

[57] The Preface to the Bank of Scotland's *Code of Banking Practice* (1994) declares that
its contents represent good banking practice and para, 8.1 sets out the Bank's observance
of the duty of confidentiality and the exceptions thereto. In its 1994 code of practice, *Good
Banking*, the British Bankers' Association did likewise and continued to do so (para 4.1)
in its 1997 replacement, *The Banking Code*. The 1998 revision of *The Banking Code*, which
came into effect on 31 March 1999 gives the same commitment and undertaking. In
Mumford and Smith v. *Bank of Scotland* 1995 SCLR 839 the Inner House disregarded the
provision of the then current version of the B.B.A. code of practice, to the effect that
banks had a duty to warn intending guarantors to take independent advice, because, it was
said, the law imposed no duty to that effect on creditors: Lord President Hope at 849B-
C.
[58] 1997 SC (HL) 111.
[59] 1994 SCLR 856 and 1995 SCLR 839 respectively.
[60] *Sharp* v. *Thomson* 1997 SC (HL) 66.
[61] See n. 18 above. Gretton in particular castigates the decision as representing judicial
legislation and one in which the ratio is difficult to find.

extent it was the (surely unavoidable) linkage with an English decision on similar facts, *Barclays Bank plc* v. *O'Brien*,[62] that fed critics with ammunition, and it is undoubtedly correct that this last case is clearly incompatible with existing principles of Scots law in several respects.[63] However, on policy grounds there is no reason why the position of an English surety should be better protected than that of a Scottish guarantor and on that basis alone the decision has much to commend it. Moreover, it would be a curious and unfortunate rule of law which sought to deprive cautioners of a protection which banks themselves consider it good practice to observe.[64] For present purposes, however, we need only concentrate on that portion of the leading judgment,[65] that of Lord Clyde, pertaining to good faith and which reads:

> [I]t seems to me preferable to recognise the element of good faith which is required of the creditor on the constitution of a contract of cautionry and find there a proper basis for decision. The law already recognises . . . that there may arise a duty of disclosure to a potential cautioner in certain circumstances. As a part of that same good faith which lies behind that duty it seems to me reasonable to accept that there should also be a duty in particular circumstances to give the potential cautioner certain advice. Thus in circumstances where the creditor should reasonably suspect that there may be factors bearing on the participation of the cautioner which might undermine the validity of the contract through his or her intimate relationship with the debtor, the duty would arise and would have to be fulfilled if the creditor is not to be prevented from later enforcing the contract.[66]

This approach is overtly predicated upon the view that Scots law recognises good faith as a principle which underwrites our law of contract.[67] It has, however, been objected that one of the two cases relied

---

[62] [1994] 1 AC 180. McKendrick, "The Undue Influence of English Law" in H.L. MacQueen (ed.), *Scots Law into the 21st Century* (Edinburgh, 1996), 214.

[63] Although as Dickson, n. 18 above, 41, points out, the principles upon which *Barclays Bank* v. *O'Brien* were decided were not applied in *Smith* v. *Bank of Scotland*. For a comparison, see McKendrick, n. 62, above.

[64] The British Bankers' Association's 1994 code of practice, n. 57 above, (para 14.1) required banks to advise "private individuals" who had been asked to act as guarantors, to obtain independent legal advice before agreeing to do so. The 1997 code of practice (para 3.14) enlarged this obligation by emphasising that the purpose of taking such advice is to ensure that the prospective guarantor understands the possible consequences of acting as such. The 1998 code of practice (para 3.14) does the same.

[65] Which, *pace* Gretton, does contain the ratio which is said to be so elusive: cf., Dickson, n. 18 above, at 42.

[66] At 121E-G.

[67] At 121B-C.

on by Lord Clyde (*Rodger* (*Builders*) *Ltd* v. *Fawdry*)[68] in support of this
contention is not only an "isolated authority" but also a case dealing
with the sale of land.[69] This ignores, however, the significance of the
second of the cases (*Trade Development Bank* v. *David W. Haig* (*Bellshill*)
Ltd)[70] prayed in aid by the judge: where the First Division were
unequivocally of the opinion that *Rodger* (*Builders*) *Ltd* v. *Fawdry*
"rested upon the broad principle in the field of contract of fair dealing
in good faith".[71] The objection also ignores other judicial articulations
to the same effect.[72] Perhaps what lies (implicitly) at the root of the
unease felt here is the very real issue of how good faith is to be tested.
In property cases, for example, where the problem relates to title, good
faith is assessed on a subjective rather than objective perception of
knowledge:[73] what the Uniform Commercial Code (UCC), for example,
terms "honesty in fact".[74] In the case of commercial contracts, however,
an objective standard, such as "the observance of reasonable commercial
standards of fair dealing",[75] would seem preferable on purely linguistic
grounds. Indeed the application of an objective standard is consistent
with *Smith* v. *Bank of Scotland*, where it was not argued that the bank
actually knew that the cautioner's consent had been obtained by her husband's misrepresentation, but rather that it ought to have realised that
the wife of the principal debtor would rely on her husband to take financial decisions, and that it ought, therefore, to have advised (or warned)
her to take independent legal advice before assuming liability as a cautioner. These warnings would have been consistent with the observation
of reasonable commercial standards. Perhaps it would have been neater
to have defined good faith in both subjective and objective senses, as do
both the UNIDROIT *Principles of International Commercial Contracts*
and the *Principles of European Contract Law*,[76] but no damage is done to
the principle of good faith by accepting that it may be assessed by different standards in different contexts.

[68] 1950 SC 483.
[69] Macgregor, n. 18 above, 92.
[70] 1983 SLT 510.
[71] At 517 per Lord President Emslie and noted by Lord Clyde at 121B-C. Note also
the supportive comments in *Steel* v. *Bradley Homes* (*Scotland*) *Ltd* 1974 SLT 133 and
Angus v. *Bryden* 1992 SLT 884.
[72] See the cases cited in notes 13, 14 and 71 above.
[73] See K. Reid, *The Law of Property in Scotland* (Edinburgh, 1996), para 137.
[74] UCC ss 1–201(19); 3–103(a)(4).
[75] UCC ss 2–103(1)(b); 3–103(a)(4).
[76] See arts 1.7 and 1.106 respectively.

Lord Clyde's judgment starts with the propositions that (a) there is a general duty of disclosure imposed on creditors vis-à-vis prospective cautioners in certain contexts, which, as I have suggested, is demonstrably correct, and (b) that this duty is grounded on a requirement of good faith. But if good faith requires disclosure in some situations, so this line of reasoning is continued, then might it not be reasonable to suppose that it can also assume the shape of other duties? Where, for instance, the proposed cautioner is emotionally involved with the principal debtor is it entirely unreasonable to suspect that the cautioner's will may have been prevailed upon by virtue of that relationship?[77] The perspective suggested here is the objective one of the reasonable person. If that paradigm would consider that "owing to the personal relationship between the debtor and the proposed cautioner the latter's consent may not be fully informed or freely given",[78] then it is surely unobjectionable to require the bank to warn the cautioner of the possible adverse consequences of guaranteeing his or her partner's debts and to advise him or her to take independent advice before so doing. Nor should it be thought objectionable to predicate these duties, in these circumstances, upon a principle of good faith and fair dealing. There is no crude abrogation here of the principle which justifies the bank in not, on its own initiative, disclosing to the cautioner the state of a customer's financial affairs. Indeed, there is no extension here of the duty of "disclosure" (at least in any meaningful sense of that word) at all. *Smith* v. *Bank of Scotland* recognises three crucial things in relation to cautionary obligations: (1) that these are obligations *bonae fidei*; (2) that good faith manifests itself by imposing a disclosure duty in most situations; and (3) that good faith also manifests itself through the requirement in appropriate cases of a duty to warn. One can only disclose that which one knows. About one's suspicions or concerns, however, one can only give warning. But although we can observe here good faith being manifested in two ways, the latter manifestation shares a common basis with the former, namely, involuntary reliance. What *Smith* v. *Bank of Scotland* does not do, however, is explain why it is that this reliance is justified.

Consider the circumstances in which a cautionary undertaking may be given. Creditor, debtor, and cautioner may all be experienced

---

[77] Emotion rather than gender is a more suitable premise for the recognition of a duty to warn or to give advice. See M. Kaye, "Equity's Treatment of Sexually Transmitted Debt" (1997) *Feminist Legal Studies* 35. It was recognised in *Smith* that emotional relationships need not be confined to those of husband and wife.

[78] At 12IH-I.

business parties for whom dealing at arm's length is the golden rule. Here the prospective cautioner may need convincing before risking his money. The cautioner can also be expected to appreciate that it is safest first to ascertain the facts about the debtor's financial affairs before giving an undertaking in financial support of the debtor. This may be contrasted with the situation where a spouse, partner, or lover is asked to stand caution. Although hard-headedness in a social companion cannot be ruled out, it is not unreasonable to surmise that a cautioner, in these circumstances, may act as such out of considerations of love, loyalty, or perhaps even on a misplaced belief that gender difference dictates that one sex should handle the family's business affairs and finances and the other its domestic arrangements. Nor is it unreasonable to think that banks, with a wealth of lending experience to draw upon, cannot appreciate that these two situations are very different and, further, that in the second there is always the possibility that the cautioner's consent was not "fully informed or freely given". But we do not have to speculate about these matters for there is concrete evidence, in the shape of *The Banking Code* that banks appreciate the risks run by non-business customers asked to stand caution. Consequently, it is articulated as an article of best banking practice that potential guarantors must be warned about their exposure to liability if they act as such and that they must also be encouraged to seek independent legal advice.[79] The banks also appreciate that emotionally connected cautioners are unlikely to know that they can access confidential information regarding a debtor's finances by asking that debtor to waive confidentiality. As a result of this awareness *The Banking Code* empowers banks to ask customers to waive their right to confidentiality and consent to the disclosure of their financial affairs to either the potential cautioner or to his or her legal adviser.[80] In the light of what constitutes best banking practice therefore, the banks' own perception of failure to encourage the taking of independent legal advice[81] is that this constitutes the taking of an unfair advantage in certain circumstances. Those circumstances exist where the

---

[79] para 3.14 of the 1998 code, replicating para 3.14 of the 1997 version. In addition to an oral warning, all relevant documents should also encourage the taking of independent legal advice.

[80] The possibility of requesting customers to consent to disclosure was introduced by the 1997 code of practice. See now para 3.14 of the 1998 code.

[81] That advice would almost certainly be that the cautioner should not jeopardise the family home or his or her personal savings without knowledge of the true state of the other partner's finances.

cautioner must rely on the bank to appreciate his or her vulnerability and to take the appropriate action.

The observance of good faith in the formation of insurance contracts is, as already noted, a mutual or bilateral duty, and non-disclosure may be pleaded against the insurer as well as the insured.[82] The bilateral nature of the principle, however, is a point which was overlooked in a recently reported Outer House decision which critics of good faith have happily seized on.[83]

In *Braithwaite* v. *Bank of Scotland*,[84] part of the pursuer's case for reduction of the obligation contained in a letter of pledge which she had granted in support of an addition to her husband's overdraft, was that the defenders had failed in their duty to warn of the consequences of her actions and to advise her to seek independent advice. These failures, it was argued, put the defenders in bad faith. The matter turned on the passage from Lord Clyde's speech in *Smith* v. *Bank of Scotland* which was examined above.[85] The defenders' argument, and the one which found favour with the Lord Ordinary (Hamilton), was that the passage proceeded "on the assumption that some vitiating factors (undue influence, misrepresentation or otherwise) had in fact occurred and had induced the pursuer to act to her disadvantage".[86] In *Smith*, good faith was said to be "used in the sense that a party may not be entitled to enforce his apparent rights because he is aware of or is put on inquiry to discover some prior vitiating factor".[87] With respect, this restricted interpretation of what was said in *Smith* v. *Bank of Scotland* does not appear to be justified. What activates the duty is a situation which should generate a reasonable *suspicion* (not an actual *awareness*) that the cautioner's consent to act may have been obtained by potentially vitiating means. *Smith*, on a true reading, invokes a duty to warn, etc., despite absence of misrepresentation or undue influence.

One can nevertheless understand the concern which lies at the heart of the judgment in *Braithwaite* v. *Bank of Scotland*. Should a cautioner be allowed to evade her or his responsibility simply by pleading the bank's failure to warn or to give the necessary advice when, in fact, no substantive grounds exist for setting the contract aside? To permit this

---

[82] See n. 39 above.

[83] Professor Thompson, in this volume, sees the decision as restricting the application of the principle.

[84] 1999 SLT 25.

[85] See n. 66, particularly the portion at 121F.

[86] At 32L.

[87] At 33B–C.

would allow the cautioner a technical defence but one without real merit.[88] But this is to view good faith as a unilateral obligation, incumbent on only the creditor in a cautionary obligation, when it is really a bilateral obligation incumbent on the cautioner as well. The purpose of the bank's duty is to warn against possible misconduct by the principal debtor, and, if there is no misconduct, then no harm has been caused by the breach. Consequently, a cautioner who points to the breach is, in effect, seeking to use this as a means of escape from an economically disadvantageous transaction. That, it is submitted, puts the cautioner in bad faith and does not justify the reduction of the cautionary obligation.

Good Faith Beyond Insurance and Caution?

This essay has argued that in contracts of insurance and cautionary obligations it is good faith which imposes a requirement of disclosure or some analogue. It has also argued that good faith, in these contexts, is explicable in terms of justifiable reliance by one party on the knowledge of the other. There is no good reason to believe, however, that good faith should only apply to contracts of insurance and caution, that its role is exclusively interstitial rather than pervasively fundamental. Indeed, once the relevance of good faith is acknowledged in the particular, there is a logical imperative that its relevance to contracts generally should be accepted. Moreover, there is not the dearth of Scottish support for this view as some might suggest. Writing on insurance towards the end of the eighteenth century, John Millar (junior) recognised the general principle when he wrote: "material concealment vitiates all contracts upon principles of natural law",[89] and his observation that insurance "imposes mutual confidence and good faith *in a particular degree*"[90] serves to emphasise that view. And Bell is not to be confined merely to recognition of insurance contracts as being *bonae fidei*, but is equally supportive of the view that, in certain circumstances, a positive duty of disclosure (an aspect of the observance of good faith) is incumbent on parties to all contracts:

---

[88] Though it may be observed that in insurance such a technical defence would be acceptable. Thus non-disclosure of a material fact will justify the insurer avoiding the contract even though there is no nexus between the undisclosed fact and the actual cause of harm or loss to the insured. If the role of good faith were properly recognised and applied in insurance then such anomalies would disappear.

[89] John Millar, *Elements of the Law Relating to Insurances* (Edinburgh, 1787), 59.

[90] *Ibid.*, 39–40. Emphasis added.

Concealment of circumstances may often as strongly deceive a purchaser as the most express misrepresentation. But it is not every concealment which will taint a contract . . . Where the circumstances left untold are such as the purchaser ought to know, or easily may become acquainted with, and for information regarding which he has no occasion to rely upon the other contracting party, concealment will not be held to injure the contract. But whenever the circumstances are of a secret nature, or such as a purchaser does not usually or naturally think of inquiring into, or which he can learn only from the seller's information, the concealment is a fraud; and if that concealment has given birth to the contract, it will annul it.[91]

What has happened is that the existence of a general principle, which had crystallised by the mid-nineteenth century, came to be increasingly misunderstood as that century continued. *Broatch* v. *Jenkins*,[92] for example, stands for the principle that concealment cannot be an issue where there is no duty to disclose. But all that this requires us to accept is that in some *circumstances* there will be a duty to reveal what one knows and in others there will not. The decision does not, however, support the contention that such a duty exists in the case of some *contracts* but not others.[93] That is a misconception which has led to the present position of designating certain contracts as being *uberrimae fidei* with all that this flawed concept is thought to entail.

A substratum of good faith continues, however, to pervade the Scots law of contract. It is true that the courts have not always recognised that they are applying the principle, and they have not always applied it consistently (indeed, they may sometimes be reluctant to apply it at all), but there are decisions which can only be satisfactorily explained in terms of the observance of good faith. Where, for example, one party to a contract for the sale of land realises that the other is acting under an error regarding one of the burdens over the property, he or she acts in bad faith and exploits an unfair advantage by not disclosing that error to the other party.[94] And if a claim lies for reimbursement of expenses, incurred in reliance on an *implied* assurance, not a misrepresentation,

---

[92] (1866) 4 M 1030.

[93] W.W. McBryde, n. 5 above, paras 10.35–10.36.

[94] See *Steuart's Trs* v. *Hart* (1875) 3 R 192 which was recognised as binding in *Angus* v. *Bryden* 1992 SLT 884. This last overtly recognises the situation in the text as turning on good faith. However, doubt was cast on *Steuart's Trs* v. *Hart* in *Brooker-Simpson Ltd* v. *Duncan Logan* (*Builders*) *Ltd* 1969 SLT 304 and *Spook Erection* (*Northern*) *Ltd* v. *Kaye* 1990 SLT 676. *Steuart's Trs* v. *Hart* remains, however, the decision of a court of authority.

that a contract exists, that remedy would rest on an application of the principle of good faith.[95]

Recognition of the role of good faith is not, however, to be limited to episodic judicial pronouncements. Good faith, as reflective of business morality, in the sense of best practice or fair dealing, is a norm lying at the very heart of banking and insurance business as reflected in *The Banking Code* (1998) and the *Statement of Long-Term Insurance Practice* and the *Statement of General Insurance Practice* (1986). In the case of insurance, the law recognised from a fairly early stage that the information dice were heavily loaded against insurers.[96] More recently, however, it is the insurance industry which has accepted that non-business proposers may not always appreciate the effect of non-disclosure and, therefore, that it is good insurance practice for proposal forms to warn of the consequences. The requirement in successive editions of *The Banking Code* since 1992, that potential cautioners must be warned of the risks which they may run and advised to take independent legal advice, is equally reflective of a desire to do business in a fair way. What the House of Lords did in *Smith* v. *Bank of Scotland* was to restore a necessary equilibrium between the law and banking business practice. One may of course object that the insurance and banking codes of practice apply only to parties dealing with the providers of these services in a private capacity and are, therefore, in common with the Unfair Contract Terms Act 1977 and the Unfair Terms in Consumer Contracts Regulations 1994,[97] consumer protection measures reflecting a departure from the commercial norm of permitting parties to contract on whatever terms they can impose. In a strictly commercial context, therefore, good faith may be viewed as a destabilising factor, a random element to be plucked out of the air by someone who, from a self-perspective, has made a bad bargain. It would indeed be unfortunate if loosely articulated concerns about fairness were to violate the important requirement that the outcome of arm's length negotiations between business parties should not be subjected to an unacceptable degree of uncertainty. Consequently, there is no shortage of expressions of misgivings or hostility to the subjection of commercial contracts to a requirement of good

---

[95] In *Dawson International plc* v. *Coats Paton plc* 1988 SLT 854, affirmed 1989 SLT 655 (merger negotiations), and *Bank of Scotland* v. *3i plc* 1990 SC 215 (loan), this possibility was not ruled out.

[96] See R. Hasson, "The Doctrine of Uberrima Fides in Insurance Law—A Critical Evaluation" (1969) 32 *Modern Law Review* 615; A.D.M. Forte, "Marine Insurance and Risk Distribution in Scotland before 1800" (1987) 5 *Law and History Review* 393.

[97] SI 1994/3159.

faith.[98] For example, an obligation to negotiate in good faith has been described as being "inherently repugnant to the adversarial position of the parties when involved in negotiations",[99] and "cunning, craft, and even deceit" have been judicially acknowledged as part of commercial life.[100] In relation to priority conflicts between secured creditors, a leading work on the Uniform Commercial Code, has criticised the application, of general principle of good faith in equally vehement tones:

> Better to leave an occasional widow penniless by the harsh application of the law than to disrupt thousands of other transactions by injecting uncertainty and by encouraging swarms of potential litigants . . . to challenge what would otherwise be clear and fair rules. . . . The courts should not believe that they serve society by taking in pitiful strays such as good faith, estoppel, and the equitable lien, for these strays carry the lice that will infest us all.[101]

Strong words indeed—though not all judges think this way. It has, for instance, been suggested that even in the purely commercial context there must be limits to the pursuit of "self-interested or exploitative conduct".[102] And Lord Steyn has expressed reservations about Lord Ackner's too ready dismissal of the concept of good faith.[103] Moreover, if good faith is so abhorrent and unworkable a principle, one is surely entitled to the observation that it is curious that it should have found its way into both the Restatement of Contracts (2nd)[104] and the Uniform Commercial Code[105] in the United States, as well as into the 1994 UNIDROIT *Principles of International Commercial Contracts*[106] and the

---

[98] For a trenchant rejection of the need for a doctrine of good faith, see Bridge, in Brownsword *et al*, n. 17 above.

[99] *Walford* v. *Miles* [1992] 2 AC 128, at 138 per Lord Ackner.

[100] *Gillespie* v. *Russell & Son* (1856) 18 D 677, at 686 per Lord Curriehill.

[101] J.J. White, R.S. Summers, *Uniform Commercial Code* (St. Paul, 4th edn, 1995), 895. The passage quoted, however, represents the view of only one of the authors. Summers' attitude to good faith is more positive: Summers, "Good Faith in General Contract Law and the Sales Provisions of the Uniform Commercial Code" (1968) 54 *Virginia Law Review* 195.

[102] P.D. Finn, "The Fiduciary Principle" in T.G. Youdan (ed.), *Equity, Fiduciaries and Trusts* (Toronto, Calgary, Vancouver, 1989), 1, at 4.

[103] J. Steyn, "Contract Law: Fulfilling the Reasonable Expectations of Honest Men" (1997) 113 *Law Quarterly Review* 433, 439. Note also the comments made by McKendrick in this volume regarding *Re Debtors* (*Nos 4499 and 4450 of 1988*) [1999] 1 All ER 149.

[104] Section 205.

[105] Section 1–203: "[E]very contract or duty within this act imposes an obligation of good faith in its performance or enforcement". "Good faith" is defined (s. 1–201(19) as "honesty in fact in the conduct or transaction concerned". In the context of sales, however, in addition to honesty in fact, good faith also requires "the observance of reasonable commercial standards of fair dealing in the trade" (s. 2–103).

Principles of European Contract Law.[107] Furthermore, if codes of practice can set standards of behaviour for carrying out business in a consumer context, then why should there not be discernible standards
reflecting good faith or its cognate, fair dealing, in a strictly commercial
context? In the context of sales, section 2–103 of the UCC requires, in
addition to "honesty in fact", the "observance of reasonable commercial
standards of fair dealing in the trade", and it is interesting to note that
recent additions and revisions to the UCC have also sought to define
good faith not only in terms of honesty but also in terms of fair dealing.[108]

The bully boy approach to the making of commercial contracts, which
appears to have found favour with Lord Ackner, and in which anything
short of misrepresentation is to be viewed as legitimate, is a grotesque
parody. There is no reason to believe that business morality would
not perceive the distinction between the situation where A exploits B's
ignorance of information which B might easily have discovered and
that where B cannot know what A does. Moreover, not all commercial
transactions give both parties equal room to manoeuvre to their best
advantage during the pre-contractual phase. Bargaining power is never
inherently equal and may be sufficiently one-sided to justify intervention in the enforcement of particular terms in the resulting contract.[109]
If codes of practice address problems faced by persons acting in a private capacity, it does not follow that those problems may not also be
faced by businesses.[110] In fact the law is already peppered with specific
examples of the application of good faith in a business-to-business context. The reciprocal nature of the duty of disclosure in insurance transactions, for example, is recognised and occasionally arises an issue
against insurers.[111] Good faith lies at the heart of the disclosure requirement in the Marine Insurance Act 1906 which was specifically drafted

---

[106] Articles 1.7 and 2.15

[107] Article 1.106. Note also art. 2.117.

[108] The new provisions are ss 2A (leases) and 4A (electronic transfers) and the revised
ones are ss 3 (negotiable instruments) and 4 (bank collections). On the matter of good faith
in the UCC, see J. Neff, "Bad Faith Breach of Contract in Consumer Transactions" in
Brownsword *et al*, n. 17 above, 115.

[109] Witness ss 3 and 17 of the Unfair Contract Terms Act 1977 dealing with exclusionary terms in standard form contracts and by virtue of which business contracts are
brought within the scope of the legislation.

[110] A point noted by the Law Commission in its criticism of the 1977 Association of
British Insurers' statements of practice. See Law Com. No. 104, *Insurance Law: Non-disclosure and Breach of Warranty*, Cmnd. 8064 (1980) para 3.29.

[111] *Banque Financière de la Cité SA* v. *Westgate Insurance Co.*, n. 39 above.

with commercial parties in mind. Good faith is also allocated a role in commercial agency[112] and informs the statutory law on sale of goods and negotiable instruments. Even the severest critics of good faith are reluctant to concede that commerce "repel[s] all notions of good faith".[113]

Good faith as a concept or as a general principle is difficult to define. Neither the UNIDROIT *Principles of International Commercial Contracts* nor the *Principles of European Contract Law* attempts to do so: although the clear identification of an objective standard, namely fair dealing, represents a good foundation for application in purely commercial transactions. But good faith is no different from other principles and absence of a definition does not deprive the concept of significance. In this essay I have argued from specific applications of good faith to the existence of a general principle which, in my view, applies to commercial transactions in Scotland. Gow described it as an "animating principle" of the law of sale. I think that Scots lawyers should be more adventurous and recognise that good faith is "like the wind; we cannot see it, but feel its force".[114] As we move into the next millennium, perhaps the greatest challenge to be faced, whether in a devolved or independent Scotland, will be to adapt our domestic law to models of commercial contract law which are not exclusively indigenous and in which good faith will play a central role.[115] And so we now face a simple choice of action. We can bury our heads in the sand and hope that good faith will go away, which it will not, or we can acknowledge its operation and, as Scots law has done in recent years with the principle of unjustified enrichment, make a start on a systematic analysis and statement of its application. If arguments of principle do not appeal as motivating factors, utilitarian ones must.

---

[112] Commercial Agents (Council Directive) Regulations 1993, SI 1993/3053. Note in particular, regs 3 and 4.

[113] Bridge, in Brownsword *et al.*, n. 17 above, 154, discussing commodities contracts and GAFTA 100.

[114] D. Cannadine, "Divine Rites of Kings" in D. Cannadine, S. Price (eds), *Rituals of Royalty, Power and Ceremonialism in Traditional Societies* (Cambridge, 1987), 1. I have substituted "good faith" for "power" in the original.

[115] I am thinking here of the resolutions of the European Parliament regarding the unification of private law in the European Union and in which contract law is singled out for specific attention: Resolution of 26 May 1989, OJEC 1989 C158/401; Resolution of 6 May 1994, OJEC 1994 C205/518. The *Principles of European Contract Law* are intended to serve "as a basis for any future European Code of Contracts": Lando and Beale, n. 20 above, xvii.

6

Good Faith in Scots Property Law

D.L. Carey Miller*

Introduction

Within the context of property, Scots law has largely inherited the civilian use of good faith as a potential "control device". In this role the question whether a party is in good faith arises in various diverse contexts concerning entitlement to property. Where the possible acquisition of a property right occurs in circumstances which are in some way exceptional, or involving some form of competition as to entitlement, it is probably to be expected that a claimant's conduct should be subject to scrutiny by reference to a norm of honest conduct. Good faith in the Scots law of property tends to be an issue in association with possession, or claims based on possession, in the context of a system of property in which possession is generally subsidiary to title. The civilian structure of Scots property law, in which the right of ownership is different in kind from the right of possession, means that good faith has potential application in disputes involving, on the one hand, a title-holder and, on the other, a possessor aspiring to title. The question of good faith may also arise between holders of personal rights in competition for acquisition of a real right: a standard instance being that of the two buyers in a double-sale situation each seeking ownership in the item of property concerned.

In different contexts distinct legal consequences follow from the circumstances of possession of a thing in good faith. This chapter will consider the role of good faith in six common law and four statutory contexts with a view to arriving at a conclusion concerning, first, the extent to which it is plausible to contend for the existence of a general

* Professor of Property Law, University of Aberdeen. I should like to thank Professor D.J. Cusine, Faculty of Law, University of Aberdeen, for commenting on an earlier draft of this essay. Responsibility for the views expressed here, however, is mine alone.

concept of good faith in Scots property law and, secondly, whether the
different forms examined are open to rational classification in any way.
Through this survey of a sample of areas of application the chapter will
seek to establish whether the operation of good faith in property can be
defined somewhat more precisely than as a "control device".

The common law situations which will be looked at are: (1) acquisition arising from a voidable title; (2) duplicated personal rights leading
to competing claims to title; (3) acquisition arising from voluntary transfer *a non domino*; (4) the role of good faith in acquisitive prescription;
(5) the role of good faith in specification; and (6) the possessor's entitlement to fruits as against the owner. The statutory contexts are: (1) sections 24 and 25 of the Sale of Goods Act 1979; (2) section 17 of the
Succession (Scotland) Act 1964; (3) section 2 of the Trusts (Scotland)
Act 1961; and (4) section 8 of the Prescription and Limitation (Scotland)
Act 1973.

In this chapter some reference will be made to South African law as
a well-developed kindred system of property, although constraints in
length preclude any systematic comparison. The focus in the various
cases considered will be upon the meaning, role and scope of the
requirement of good faith, without any attempt to set the full scene in
respect of the particular situations within which the doctrine operates.
The situations considered are all dealt with sufficiently in the relevant
authorities but good faith tends to be referred to there as a requirement
with little elaboration on or analysis of its role in the context concerned.
The position taken in the chapter will be more focused and, accepting
that good faith is admitted to play a role in context X, it will seek to
explore its meaning and operation in that particular context.

Common Law Contexts

(1) *Acquisition Arising from a Voidable Title*

Consistent with a definite priority given to recognising and protecting
the right of ownership,[1] in a manner which accords with the Civil law,
Scots law does not readily depart from the axiom that a party purporting to transfer property can convey no more than is actually held. As

---

[1] Stair, *Institutions of the Law of Scotland* (1681), II.1.28, D.M. Walker (ed.),
(Edinburgh, 1981): "The main real right is property".

Hume[2] noted, concerning one who purports to transfer ownership in the thing of another:

> [I]f he had not the property, as little can any of the after acquirers, how fair and onerous soever they be: since no one can convey a better or more ample right to another, than he has in his own person.[3]

This principle is not infringed by recognition that a transferee, having acquired on a basis giving a title which is defective only to the extent of being voidable at the instance of the transferor, is in a position, pending reduction of the voidable title, to pass a good title. What is significant for present purposes is that derivative title will only pass from a voidable title to a *bona fide* party: i.e., one unaware of the circumstances of the defect.

We may take the case of property acquired in good faith by A from B who held on a basis open to reduction at the instance of his or her transferor C: the typical case being that C's consent was induced by B's fraud thereby giving B a voidable title only.[4] In principle, pending the reduction of B's right, a purported transfer to a third party will be effective. Stair notes this consequence in the context of both land and moveable property and, in respect of the former, he states:

> to secure land-rights, and that purchasers should not be disappointed . . . no action can be effectual against them, upon the fraud of their authors, unless they were accessory thereto, at least by knowing the same when they purchased.[5]

In the same passage Stair says that purchasers of moveables are "not quarrellable upon the fraud of their authors, if they did purchase for an onerous equivalent cause".[6] According to Hume, however, the principle applies to moveables with both the requirement of good faith and payment of a price by A:

[2] G. Campbell H. Paton (ed.), *Baron Hume's Lectures 1786–1822*, (Edinburgh, 1952), Stair Society, vol. 15, 232.

[3] This is consistent with the civil law. See R. Zimmermann, *The Law of Obligations: Roman Foundations of the Civilian Tradition* (Cape Town, 1990), 279: " 'Nemo plus iuris transferre potest quam ipse haberet' (no-one can transfer a greater right than he himself has) was the rule of Roman law, and acquisition of ownership in good faith on the part of the purchaser was therefore out of the question".

[4] "Property" in *The Laws of Scotland. Stair Memorial Encyclopaedia* (Edinburgh, 1993), vol. 18, para. 601.

[5] *Institutions*, IV.40.21.

[6] *Ibid.*

If, therefore, in the mean-time, and before any challenge is moved, he shall sell and deliver the subject to another, who buys it of him, *bona fide*, and pays a price, the property must necessarily pass to this second purchaser.[7]

In the standard modern interpretation good faith is required in respect of both land and moveables. As Gordon puts it: "The fraud can be pleaded only against the person using it and if the property has been passed to a third party before the transfer is set aside it cannot be recovered except where the third party has notice".[8] In this situation it is indeed the case that notice of the defect is synonymous with an absence of good faith, and Hume is to like effect in identifying the corollary situation of a *male fide* purchaser as "one who knew the true state of the property at the time".[9]

How do we analyse the role of the requirement of good faith in the context of acquisition deriving from a voidable title? Where the transferee (A) knows that the party from whom he or she obtained the thing (B) acquired it on a fraudulent basis from C, any intention to become owner is tainted by knowledge of the fraud. In these circumstances A acquires subject to the defect affecting B, his or her transferor, and, on this basis, is also vulnerable to reduction at the instance of C, the deprived owner.

Arguably, the better view is that the result in this case is simply an instance of the operation of the abstract system[10] in terms of which ownership passes on the basis of a "real agreement":[11] a *"Realvertrag"* in Savigny's sense of "a contract relating to transfer of a thing"[12] and which is open to vices of consent[13] in the normal way.[14] In the circumstances of a transferee being aware of the defect inherent in the transferor's title he or she is simply not in a position to entertain the requisite intention to acquire an unimpeachable title: the transferee's knowledge of the defect which makes the transferor's title vulnerable to reduction in this way excludes the possibility of the former being in any better

[7] Hume, n. 2 above, 236–7.
[8] W.M. Gordon, *Stair Memorial Encyclopaedia*, n. 4 above, para. 616.
[9] Hume, n. 2 above, 234.
[10] See R. Zimmermann, "The Civil Law in European Codes" in D.L. Carey Miller, R. Zimmermann (eds), *The Civilian Tradition and Scots Law: Aberdeen Quincentenary Essays* (Berlin, 1997), 274–5. See also *Stair Memorial Encyclopaedia*, n. 4 above, paras 608–13.
[11] D.L. Carey Miller, *Corporeal Moveables in Scots Law* (Edinburgh, 1991), paras 8.06–8.10.
[12] Gordon, *Stair Memorial Encyclopaedia*, n. 4 above, para. 608. See also D.L. Carey Miller, *The Acquisition and Protection of Ownership* (Cape Town, 1986), 9.2.2.3.
[13] See *Stair Memorial Encyclopaedia*, n. 4 above, para. 614.
[14] Carey Miller, n. 11 above, para. 10.17.

position than the latter. On the other hand, when the transferee is innocent of the circumstances, his capacity to receive the thing with the intention of becoming owner is unaffected.

(2) *Duplicated Personal Rights Leading to Competing Claims to Title*

It is trite that the standard civilian format for the acquisition of property involves a preliminary contractual act, giving only a personal right, followed by an act of delivery (or conveyance) on the basis of which a real (or proprietary) right, comes into being.[15] In principle, delivery trumps (in the sense that the first party to obtain a real right defeats the holder of an existing competing personal right—even an earlier one), hence the "race to the register". The basis of this is, of course, the superiority of a real right, as a right available against the whole world, over a personal right which is only available against a particular individual. But the trumping principle does not apply where the party receiving delivery is aware of the existence of the earlier competing claim. Scots law has come to label this exception, which is based on an absence of good faith, in terms of a footballing metaphor; identifying it with what would be a scoring act were it not disallowed because execution has been tainted by culpability: i.e., the "offside goals rule".[16] As Professor Reid has shown, Stair's[17] reference to good faith as a prerequisite to the obtaining, in appropriate circumstances, of an unassailable title by a party receiving delivery "is an acknowledgement that at common law the rule against 'offside goals' applied".[18] It may be noted that in South African law[19] the same exception is prosaically designated as

[15] See W.M. Gordon, *Studies in the Transfer of Property by Traditio* (Aberdeen, 1970). See also D.L. Carey Miller, "Derivative Acquisition of Moveables" in R. Evans-Jones (ed.), *The Civilian Tradition in Scotland* (Edinburgh, 1995), 128.

[16] *Rodger (Builders) Ltd* v. *Fawdry* 1950 SC 483, at 501 per Lord Justice-Clerk Thomson: "The appellants assumed that their title would be safe once the goal of the Register House was reached. But in this branch of the law, as in football, offside goals are disallowed".

[17] *Institutions*, I.13.7.

[18] See *Stair Memorial Encyclopaedia*, n. 4 above, para. 691. Judicial authority for the rule antedates Stair by a century: see *Stirling* v. *White and Drummond* (1582) Mor 1689. The case is reported in *Morison's Dictionary* under the heading "Private Knowledge of a Prior Right".

[19] In which the various common law instances of the role of good faith in property covered in this chapter can be found. The definitive modern text is that of C.G. van der Merwe, *Sakereg* (Durban, 2nd edn, 1989). See also D.G. Kleyn, A. Boraine, *Silberberg and Schoeman's The Law of Property* (Durban, 3rd edn, 1992); Carey Miller, n. 12 above.

an application of the "the doctrine of notice" or, in Afrikaans, "*ken-nisleer*".[20]

What is the basis of the requirement of good faith in this situation? The case is distinguishable from that of a voidable obligation insofar as the transferor's right is not defective and the situation is not one in which the transferee cannot entertain an intention to acquire what he knows is not available. In this case the transferor (A) has created a situation in which a first party (B) and a second party (C) are in competition. If delivery is effected by A to C, who is aware of B's prior claim, on what basis is C precluded from acquiring? On one view C should be able to say "I am in competition with B and I am entitled to move to consolidate my position by seeking delivery before he (or she) does".[21] But Scots law, conforming to a standard civilian approach,[22] takes a more moralistic stand and holds acquisition by C to be defective and open to reduction at the instance of B by reason of being tainted by the knowledge of B's prior claim. As Stair notes, what might otherwise be unchallengeable acquisition is affected by knowledge inducing *malam fidem*, "whereby any prior disposition or assignation made to another party is certainly known" and is accordingly reducible because "the acquirer is partaker of the fraud of his author, who thereby becomes a granter of double rights".[23]

This case is distinguishable from the previous one in terms of the focus of the transferor's knowledge concerning what actually constitutes bad faith. However, the two situations are analogous in that both are concerned with receiving delivery subject to knowledge which is taken to affect the right to acquire. Arguably, the present case is also a situation in which the correct analysis is that C's defective title comes about as a consequence of the operation of the abstract system.[24] In this case, the legal basis of the act of delivery involving A and C is open to attack

---

[20] Van der Merwe, n. 19 above, 61–2.

[21] The "race to the register" label is consistent with this sort of attitude because the minimum for a race is one party competing against another who, of course, can be passive.

[22] See generally J.E. Scholtens, "Double sales" (1953) 70 *South African Law Journal* 22, who states (22, fn. 2) that although the leading Roman text (*C.* 3.32.15) "does not make distinction between the second purchaser with and without notice, the Glossators already require the good faith of the second purchaser".

[23] *Institutions*, I.14.5.

[24] Arguably, this proprietary explanation is more compelling than the suggestion that the basis is a matter of personal bar: see *Petrie* v. *Forsyth* (1874) 2 R 214, at 223, per Lord Gifford. In Reid's view, *Stair Memorial Encyclopaedia*, n. 4 above, para. 695, that is a position arrived at "not perhaps very convincingly".

at the instance of B, the basis being C's knowledge of B's prior claim to delivery. The claim is based upon B's personal right being in competition with the right granted to C, in the sense that each party has a right capable of being made real.[25] Accordingly, the fact that C was unaware of the existence of B's right at the time he or she obtained a personal right from A is irrelevant, and not a defence available to C, against B's claim. That the requirement is knowledge prior to the perfection of the right is implicit in Professor Reid's summary of the relevant requirement "either that the grantee knew of the antecedent obligation *prior to the completion of his own right* or that the grant was not for value".[26]

The case law is not wholly satisfactory in elucidating the basis upon which the rule against "offside goals" operates.[27] The standard approach in both the institutional literature and the case law is that B's remedy against C follows as a result of C's participation in the "fraud"[28] of his author (A). Stair[29] speaks of the acquirer with knowledge as being a "partaker of the fraud of his author"; similarly Lord Kinloch identifies the party who takes a right in the knowledge that the same right has already been granted to another as "an accomplice in the fraud".[30] The difficulty with this sort of analysis, however, is that it is inconsistent with the fact that C's conduct does not need to amount to participation in the fraud in any meaningful sense because mere knowledge ascertained at the last possible moment in advance of delivery will suffice to render the act of delivery ineffective.

The "not for value" aspect, it may be noted, can be explained as a matter of policy which gives priority to the party who has given value. But although the bases are surely distinct, the law recognises the same

[25] *Wallace* v. *Simmers* 1960 S.C. 255, at 259–60, per Lord President Clyde.
[26] See *Stair Memorial Encyclopaedia*, n. 4 above, para. 695: emphasis added. The analysis which focuses on the second grantee's knowledge at the time of perfection is also supported by South African authority: see the dictum of F.S. Steyn R in the Transvaal Full Bench decision in *Strydom* v. *De Lange* 1970 (2) SA 6 (T) 6, at 14: "Sou Nel geslaag het om ter goeder trou transport te neem, sou sy title onaantasbaar gewees het". This may be rendered: "Had Nel taken transfer in good faith, his title would have been unimpeachable".
[27] See, for example, *Petrie* v. *Forsyth*, n. 24 above. Note also Reid's comments, *Stair Memorial Encyclopaedia*, n. 4 above, para. 695.
[28] With the term used in the original somewhat loose moralistic sense which identified "fraud' as a state or condition equated to *mala fides* rather than as a wilful act of deceit. See T.B. Smith, *A Short Commentary on the Law of Scotland* (Edinburgh, 1962), 838–839. A difficulty, in the present context, with fraud defined in this manner is that it amounts to no more than an unhelpful metaphor for bad faith.
[29] *Institutions*, I.14.5.
[30] *Morrison* v. *Somerville* (1860) 22 D 1082, at 1089.

effect in bad faith and absence of value. On this basis the two factors, in the positive requirement role, are treated as operating in tandem[31] or, in the negative mode, are taken as equal alternative bases for an attack on the grantee's position.[32]

In double sales' cases the question of the first transferee's good faith will clearly only come into issue if raised by the thwarted party and, of course, it will be up to that party to establish that the transferee was in bad faith through knowledge of the other party's prior right. This is also true in respect of the knowledge of defective title case where the potentially active factor is bad faith through knowledge of the defect. Identifying acquisition in these cases as being subject to good faith is to do with the state of knowledge of the party in consideration, but in a passive rather than an active sense because the issue is whether the basis of delivery is defective due to the transferee's knowledge of the true circumstances. Moreover, on a more sophisticated analysis, these are simply instances of the application of the abstract system of transfer of ownership on the basis of which the act of delivery may be challenged from the point of view of a contractual defect in the "real agreement" of the parties that title should pass.

(3) *Acquisition Arising from Voluntary Transfer a non domino*

It is trite that in the context of derivative acquisition the principle *nemo plus juris ad alium transferre potest quam ipse habet*, or simply *nemo dat quod non habet* rules,[33] is subject to only a very limited class of exception.[34] The exceptions which allow title to pass despite the fact that the act of transfer is not motivated by the owner (hence the alternative label of "involuntary transfer")[35] all require that the transferee receives the

---

[31] Hume, n. 2 above, vol. 17, 317: "onerously and *bona fide*".

[32] See *Stair Memorial Encyclopaedia*, n. 4 above, para. 699: "[b]ad faith or absence of value".

[33] J.J. Gow, *The Mercantile and Industrial Law of Scotland* (Edinburgh, 1964), 118, fn. 5, regards the unabbreviated version of the *Digest* as the correct Scottish form but the truncated *nemo dat quod non habet* has come into widespread general use: e.g., see n. 4 above, where the heading to paras 669–83 is "The Rule *Nemo Dat Quod Non Habet*".

[34] While the brocards are civilian, the principle must apply on a universal basis where ownership is protected as the primary right. See D.L. Carey Miller, "Stair's Property: a Romanist System?" 1995 *Juridical Review* 70, 71.

[35] See *Stair Memorial Encyclopaedia*, n. 4 above, para. 672, and the heading, "Involuntary Transfer: Personal Bar in the Sale of Goods", to paras 680–3.

subject concerned in good faith.[36] For present purposes it is not necessary to consider the nature and scope of the common law and statutory exceptions on the basis of which ownership may pass *a non domino* in circumstances of apparent derivative acquisition: the different forms have been examined in recent works, under the alternative heads of, respectively, exceptions to *nemo dat quod non habet*[37] and exceptions to the owner's right to restitution.[38] It is submitted that the correct analysis of the role and relevance of the good faith requirement in the *a non domino* situation is the same as that urged in respect of the two cases of derivative acquisition already considered. Applying an abstract basis template, the absence of an honest belief by the transferee that property was being acquired would, perforce, negate the capacity to exercise the necessary intention to acquire ownership with possession. There is clearly a policy justification for such a result but, on a correct analysis, the rationale is principle rather than policy. To this extent the requirement of good faith would appear to be distinguishable from the requirement of onerosity: absence of the latter does not *per se* preclude a state of mind consistent with the acquisition of ownership.[39]

In the context of moveable property, it may be noted that Scots law recognises a presumption that the possessor is owner.[40] Arguably, the presumption is relevant in the present context because, although it cannot give title as such, it operates to put the possessor in as good a position as an owner by immunising against a claim by or deriving from the true owner. The presumption is rebuttable by one who can establish, first, the right of ownership and, second, that the thing concerned was parted with, removed or lost on a basis inconsistent with the transfer of ownership.[41] Good faith does not have a primary role in relation to the operation of the presumption. However, it is submitted that it necessarily has a residual role. The potential role of the good faith factor may

---

[36] See generally *Corporeal Moveables: Protection of the Onerous Bona Fide Acquirer of Another's Property*, Scot. Law Com. Memorandum No. 27 (1976).

[37] See n. 4 above, paras 680–3.

[38] Carey Miller, n. 11 above, paras 10.15–10.22. See also my general discussion in "The Owner's All-conquering Right? Scottish version" in C. Visser (ed.), *Essays in Honour of Ellison Kahn* (Cape Town, 1989), 87.

[39] It may be noted that onerosity is not a prerequisite in all the relevant cases: see Reid's treatment, n. 4 above, paras 681–2. Arguably, as a policy requirement, it is optional, while good faith, as a requirement of principle, is not.

[40] Stair, *Institutions*, III. 2. 7; Erskine, An *Institute of the Law of Scotland* (Edinburgh, 8th edn, 1871), II.1.24. For a modern account see *Stair Memorial Encyclopaedia*, n. 4 above, para. 130.

[41] Stair, *Institutions*, IV.45.17 (VIII).

be illustrated by reference to a three-party situation. A, the owner, parts
with possession by loan to B who, acting in bad faith, sells and delivers
to innocent party C. C's possession is protected by the presumption, but
it is open to A to recover the thing on proof of ownership and the fact
of the loan to B. If, however, C, being aware of A's ownership all along,
did not receive possession in good faith, it would be equally open to A
to recover on the basis of proof of B's lack of good faith.

In the presumption of ownership context good faith simply operates
as a control device, in that its absence bars the possessor from access to
the benefit of the presumption. In this case, the question of good faith
in a role in the context of acquisition on the basis of the abstract system
simply does not arise, because the situation is not one in which there is
scope for ownership to pass.[42] In the context of a property system such
as the Scottish one, which gives primacy to a right of ownership which
is different in kind from lesser proprietary rights, it is only rational to
protect the right of ownership.[43] It is suggested that, even in relation to
moveable property, the protection should at least be against loss arising
from a bad faith act.

(4) *The Role of Good Faith in Acquisitive Prescription*

Acquisitive prescription is treated here as a matter of common law principle although, of course, there was early legislation on the subject and
the only significant form in modern law is statutory.

Stair states: "because our prescription is so long, there is little question with us, *de bona fide*".[44] This cryptic statement is an allusion to the
distinction between the models of short prescription, specifically
directed towards the rectification of a defect in title, as developed in the
Roman law of *usucapio*, and the later civilian development of long pre-

---

[42] Bell, *Commentaries on the Law of Scotland in relation to Mercantile and Maritime Law,
Moveable and Heritable Rights and Bankruptcy* (Edinburgh, 7th edn), I, 305. Bell's inter-
pretation of Stair to this effect was shown by Lord McLaren to be too wide: see Carey
Miller, n. 11 above, para. 10.16.

[43] In contrast, at least as a matter of degree, to English law and the systems developed
from it. See W.W. Buckland, A.D. McNair, *Roman Law and Common Law* (Cambridge,
2nd edn, 1952), F.H. Lawson (ed.), 68–9.

[44] *Institutions*, II.12.11. While the feudal basis of landownership in Scotland remains,
all land ultimately vests in the Crown. This complicates the application of a doctrine of
good faith because a claimant to title would be assumed to recognise that, even if no one
could be identified as owner, the Crown would always have a residual right.

scription, based on the idea that it should be possible for long-standing possession "as owner" to give title.[45]

Stair prefaces his comments on the common law of Scotland with an account of the Civil law:

> As to *bona fides*, or innocent possession required in prescription, it is commonly agreed, that it is requisite at the beginning of the possession in shorter prescriptions, but that it is presumed in the longest prescription.[46]

One can see that the idea of short prescription to cure a formal defect in title should be limited by a requirement of good faith because a *usucapio* type device is a concession to the norm and, logically, the transferee's knowledge of what is required to obtain title should be a bar to any concession to failure to conform. On this basis, the requirement of good faith is only strictly necessary at the commencement of possession, because its proper role lies in supporting an intention to become owner which is objectively justifiable. In contrast, the canon law requirement of good faith throughout appears to be founded on normative rather than technically rational grounds. Stair noted this in saying that the canonist position was: "if the right of another appear" then "*in foro conscientiae* . . . the possessor is obliged to restore".[47]

Another perspective on the absence of a requirement of good faith in the Scots law of prescription is from the point of view of the absolute bar to the acquisition of stolen property, which was recognised in Roman law and came to be established in Scots law under the *vitium reale* label.[48] Stair's position,[49] regarding the Roman law rule against the acquisition of stolen property by *usucapio*, is that the circumstances of "real vitiosity", as a matter of necessary policy, rendered irrelevant the incidence of requirements for prescription, including the good faith aspect.[50] The bar made complete sense because it was unacceptable to give priority to an honest acquirer in the context of derivative acquisition (by recourse to an easy title through *usucapio*) against the owner deprived by theft. In Scots law, as a matter of principle, the *vitium reale* of theft protected an owner against acquisition by a *bona fide* subsequent

---

[45] Van der Merwe, n. 19 above, 271–3.

[46] *Institutions*, II.12.5.

[47] *Ibid.* On the canon law requirement of good faith in prescription, see R.H. Helmholz, *The Spirit of Classical Canon Law* (London, 1996), 188–89.

[48] Stair, *Institutions*, I.9.16, notes that: "Spuilzie . . . is the taking away of moveables without consent of the owner or order of law" and that "Spuilzie *inurit laben realem*, whereby the goods may be recovered from purchasers *bona fide*".

[49] *Institutions*, II.12.10.

[50] *Ibid.*

party through derivative acquisition:[51] meaning in effect that the presumption that the possessor of a moveable was its owner would be open
to rebuttal. But Scots prescription, being, at common law, based on
forty years' possession, was not subject to any bar from the point of view
of the property being stolen.[52] Its purpose was not to deal with defective title arising in the context of derivative acquisition, but simply to
accord a title on the basis of the assertion of one over a continuous
period of long possession.

Modern Scots law is consistent with the idea that good faith is irrelevant to prescription[53] as a process giving title on the basis of a long-
standing assertion of a right of ownership with associated possession. By
far the most important modern application of prescription is the device
on the basis of which an unimpeachable title to land may be acquired
by a continuous period of possession for ten years—"openly, peaceably
and without any judicial interruption"—which is founded on and follows the recording and registration of an *ex facie* valid deed in favour of
the possessor.[54] It is possibly open to argument that the reductions in
the requisite period of possession which have occurred in the development of this device[55] make the absence of any requirement of good faith
an issue. But, of course, as the device is incompatible with any requirement of good faith, the real issue is to determine, as a matter of policy,
what the period of possession should be.[56]

In the rules concerned with prescription, whether positive or negative, as well as in the more particular provisions directed at the protection of the *bona fide* purchaser, there is considerable scope for variation

[51] Stair, *Institutions*, I.9.16.

[52] Stair, *Institutions*, II.12.11. See also II.12.19: "In neither of the statutes introducing
long prescription by forty years, is there any mention or provision, concerning the manner of the entry in possession, whether it was bona fide peaceable or lawful, but only that
it have a title and continue without interruption".

[53] Regarding the purpose of positive prescription see *Scott* v. *Bruce-Stewart* (1779) 3
Ross's Leading Cases, 334, at 335 per Lord Braxfield: "It is the great purpose of prescrip-
tion to support bad titles. Good titles stand in no need of prescription". See, generally,
W.M. Gordon, *Scottish Land Law* (Edinburgh, 1989), 353–60: the dictum of Lord
Braxfied is cited at 353–4.

[54] Prescription and Limitation (Scotland) Act 1973, s. 1.

[55] Under the Prescription Act 1617 the period was 40 years. The Conveyancing
(Scotland) Act 1924 reduced the period to 20 years and the Conveyancing and Feudal
Reform (Scotland) Act 1970 substituted 10 years, this period being retained in the cur-
rent Prescription and Limitation (Scotland) Act 1973.

[56] It may be noted that the obsolete "possessory judgement" based on seven years' possession (Stair, *Institutions*, IV.26.3) also did not require good faith. However, a successful
claimant was deemed to be a *bona fide* possessor until judicial termination of the title. See
n. 4 above, paras 133, 146.

of particular requirements, as to state of mind and period, within an integrated context in which the paramount consideration is policy. Continental European systems tend to feature this sort of approach, especially in respect of moveable property.[57]

(5) *The Role of Good Faith in Specification*

The question whether good faith should be a prerequisite to acquisition by *specificatio* was debated in Roman law[58] and remains an issue in modern Scots law.[59] Approaching the matter from the point of view of specification as a rational solution to the problem of allocating title in respect of a new thing, it is open to argument that the creator should acquire property subject to a possible obligation to compensate the deprived party. Against this, there is the view that, as a matter of sound policy, the law should not give a proprietary reward for a manifest act of bad faith by which the actor seeks to benefit. While the first solution may be attractive to the typical mode of thinking of private law (a primary proprietary solution possibly subject to a complementary personal claim), it is not the only possible rational solution.

Regarding the scope for departure from a property outcome in circumstances of bad faith, the problem of *specificatio* appears to differ from that of *accessio*. In any final instance of the latter the accessory thing must necessarily become part of the principal thing regardless of the motive or intention of the party effecting the accession. Given the obvious controlling feature of *accessio*, namely, that the identity of the accessory is subsumed under that of the principal, any policy-based deviation from this position on account of bad faith would be an aberration. The only rational solution, from the point of view of private law, is to deal with a *mala fide* act of accession by according a claim for compensation to the deprived party. The moral outrage of the matter is the territory of the criminal law: a position well established in Roman law.[60]

[57] See the surveys in the Scottish Law Commission memoranda on corporeal moveables: *Protection of the Onerous Bona Fide Acquirer of Another's Property*, Memorandum No. 27 (1976); *Usucapion, or Acquisitive Prescription*, Memorandum No. 30 (1976). See, generally, T.B. Smith, *Property Problems in Sale* (London, 1978).

[58] See the texts and authorities referred to in W.W. Buckland, *Text-book of Roman Law* (Cambridge, 3rd edn, 1963), P.G. Stein (ed.), 216–18.

[59] See n. 4 above, paras 561–2.

[60] Buckland, n. 58 above, 210, citing *Inst.* 2.1.26, notes: "[i]f it was done in bad faith by the acquirer and he had possession, the loser could proceed for theft". The comment following this one, concerned with the unlikely situation of the deprived party being in

In the case of *specificatio*, although, as a matter of strict principle, the deprived owner cannot vindicate,[61] one can hardly say more regarding entitlement to the new thing than that the balance of argument points to acquisition by the maker. At the same time, there is a strong case to be made for denying a proprietary right to one who, in bad faith, seeks to benefit by making a new thing from the property of another.[62]

The difference between accession and specification shows that the scope for good faith as a control device is not necessarily simply a matter of arriving at an appropriate adjustment in terms of policy, because particular outcomes may be dictated by overriding considerations. In these two forms of original acquisition the policy considerations respectively applicable to good and bad faith scenarios cannot be distinguished but, arguably, as a matter of what is rationally possible, *specificatio* leaves scope for a consideration of *fides* which *accessio* does not. This is consistent with the "control device" role of good faith as one which is subsidiary to principle in the area of property. Consequently, as demonstrated by *accessio* and *specificatio*, even in contexts which are essentially similar, outcomes may be different.

(6) *The Possessor's Entitlement to Fruits as against the Owner*

Buckland describes the *bona fide* possessor's entitlement to fruits as "the most important and most discussed case"[63] of *fructuum separatio* (acquisition of fruits), on the basis of their separation by one not the owner of the parent thing. It is also the most obvious case of the role of good faith as a basis for acquisition by a possessor. In the context of prescription Stair identifies the distinctive basis of the acquisition of fruits as being "by that right that followeth possession *bona fide*".[64] Comparing this application of good faith with other property contexts, it would appear

possession, demonstrates the irresistibility of the property factor in the case of *accessio*: "If on such facts the loser was still in possession, the owner [i.e. the acquirer by *accessio*] could no doubt vindicate subject to payment for the added value, but he would still be liable to the *actio furti*".

[61] *Gaius.* II.79. See F. de Zulueta, *The Institute of Gaius* (Oxford, 1946), vol. 1.

[62] *McDonald* v. *Provan (of Scotland Street) Ltd*, 1960 SLT 231, at 232 per Lord President Clyde. For comments on this case see *Stair Memorial Encyclopaedia*, n. 4 above, para. 562 and n. 11 above, para. 4.04.

[63] See n. 58 above, 224.

[64] *Institutions*, II.12.10. Stair is concerned in this passage with the civilian *vitium reale* of theftuous or violent dispossession, which precluded acquisition by prescription by an innocent party but which did not affect the *bona fide* possessor's right to acquire fruits.

that here the role of good faith is less incidental and more a matter of basis than that of a control device.

Stair certainly sees the rule that a *bona fide* possessor acquires fruits on the basis of consumption as an inevitable result, in the sense of being the only possible appropriate solution:

> [T]he reason whereof is, because they who enjoy that which they think their own, do consume the fruits thereof without expectation of repetition or accompt, else they are presumed to reserve them, or employ them profitably for restitution; and if it were otherwise, there could be no quiet or security to men's minds, who could call nothing securely their own, if the event of a dubious right might make them restore what they had consumed *bona fide*; and as this is in favours of the innocent possessor . . . so it is in hatred of the negligence of the other party not pursuing the right.[65]

Stair's rationality means that a complementary rule allows the claimant to restitution of the parent entity the right to recover unconsumed fruits.

> And as to the fruits of that which is another's, the obligation of restitution takes only place against the haver, where they are extant; and therefore, where they are neglected, or being reaped have perished.[66]

Other Scottish authorities justify the acquisition of fruits on the traditional civilian basis of separation. The obvious question, however, is whether this is the appropriate basis because, if it is, *bona fide* consumption should be seen as an *a fortiori* situation subsumed under *bona fide* separation. This issue is material to how the good faith factor operates in the context of fruits, which, of course, is a relevant issue for present purposes.

Erskine contends for the acquisition of fruits by a *bona fide* possessor upon separation: i.e., when the fruits becomes a separate entity of property open to acquisition. The rationale is the possessor's essential contribution to production, made in the context of a state of mind only consistent with acquisition by reason of an honest conviction of ownership of the parent thing:

> This doctrine has been introduced, that the minds of men would bestow their pains and money on what they believe their own, and who afterwards enjoy the profits thereof, may be secured from the continual apprehensions under which they might labour, if the event of a doubtful right should lay them under a necessity of accounting for what they had thus possessed *bona fide*.[67]

---

[65] *Institutions*, II.1.23.
[66] *Institutions*, I.7.11.
[67] Erskine, *Institute*, II.1.25.

Hume saw "the most material consideration of any" as being "that
though the defender have saved and profited, yet still his plan of life and
expense must have been calculated, upon the whole, on the footing of
the revenue which he truly believed himself to have right to".[68]
Rankine, the most valuable nineteenth century Scottish authority on
property, also analyses the *bona fide* possessor's right to fruits on a basis
of acquisition by reference to possession:

> as never having been, in their character of independent subjects, the prop-
> erty of the true owner of the land; but, on the contrary, as belonging to the
> person who, being in possession of the principal subject for the time being,
> also possesses its fruits as soon as they come to have an independent exis-
> tence in the eye of the law.[69]

The conclusion that the *bona fide* possessor acquires, *ipso facto*, on the
basis of obtaining possession, as a consequence of separation, is consistent with the Scots common law presumption that the possessor of a
moveable is its owner.[70] Indeed, on the basis of the presumption, one
might venture that separated moveable fruits must necessarily be
absolutely acquired.[71]

The issue whether consumption should be a prerequisite to acquisition is not resolved by the case law, which does not offer significant
assistance with the problem of analysis.[72] One judicial view which may
be noted is that of Lord Gifford in *Houldsworth* v. *Brand's Trustees*[73] to
the effect that the *bona fide* possessor's right to fruits arose "[f]rom considerations of equity". The difficulty with the equity theory, however,
as the present writer has noted,[74] is that it can be applied only with
hindsight; because at the relevant point in time of separation the possessor is alone in the position of owner.

Arguably, the *bona fide* possessor's entitlement to fruits is a matter of
rational principle involving three aspects, namely: (1) the coming into
being of a new thing on separation of the fruit; (2) its falling into the

---

[68] See n. 2 above, 241.
[69] J. Rankine, *Landownership* (Edinburgh, 4th edn, 1909), 76.
[70] See, for example, Erskine, *Institute*, II.1.24.
[71] Rankine, n. 69 above, 78, acknowledges the relevance of the presumption. See also
Carey Miller, n. 11 above, para. 6.04.
[72] Carey Miller, n. 11 above, para. 6.07, provides a brief survey of the main decisions.
[73] (1876) 3 R 304, 316.
[74] "Logical Consistency in Property" 1990 *Scots Law Times* (News) 197.
[75] In the traditional civilian breakdown of ownership into consitutional rights of use,
fruits, and disposal (*usus, fructus, abusus*) the right of disposal (*abusus*) is the most fundamental feature.

possession of the possessor of the parent entity; and (3) the possessor's assumption (actual or inferred) of ownership of the fruit, justified by an honest belief in ownership of the parent thing. On this basis, policy considerations in support of the *bona fide* possessor's entitlement are superfluous. Moreover, logically, the right to consume the fruit, should be seen as a consequence of acquisition on the above basis because consumption is the exercise of the most fundamental right of ownership[75] rather than a mode of acquisition.[76]

A distinctive Scottish application,[77] amounting to an exception to the normal operation of the principle of accession, extends the right to fruits to a stand of annual crops sown in good faith on another's land. Thus Stair notes that "by our custom, corns and industrial fruits are esteemed as distinct moveables, even before they be separated or ripe, and belong not to the purchasers of land or heirs".[78] Erskine explains the sound policy justification for the rule, *messis sementem sequitur* (the harvest goes to the sower), as being

> because the seed, and the labour in preparing the ground, cannot be said to be employed on the lands for their perpetual use, but for the immediate profit of the possessor.[79]

In this context good faith operates, as it were, to validate entitlement in anticipation of separation through the normal harvesting process. This justification, deriving from the coexistence of an honest belief in a right to the land and the equitable policy of the sower's right to the harvest, is implicit in the late nineteenth century dictum of Lord Adam: "if the crop was sown in *bona fide*, then the general rule *messis sementem sequitur* applies".[80] It would appear that the operation of good faith involved in this rule may be identified as a variant of the standard position relating to fruits.

---

[76] It is submitted that this is a preferable analysis to the consumption basis adopted by Stair. Although consumption puts the matter beyond any possible practical doubt, it is a flawed basis since the exercise of a right of consumption presupposes the right of ownership which, obviously, cannot be made pending the completion of an act of consumption.

[77] See T.B. Smith, n. 28 above, 296. See also *Stair Memorial Encyclopaedia*, n. 4 above, para. 595, fn. 4.

[78] *Institution*, II.1.34. See also II.1.2, citing *Somervel* v. *Stirling* 1627 Mor 5074.

[79] Erskine, *Institute*, II.2.4.

[80] *Swanson* v. *Grieve* (1891) 18 R 371.

Statutory Contexts

(1) *Sections 24 and 25 of the Sale of Goods Act 1979*

Sections 24 and 25 of the Sale of Goods Act 1979 both provide for
exceptions to the principle *nemo dat quod non habet* which is given effect
in the Act by the formulation:

> where goods are sold by a person who is not their owner, and who does not
> sell them under the authority or with the consent of the owner, the buyer
> acquires no better title to the goods than the seller had.[81]

The sections concerned make provision for possible exceptions to the
nemo dat rule in situations in which a subsequent buyer, from, respectively, the original seller still in possession[82] and the original buyer now
in possession,[83] might rely upon the circumstances to assume the title
holder's involvement or authorisation. What is significant for present
purposes is that in both cases the Act expressly limits the availability of
the exception to the case of a person (i.e. the subsequent buyer) "receiving the same in good faith".[84]

Arguably, these two cases simply represent statutory contexts of the
application of the abstract approach to the passing of ownership considered above in certain common law contexts. Given the Sale of Goods
Act's identification of the parties' intention as the basis under which
property passes,[85] it would seems clear that there could be no question
of property passing to one who was aware that the other party was not
the owner or someone with the owner's authority to sell.

It may be noted that the general exception in the Act which qualifies
the *nemo dat* statement quoted above,[86] from the point of view of personal bar, is not formulated subject to any specific requirement that the
party relying upon the owner's conduct be in good faith. The better
view is that this is not necessary. And it would appear to be plain that
there could hardly be reliance upon conduct sufficient to preclude the

---

[81] Section 21(1).

[82] Section 24: essentially reproducing s. 8 of the Factors Act 1889.

[83] Section 25: essentially reproducing s. 9 of the Factors Act 1889.

[84] In the case of s. 24 this requirement is amplified by the clause "and without notice
of the previous sale", while in the case of s. 25(1) the amplifying words are "and without
notice of any lien or other right of the original seller".

[85] Section 17(1): "at such time as the parties to the contract intend it to be transferred".

[86] See n. 81 above.

"denying [of] the seller's authority to sell"[87] in the context of knowledge that the party purporting to sell did not have the right or authority to do so. As an essential requirement for the intended operation of the statute a stipulation of the buyer's good faith is not necessary. That it appears in sections 24 and 25, but not in section 21, is probably because the former are codified rules while the latter is simply an invocation of the common law.

(2) *Section 17 of the Succession (Scotland) Act 1964*

Section 17 of the Succession (Scotland) Act 1964 provides for the protection of a party who has "in good faith and for value acquired title to any interest in or security over heritable property which has vested in an executor". The scope of the provision is described as follows in the standard work on the Act:

> If the title was acquired directly or indirectly from the executor or from a person deriving title directly from the executor, no challenge to the acquirer's title may be made on the ground that the executor's confirmation was reducible or even that it has been reduced. Equally where the title was acquired from a person who himself derived title directly from the executor, it is not a competent ground of challenge that the executor should not have transferred the property to him. This means that there is no need for third parties to investigate the validity of a confirmation.[88]

It is submitted that this is simply another instance of the necessary requirement of good faith in the context of derivative acquisition, in which a transferee must be unaware of circumstances which render the transfer defective to be in a position to acquire title.

(3) *Section 2 of the Trusts (Scotland) Act 1961*

Possibly anomalously,[89] the counterpart to the above provision,[90] in section 2 of the Trusts (Scotland) Act 1961, does not stipulate a requirement

---

[87] Section 21(1).

[88] M.C. Meston, *The Succession (Scotland) Act 1964* (Edinburgh, 4th edn, 1993), 109.

[89] I am indebted to Professor D.J. Cusine for drawing my attention to this possible anomaly in the respective legislative provisions.

[90] See W.A. Wilson, A.G.M. Duncan, *Trusts, Trustees and Executors* (Edinburgh, 2nd edn, 1995), paras 24–5; 34–36, 37.

of good faith in denying scope, subject to certain limitations,[91] for the
reduction of a transaction by a trustee on the basis of a challenge "on the
ground that the act in question is at variance with the terms or purposes
of the trust". A statement of the authors of one text on the law of trusts,
to the effect that good faith is a necessary requirement, appears to reflect
the view that a requirement of good faith is implicit in the situation
concerned.[92] However, the position taken by Professor Reid is that a
transaction at variance with the terms is protected to the extent provided
for "regardless of questions of good faith".[93] Is it tenable to argue that a
reason why good faith cannot be inferred is that the requirement would
necessarily imply a duty to examine the trust deed? This would appear
doubtful: the possible role of good faith can only be in terms of its common law form based on actual rather than inferred knowledge.

On the view developed in this chapter concerning the requirement of
a transferee's good faith in potentially defective cases of derivative
acquisition, this case appears to be another situation in which the obtaining of an unimpeachable title should, in principle, only occur in circumstances in which the transferee was in good faith, in the sense of
being unaware of the ground of a possible challenge to the validity of
the transfer. This, however, is not to deny the capacity of the legislature to depart from principle.

(4) *Section 8 of the Prescription and Limitation (Scotland) Act 1973*

It may be noted that good faith has a role in respect of the extinctive
prescription of the right to recover property under section 8 of the
Prescription and Limitation (Scotland) Act 1973 in that the right to

[91] The section refers to transactions covered by s. 4(1)(a)–(e) of the Trusts (Scotland) Act 1921, empowering trustees "to do certain acts where such acts are not at variance with the terms or purposes of the trust".

[92] K.McK. Norrie, E.M. Scobbie, *Trusts* (Edinburgh, 1991), 158: "Only persons act-ing onerously and in good faith can rely on this section". It may be noted, however, that the late Professor J.M. Halliday, in an opinion, did not mention good faith in a context in which he would have done so had he considered it implicit. See D.J. Cusine (ed.) *The Conveyancing Opinions of J. M. Halliday* (Edinburgh, 1992), 451: "The law was signifi-cantly changed by the Trusts (Scotland) Act 1961, s. 2, which validates sales by trustees and the title acquired by the purchaser whether or not the sale was at variance with the terms or purposes of the trust".

[93] See *Stair Memorial Encyclopaedia*, n. 4 above, para. 691. Reid sees the legislation as a departure from the common law rule, stated by Stair (*Institutions*, I.13.7), which limited acquisition in a transaction in breach of trust to those acquiring *bona fide*.

recover stolen property "from the person by whom it was stolen or from any person privy to the stealing thereof" is imprescriptible.[94] This, of course, means that the possessor of property who is in bad faith, on the basis of knowledge that the subject matter concerned is stolen property, does not have recourse to the defence under section 8 of the Act that a claimant's right to recover has been extinguished by the passage of a twenty year period. The position under the Act would appear to represent the minimum limitation consistent with the common law[95] in respect of the *vitium reale* of theft. However, as a matter of policy, it would be difficult to justify a denial of the *bona fide* possessor's right to resist the owner's claim after the passage of so long a period and, on this basis, the logical approach, followed by the 1973 Act, is that the *vitium reale* may be erased by the passage of time in the circumstances.

The presence of good faith operating in the manner considered in the context of negative prescription can be contrasted with positive prescription, both under the common law and on the basis of the statutory form applying to heritable property, in which there is no requirement of good faith. Arguably, in the context of negative prescription, it is appropriate, as a matter of policy, that a party in bad faith—in the sense of being aware that the thing concerned was stolen—should be denied any defence based upon the passage of time against a claimant able to establish title.

Conclusions

(1) *The Existence of a General Concept of Good Faith in the Law of Property*

Do the samples of contexts in which good faith operates point to there being a general concept of good faith in Scots property law? While the meaning and definition of good faith for the purposes of its application in our law of property is presented in the sources in terms of general propositions,[96] it cannot be said that there is a general concept of good

---

[94] Sched. 3 (g).

[95] See, for example, Stair, *Institutions*, I.9.16.

[96] Stair, *Institutions*, II.1.24, with characteristic succinctness, identifies possessors in good faith as those "who do truly think that which they possess to be their own, and know not the right of any others". Erskine's definition (*Institute*, II.1.25) introduces an objective element: "A bona fide possessor is one who, though he be not truly proprietor of the subject which he possesses, yet believes himself proprietor on probable grounds, and with

faith in terms of anything approaching a uniform basis of operation. Moreover, short reflection tells one that in the property context there could not be a general doctrine of good faith in the sense that may apply in the law of contract in certain legal systems.[97] While a general uniform concept of good faith may be applied in contract to control outcomes in issues between the parties which are open to control by reference to policy considerations, there is simply not the same scope for this in the diverse aspects of the law of property in which good faith may have a role. The position in Scots law in this respect would appear to match that of the civil law in respect of which Buckland and MacNair noted that "[i]t is clear that *bona fide* possession is not the same in these various cases, and it is impossible to form out of them a coherent concept".[98] One finds in the sources various generalisations about good faith in the context of issues relating to property. Do these stand up to scrutiny? It would appear to be necessary to distinguish certain different forms which statements may take.

One particular category does no more than present well-established principles applied to good faith. Erskine's statement that "the strongest *bona fides* must give way to truth"[99] is correct but does not go beyond the trite point that established property rights trump lesser interests regardless of the fact that the holder of a lesser right has an honest belief in its superiority. A second category seeks to clarify the issue of the possible superior nature and enhanced scope of a right held on a basis of good faith. Thus, in a late eighteenth century case, Lord President Millar commented: "As to *bona fides*, although *mala fides* may cut down a right, *bona fides* cannot establish a right".[100] Clearly there are certain property rights associated with possession (e.g. the right to fruits) which are open to defeat on the basis of the possessor's bad faith. But is it

a good conscience". The relevant case law is reviewed in the modern writings. Regarding the meaning of good faith and the significance and interpretation of knowledge (actual and constructive) see Reid's valuable treatment, n. 4 above, paras 131–5. Note also Carey Miller, n. 11 above, para. 6.05.

[97] As is clear from several of the contributions to the present volume, the concept of good faith in the law of contract is something entirely different from good faith in property. MacQueen notes that good faith operates as an objective concept in the contractual context but from a subjective perspective in property cases. Forte argues to similar effect but would leave some role for subjective good faith. Thompson identifies various perceived aspects of good faith in contract but none would appear to have any role or relevance in the property context.

[98] See n. 43 above, 85.

[99] Erskine, *Institute*, II.1.25.

[100] *Mitchell* v. *Fergusson* (1781) 3 *Ross's Leading Cases*, 120, 127. I am grateful to Niall Whitty, Scottish Law Commission, for drawing my attention to this dictum.

accurate to say that "*bona fides* cannot establish a right"? It is true that the mere presence of good faith cannot *per se* establish a right: if that were the case the proposition in the second sentence of the preceding paragraph would not be tenable. At the same time, however, good faith may operate to establish a particular right where other requirements are met, as in the case of fruits. Insofar as good faith is a critical requirement in a number of situations in which property rights are acquired, it would appear to be somewhat misleading to deny its active capacity in the way in which Lord President Millar appears to do.

In view of the affinity between Scots and South African property law (a position which is being increasingly recognised and probably only subject to the exclusion of the feudal factor) a source from the latter system, relevant to the issue of a general basis for good faith, may be considered. In the most widely used English language text on modern South African property law the authors contend for a general basis for good faith in the area of the "doctrine of notice":

> The general principle *nemo ex suo delicto meliorem suam conditionem facere potest* operates in the law of property to the same extent as it governs every other sphere of law. This means inter alia that nobody will be permitted to defeat another person's potential real right for his own individual benefit if he knows of its existence.[101]

The maxim is rendered as: "[n]obody will be allowed to derive a benefit or advantage from his own bad faith".[102] In a subsequent footnote, reference is made to the theory that the operation of a requirement of good faith, in the context of competing claims to acquisition on a derivative basis, may be explained as an application of the principles of delict, there being no room in South African law for the operation of an independent "doctrine of notice".[103] As Kleyn and Boraine point out, a difficulty with this theory is that while the law allows a claim for specific implement[104] in the context of a claim based on the doctrine of notice, this remedy would not be available for a claim based on delict.[105]

It is clearly plausible to argue that the consequence of a state of bad faith in barring the right to a property entitlement or benefit which

[101] Kleyn and Boraine, n. 19 above, 68.

[102] *Ibid.*, fn. 19.

[103] N.J. van der Merwe "Die Aard en Grondslag van die Sogenaamde Kennisleer in die Suid-Afrikaanse Privaatreg" (1962) *Tydskrif vir Hedendaagse Romeins-Hollandse Reg* 155, 172.

[104] "Specific performance" in South African law.

[105] Kleyn and Boraine, n. 19 above, 68–9, fn. 21.

would otherwise be available, may be ascribed to a general position taken by the law that no party manifesting bad faith in a particular context should benefit therefrom.[106] On the other hand, however, without detracting from the notion of an umbrella justification of the type just described, one would assume that analysis might show that the requirement of good faith operated in a particular way in a given context. Identifying any such differences has potential utility for the application and development of the law: a potential which is not easy to see in the generalised forms of justification referred to above.

The answer to the question implicit in the heading of this section would appear to be that the different property cases do reflect the recognition of a broad, general, concept of good faith. However, there is limited utility in identifying a broad general basis such as "control device" or "no benefit from wrongful position". It is more useful to identify, as far as possible, the particular bases appropriate to the distinct situations with a view to arriving at some form of rational classification.

(2) *The Scope for Rational Classification*

It would appear that a measure of classification can be contended for. There is probably scope for identifying at least two and possibly three groupings, *viz*.: (1) the "fundamental basis" of acquisition of fruits; (2) the "necessary in context" derivative acquisition cases; and, possibly, (3) the policy based "control factor" cases, as in specification, insofar as good faith is required.

In the case of fruits, the *bona fide* possession factor is the active driving consideration on the basis of which acquisition proceeds. It is an integral consideration in the sense that the physical and mental elements must coexist. This case may be contrasted with specification in which the fundamental factor is the coming into being of a new thing with good faith having no more than a "control factor" role in terms of property consequences.

The common law and statutory cases concerned with derivative acquisition can be explained on the basis that an absence of good faith on the part of the transferee, in the form of knowledge of the true circumstances, precludes the exercise of an intention to become owner (in any final sense). This means that the abstract system of the transmission

---

[106] The writer finds it more difficult to see the case for or benefit of identifying the basis for the requirement of good faith as delictual.

of ownership, which, it is submitted, applies in Scots law, will not operate to give an unimpeachable right.

In some cases the role of good faith may be identified as that of a "control factor"[107] on the basis that there is room for a policy-based limitation of the acquisition of a right on the basis concerned. *Specificatio* would appear to fall into this category. Arguably, because acquisition by the maker is not an irresistible solution, there is scope for restricting the maker's right by reference to a requirement of good faith. This case may be contrasted with accession in which the fundamental factor, the attachment of accessory to principal, gives a property result not open to rational limitation on the basis of good faith.

---

[107] In a more particular sense than the meaning applied to the label in the introduction to this chapter.

7

Good Faith
and the Doctrine of Personal Bar

John W.G. Blackie*

Introduction

This essay examines a number of models of core principles lying behind
the examples found in Scots case law and juristic writing under the label
"personal bar". In this way it seeks to identify the extent to which good
faith in this area of Scots law does or does not provide a unifying principle.

The Ambit of Personal Bar

It is helpful at the outset to give a very basic description of the sorts of
factors that arise in situations described as ones of "personal bar". As a
minimum, they involve on the part of some person behaviour, whether
active or passive, which in law will prevent that person insisting on a
right. To this may be added for consideration the idea that it may also
cover behaviour in some situations which, though not delictual, gives
rise to a right in another *ex lege*. Roughly, the types of situation covered
would be grouped under the heading "estoppel by representation" in
Anglo-American legal systems. But it should be emphasised that the sole
purpose for stating this here is to focus on fact situations, and not on
the legal rules needed to analyse them. Indeed, for the present purpose,
that of seeking a core principle or core principles, there is a real danger
of begging the question. If one initially determines the boundaries of
personal bar by applying a particular rule to discover what it is, the field
consequentially discovered will, of course, confirm the principle applied

* Professor of Law, University of Strathclyde.

to discover it. An alternative way of describing the field avoids this problem. This is to examine anything that has been referred to by judge, jurist or legislator[1] as being an example of personal bar, and extracting a core principle or core principles from that body of material. But there are also dangers in this way of going about things. The first is of being insufficiently inclusive. But in an essay of this scope it is not possible to consider every piece of relevant material. The second danger is of being over-inclusive. Some things may have been described as personal bar which should not have been.

However, adopting this approach not only makes it possible to consider the question of analysis, which is the main purpose of this essay, but it also enables two lines to be drawn. First, it excludes public law questions. Certainly there may be many situations giving rise to public law questions where similar issues may arise. However, questions of public law are better focused within the whole field of the law relating to control of administrative action, rather than as part of personal bar. For example, the term "personal bar" is not appropriate to deal with the issues arising where the Crown has published a policy statement that it will not prosecute particular variants of a criminal offence.[2] Secondly, the approach adopted excludes cases of "waiver". Without venturing to try to determine whether these are never, or are sometimes, or are always ones of personal bar, they can at any rate be excluded from this present study on the crude ground that that there is authority that they are different.[3] That authority, whatever its merits or demerits, is not all new.[4]

The First Model—An Original Pure Principle of Personal Bar?

It might be anticipated that using the techniques of doctrinal legal history would reveal an original, clear model of principle for the law of

---

[1] It is beyond the scope of this essay to examine all of the legislation where the term "personal bar" has been used. There are also a number of "bars" created by statute that have been assumed as coming within the field, though the term as such is not used.

[2] For a recent treatment of this question, and one which suggests that questions of public policy play a particular role, see C.T. Reid, "Renouncing the Right to Prosecute" (1998) 43 *Journal of the Law Society of Scotland* 117.

[3] For an analytical discussion of waiver, see E. Reid, "Recognising Waiver" (1999) 3 *Edinburgh Law Review* 107: inter alia considering *James Howden & Co. Ltd* v. *Taylor Woodrow Property Co. Ltd* 1998 SCLR 903.

[4] See *Gatty* v. *Maclaine* 1920 SC 441 (affd. 1921 SC (HL) 1), at 453–4, per Lord Skerrington.

personal bar. That then, it might be anticipated, could be shown to have been overlaid in the course of time with confusions, complications and contradictions. Such an approach would seek to pare away the excrescences of the law as it has developed over time and so reveal at its origins a statement of principle as to what personal bar is. Unfortunately, here these techniques do not produce this result. There is no such original principle underlying "personal bar" that can be found by such a route. The problem is stark. There appears to be no label in the *ius commune* tradition which takes the form, "personal bar", or even some variant of this form. Moreover, there is no statement of general principle, before Bell,[5] that refers to the phrase or a variant of it. A Latin version of the phrase, *"personalis exceptio"*, or, alternatively, *"exceptio personalis"* was certainly commonly used into the nineteenth century. Occasionally this comes in the form, "personal objection". *Objicere* is the verb routinely used in *ius commune* literature for the pleading of an *exceptio*, and "object" was the Scots word for that.[6] These phrases all sound as if they have a good civilian ring about them. But these Latin and Latinate words are empty of content. No genus covering even the field that every Scots lawyer would recognise as personal bar is found under any such label in the *ius commune* or early Scots literature. The phrase *"personalis exceptio"* (or *"exceptio personalis"*) was known in that material, but it covered two very much narrower matters: the defence that a person acting as one's apparent procurator did not have capacity so to act either because of being female or a soldier in Roman law[7] was described using the word personalis. It can aslso be found in *ius commune* literature as the plea *"personali exceptione tu es Miles, tu es Mulier"*. In early seventeenth century Scots law "Exceptionis contrary to the persewaris person" comprehended a range of situations where a person was not entitled to access to the courts at all[8] because of some feature of his or her personal life: rebels or excommunicates were given as examples. While possibly an extension of the idea of personal

---

[5] In Bell's *Principles of the Law of Scotland*, W. Guthrie (ed.), (Edinburgh, 10th edn, 1899) all of the uses of the phrase in the parts covering the central question (paras 27, 946 and 999) are editorial. (*cf.* the heading to para. 1816, which deals with ratification or homologation on one's deathbed).

[6] For example, P.J. Hamilton-Grierson (ed.), *Habakkuk Bisset's Rolment of Courtis* (Edinburgh, 1920), vol. 1, 176: against a criminal indictment "na exceptionis may be obiected". The work was composed c. 1613–22.

[7] *Institutes* IV.13.10, *De Exceptionibus*, P. Birks, G. Macleod (eds and trans.), (London, 1987), 141: *"ex persona dilatoriae sunt exceptiones"*—"some dilatory pleas arise from the character of the parties".

[8] *"Non habet standi in iudicio"*.

exception beyond that of procurators, this clearly does not provide a background for the modern law of personal bar. An echo of this older usage, but extending it to anything preventing a person from holding an office (such as a conflict of interest), can be found in one source even in the late nineteenth century.[9]

Nothing hangs on the term "personal" in the phrase, "personal bar". Scotland seems never fully to have developed a division between exceptions in rem and exceptions *in personam*: a distinction found in some *ius commune* literature.[10] In some situations involving persons with rights or liabilities in some way connected with the rights or liabilities of another, a bar might affect only one of these parties if it were classified as in *personam*.[11] Amongst these, and building on Roman law,[12] were some situations involving cautioners: as where a cessio was made by the principal debtor.[13] Stair, possibly under reference to this, refers briefly at one point to exceptions "personal against the cedent" in cases of assignation.[14] However, this *ius commune* distinction adds nothing to what might be the central idea or ideas in personal bar.

It is, however, not too suprising that occasionally, though not very commonly, one does encounter in modern material attempts to rationalise decisions in the field of personal bar by reference to the fact that it is *personal*. There are two notable examples, both in case law rather than juristic writing, and neither gives grounds for thinking that this approach provides a workable, coherent principle for the law of personal bar. One example comes from the judgement in a Sheriff Court case where it was held that, while not incompetent for a Sheriff in summary

[9] J. Trayner, *Latin Maxims and Phrases* (Edinburgh, 4th edn, 1894) *s.v.* "*Personali objectione*". The case referred to, *Clark* v. *Wink* (1847) 10 D 117, dealing with the ineligibility of a sheriff-clerk depute to be a trustee in a sequestration, makes no use of this phrase or any other like it. Trayner, uniquely, treats the phrase, "*personalis objectio*", as covering something different from a wider idea under "*personali exceptione*" of which he gives examples that would generally be considered "personal bar".

[10] There was a third category, *exceptiones mixtae*, where the bar affected some of the connected persons but not others. See, for example, Voet, *Commentary on the Pandects*, P. Gane (trans.) (Durban, 1957), 44.1.9, who refers under this heading to the exceptio that the alleged debtor was a minor, which was available to his heirs but not to his cautioners.

[11] *Ibid.*

[12] *Institutes* IV.14, *De Replicationibus.*

[13] Voet, n. 10 above, 44.1.9.

[14] Stair, *Institutions of the Law of Scotland* (1681), III.1.23, D.M. Walker (ed.), (Edinburgh, 1981). This is part of a wider issue dealing with the modifications necessary to the doctrine of mutuality in contract where assignees were involved (*Institutions*, I.10.16). The difficulty was that an assignor might then, if the law were not adapted, be able to prevent the assignee having a valuable right by simply not performing his obligations to the debtor where these obligations arose from a mutual contract.

proceedings to raise a defence of personal bar *ex proprio motu*, it is nonetheless unwise to do so.[15] It is unwise because there would always have to be evidence from the defender relating to this matter. That point of the law of evidence was then given a justification by reference to the "personal" element in "personal bar". The Sheriff Principal put the matter thus:

> It seems to me that a plea of personal bar is not only personal in relation to the person against whom it is pleaded. It is also personal to him who pleads it.[16]

While acceptable as an application of the best evidence rule in the law of evidence, it must, however, be wrong as a statement of the rules of the law of personal bar: since, whatever model is adopted for personal bar, the law will proceed on essentially an objective view of the facts. The other context in which a reference has been made to "personal" as an essential element is in the case of an encroachment onto land of a building or some other structure. Where an action is raised by a singular successor who has come to own the land after the encroachment upon it has occurred, it is thought[17] that he or she cannot be barred by the acts or omissions of a predecessor in title.[18] However, reliance on the idea that bar is "personal" as the key to this rule rings hollow when one finds that in nuisance cases the situation is the exact opposite and singular successors are in such cases bound by any bar applicable to their predecessors in title.[19]

There is some evidence that the early Scots cases on personal bar may have been, at least to some extent, affected by working out from a core of extreme bar constituted by the *exceptio doli*.[20] As such, the experience may have parallels with that of South Africa.[21] However, in Scotland

---

[15] *Hamilton District Council* v. *Lennon* 1989 SCLR 193.

[16] *Ibid.*, at 198, per Sheriff Principal Mowatt.

[17] There is still sufficient doubt as to the law for a judge recently "with some hesitation" to allow a case of this sort to proceed to a hearing of the facts. See *Michael* v. *Carruthers* 1998 SLT 1179, at 1187B, referred to in C. Campbell, "Acquiescence and Title to Land—Part 1" 1999 *Juridical Review* 183, 187 (where the judge's name is incorrectly stated as Lord Walker) and further generally ibid. Part 2 (1999) Juridical Review 211, 211–217.

[18] *Brown* v. *Baty* 1957 SC 351, at 353, per Lord Walker.

[19] *Charity* v. *Riddell* 5 July 1808 FC.

[20] See in particular *Campbell* v. *Cochran* (1747) Mor 10456 (reversed *sub nom Kennedy* v. *Campbells* (1753) 1 Paton 519) per counsel *arguendo* at 10456: "ought to be repelled *exceptione doli et personali exceptione*".

[21] For the way in which estoppel entered South African law by this route, see R. Zimmermann, "Good Faith and Equity" in R. Zimmermann, D. Visser (eds), *Southern Cross: Civil Law and Common Law in South Africa* (Oxford, 1996), 218, 221–7.

during that earlier period, the process was to develop a wider Scottish concept of bar rather than to adopt, as in South Africa (and as happened later in Scotland by other routes), part of the English law of estoppel. It is not clear in some eighteenth century Scottish cases whether it is or is not the *exceptio doli* that is being relied on as personal bar in a wide sense. In one case,[22] for example, there was a failure to raise the point that a disposition was defective until after houses had been built on the land to which title was transferred under the disposition. This situation resulted in a finding that the pursuer was barred from challenging the disposition "*personali objectione*, as heir". But the defenders, who were successful on this ground, are reported only as having argued for bar on the apparently different basis, "*exceptione doli*".[23]

It should be stressed that to point to the lack of a secure, conceptual origin for the Scots law of personal bar does not suggest that there are no ideas within the law of personal bar that have a perfectly respectable *ius commune* pedigree. This is apparent in much of the special terminology that continues to be used within this area of law. All of the terms commonly encountered, with the exception of "acquiescence" (and possibly "waiver"),[24] are of *ius commune* origin. *Mora* almost certainly comes from the concept of *mora creditoris*.[25] This is early reflected in the requirement that creditors attaching the assets of debtors should proceed through the various stages of the process with appropriate speed.[26] In time, however, *mora* became used for so many delay contexts that it ceased to have any specific connection with *mora creditoris*. For example, the only book devoted specifically to the law of personal bar[27] includes under *mora* the rule that an offer, unless something else is specifically stated in it, is subject to an implied term that an acceptance will only bind if that acceptance is made within a reasonable time. "Taciturnity" can be found in the *ius commune* literature as a bar spe-

---

[22] *Williamson* v. *Daw* (1761) Mor 10459.

[23] *Ibid.*, 10461.

[24] For the position of waiver see Reid, n. 3 above.

[25] See R. Zimmermann, *The Law of Obligations: Roman Foundations of the Civilian Tradition* (Cape Town, 1990), 817 ff.

[26] Stair, *Institutions*, III.2.21. See the extended treatment in Kames, *Elucidations Respecting the Common and Statute Law of Scotland* (Edinburgh, 1777), (reprinted with an introduction by J.V. Price, London, 1993), Article 19 (121–3).

[27] J. Rankine, *A Treatise on the Law of Personal Bar in Scotland* (Edinburgh, 1921).

[28] See, for example, U. Zasius, *Commentaria, Seu Lecturas in Titulos Pandecatarum* (1537–43), *s.v.* "*De Damno Infecto*", para. *Si Quis Iuxta* 4 "*Quod si taciturnitas per quam praesumeretur consensus*". ("The position where there is silence from which consent may be presumed").

cifically to an action based on the *cautio damni infecto*,[28] and also in other contexts.[29] "Homologation", or at least the verb *"homologare"*, is also found in the *ius commune*.[30] This is so despite a long-standing Scots tradition that the word is our very own special word. Erskine refers to it as "in the style of our law, by acts of homologation".[31] Dirleton puts it in Latin: *"ut loquimur de homologatione"*.[32] Stair gives it an etymology.[33] The *ius commune* usage was not, it seems, confined to judicial ratification or approval, which Bell says is (and perhaps was in his day) its narrower meaning in "the Continental law".[34] In any event, there is authority from the start that homologation is a synonym for "approbation", and that word is certainly of *ius commune* origin.[35] Indeed, in accordance with this, the law of "approbate and reprobate", familiar to those acquainted with the more austere corners or the law of succession, has always been considered part of the law of personal bar, although too technical in its details for treatment under such a general heading. *Rei interventus* may also have been a term that comes from the *ius commune*, if Professor Smith's speculation that it comes from the law of real contracts is correct.[36] It is of no importance today, however, since it was confined to the setting up of contracts lacking the required formalities, and has been abolished and replaced by a new statutory set of rules.[37] Unlike homologation it never had any application outside that sphere,[38] and so its abolition (along with homologation in that

---

[29] *Ibid. De Procuratoribus et Defensoribus* 27, *"Quando autem confessio, vel taciturnitas, vel factum procuratoris noceat domino"* (i.e., Of Procurators and Defenders 27, "When the confession, silence or deed of a procurator may be to the harm of the person for whom he acts").

[30] Voet, n. 10 above, 43.1.4, refers to the defence that the parties have gone to arbitration as *"laudi seu arbitrii ex compromisso homologati"*.

[31] Erskine, *An Institute of the Law of Scotland* (Edinburgh, 8th edn, 1871), III.3.47.

[32] Sir John Nisbet of Dirleton, *Doubts and Questions in the Law Especially in Scotland* (1698), 6 *s.v.* *"Approbatio"*.

[33] *Institutions*, IV.40.29: "[It is] from a mathematical term, by which one figure does quadrate with another, having like angles thereto; so homologous triangles are these which have equal angles, severally, each of them being of equal wideness to the angles of the other". It is a curiosity of Stair's text that he uses the word at various points earlier in the work without giving this etymology there.

[34] Bell, *Commentaries on the Law of Scotland in relation to Mercantile and Maritime Law, Moveable and Heritable Rights and Bankruptcy* (Edinburgh, 7th edn, 1870), I,139.

[35] For an early example of its use in Scotland, see Bisset, n. 6 above. "Approbate and reprobate" began to be distinguished from homologation in *Lord Panmint* v. *Crockat* (1854) 17D 85.

[36] T.B. Smith, *A Short Commentary on the Law of Scotland* (Edinburgh, 1962), 293.

[37] Requirements of Writing (Scotland) Act 1995, s. 1(5).

[38] It was used by Bell in another way as a synonym for *"rebus ipsis et factis"* in the context of encroachment on land cases, but that usage did not catch on.

sphere, but in that sphere only)[39] means it will play no role in the present study.

Although the origins of our law of personal bar have connections to the *ius commune*, there cannot be uncovered through doctrinal legal historical analysis a set of principles which form its whole, or, indeed, its core, conceptual structure, and, accordingly, another approach is necessary.

English Law as a Solution?

Can English law solve our difficulty? An affirmative answer to this question would not necessarily be as stupid or as alarming as it might seem. Recently it has become common, for the first time in this area, to state from the bench that our law is a different beast from the English law of estoppel.[40] Warning is thus now given against an assumption such as Rankine's[41] that Scots law is the same as the law in England in this area. On the other hand, it has recently been reaffirmed that the law relating to agents of undisclosed principals is the same as it is in England. The basis of this aspect of the law of agency lies in bar; and so the English rule based on estoppel is the Scots rule based on personal bar.[42]

In fact to accuse Rankine of following the whole of the English law of estoppel is to misrepresent him, for he did so only in part. This is the relatively simple and "user-friendly" part of the English law of estoppel. Rankine uses the law French term, "estoppel *in pais*", which is normally referred to today in English as well as in Commonwealth material as "estoppel by representation", and does not involve referring to promissory estoppel or to estoppel by deed for example. South Africa, it may be noted, has adopted the law of estoppel by representation from

[39] The Requirements of Writing (Scotland) Act 1995 does not remove homologation from all of the law but merely in the context of setting up obligations that require writing where that is defective or lacking: W.A. Wilson, A.D.M. Forte (eds), *Gloag and Henderson, The Law of Scotland* (Edinburgh, 10th edn, 1996), 57, fn. 10a. Section 1(5) only removes, and replaces it with a statutory rule, for "constitution" of the obligations listed in section 1(3).

[40] It is notable that these statements are, however, made in the context of the question of "waiver" (which is outside the scope of this study) but seem to be being expressed more widely as to the whole area of English law. See *James Howden & Co. Ltd* v. *Taylor Woodrow Property Co. Ltd*, n.3 above.

[41] The full title of Sir John Rankine's book, n. 27 above, is *A Treatise on the Law of Personal Bar in Scotland Collated with the English Law of Estoppel in Pais*.

[42] *Bank of Scotland* v. *Brunswick Developments (1987) Ltd* 1997 SC 226, at 234E, per Lord President Rodger under reference to the "classic opinion of Diplock LJ in *Freeman & Lockyer* v. *Buckhurst Park Properties (Mangal) Ltd* [[1964] 2 Q B 480] at p. 503".

England, though there are divergent views there as to what the precise position is.[43] However, estoppel by representation has now developed fully in South Africa in more detail and depth than the equivalent here.

There are numerous references in dicta[44] to Scots law having what in England is called estoppel. These have to be taken as references to estoppel by representation, although many of the judges making these remarks may not have understood the different categories of this part of English law at all well. This is also implied in the leading, though brief, dictum of Lord Birkenhead LC expressly setting out "the familiar principles of estoppel or bar".[45] This dictum is still applied routinely[46] in personal bar cases:

> Where A has by his words or conduct justified B in believing that a certain state of facts exists, and B has acted upon such belief to his prejudice, A is not permitted to affirm against B that a different state of facts existed at the same time.[47]

Moreover, the English return the compliment. It is not this snappy formulation that is applied by them as a judicial formulation (presumably because it is only reported in Scots sets of law reports). Nonetheless, it is another Scots House of Lords case[48] that English lawyers use,[49] and one whose facts could not be more strongly redolent of Scotland. (It concerned the amalgamation of the congregation of United Seceders in Carnoustie with the Free Church). It happened to get reported in the *Law Times Reports* and it is doubtless by that route that it became known to English lawyers.

Notwithstanding this interaction with the law of England, there are two problems in assuming that this area of English law amounts to the essence of our law of personal bar. First, Scottish judges can be shown to have ranged more widely than this. Second, in both English and

---

[43] See *Johaadien* v. *Stanley Porter (Paarl) Pty Ltd* (1970) 1 SA 394, discussed in P.J. Rabie, *The Law of South Africa* (Durban, Pretoria, 1996), vol. 9, *s.v.* "Estoppel", para. 452.

[44] For example, *Newburgh and North Fife Railway Co.* v. *North British Railway Co.* 1913 2 SLT 212, at 232, per Lord President Dunedin: "personal bar—or, as it is called in the sister country, estoppel".

[45] *Gatty* v. *Maclaine* 1921 SC (HL) 1, 4.

[46] Recent examples include *Hamilton District Council* v. *Lennon*, n. 15 above, (where the question was whether a local authority was barred from not accepting the defender as a tenant) and *Unity Trust Bank plc* v. *Ahmed* 1993 SCLR 53 (where the pursuer was barred by sending a statutory notice to pay which gave one final date for payment and also intimated a petition for sequestration which gave another).

[47] *Gatty* v. *Maclaine*, n. 45 above, 7.

[48] *Cairncross* v. *Lorimer* (1860) 3 MacQ 827.

[49] See in particular *Hopgood* v. *Brown* [1955] 1 All ER 550.

Commonwealth legal writing there is now a recognition that to find the
core of estoppel involves bringing together all the aspects of estoppel,
including those that are definitely not received as part of Scots law. In
recent English and Commonwealth literature three models have been
proposed for the core principles, *viz.*, reliance, promise and unconscionability.[50] Scots law would be uncomfortable with the last of these.
It is a wider doctrine in equity in the English sense, and has been
resisted in Scotland as the key to what may be the underlying principle
for recognising a constructive trust.[51] Rejection of such a rule from
within the law of equity in England and the Commonwealth does not,
of course, mean that general ideas of fairness may not have a role to play
in the law of personal bar. A general equity model has also been considered for the law of estoppel and that, as discussed below, has also had
some currency with respect to the Scots law of personal bar. A third factor, is that for the last seventy years or so, for better or worse, there has
been no use of modern English case law on estoppel by representation.
Scots law might now consider itself personally barred from starting
again to use that material after all this time.

Consent Based Models

It is quite common to encounter "consent" referred to as personal bar
in the cases. However, before considering whether consent provides any
guiding principle in the field, it is necessary to be aware that consent
in the law of delict is a quite different idea from consent in the law of
contract and both of these ideas have become intertwined in the law of
personal bar.

(1) *Consent to Delict—Acquiescence*

One quite large sub-area of the law of personal bar deals with the effects
on the property of A by the activities of B. These situations involve the
interface of property law and the law relating to delicts of intention. The

---

[50] The literature is becoming extensive. See, recently, A. Robertson, "Reliance and
Expectation in Estoppel Remedies" (1998) 18 *Legal Studies* 360—especially the summary
at 362; and "Situating Equitable Estoppel Within the Law of Obligations" (1997) 19
Sydney Law Review 57.
[51] G.L. Gretton, "Constructive Trusts" (1997) 1 *Edinburgh Law Review* 281, 408.

situations are themselves sub-classified as encroachment, nuisance,[52] trespass and intrusion. In all of these areas personal bar cases are typically described as "acquiescence" cases. There are two principal difficulties in this field. The first is a historical one, namely, that acquiescence, as a relative latecomer into our law, does not have a self-evident core of principle.[53] The second difficulty is that the term "acquiescence" obscures the difference between consent as understood in the law of delict, and consent in the law of contract. Judicial statements such as that of Lord Inglis, that "acquiescence is nothing but implied consent",[54] sound good, but are not helpful.

During this century the word "acquiescence" has, at least in some hands, become virtually a synonym of the generic term, "personal bar". Hence it comes at first as something of a surprise to find that it was rarely used before the beginning of the nineteenth century. It was then, in one case,[55] described without challenge as "a plea not known to our law till lately".[56] It probably first came to be regularly used around that time because the much more familiar term "homologation" had by then come to be confined to inferences that could be drawn from the actings of a person *prima facie* liable.[57] It is arguable that homologation was used earlier for a wider range of situations. Stair gives one example, where he used the word "acquiescence" as well.[58] This is where a buyer in a contract of sale, where after delivery it has become apparent that the goods are defective, fails right away to offer to return them to the seller. Historically, homologation may have been a generic term into which "acts of the victim" could have been brought as a species under a label such as "acquiescence".

One unfortunate result of the very widespread use of the word "acquiescence" is that categories become blurred. The word can either have a strong meaning, such as "personally barred", or a weak meaning,

---

[52] I am assuming that no one will now argue that nuisance is a delict of strict liability also covering accidents. For the correct view, see N.W. Whitty, *Stair Memorial Encyclopaedia*, vol. 14, *s.v.* "Nuisance", especially para. 2017.

[53] See also below for the problem of the meaning of "acquiescence" in other areas of case law treated as personal bar.

[54] *Cowan & Co* v. *Lord Kinnaird* (1865) 4 M 236, at 241.

[55] *Hart* v. *Taylor* (1827) 4 Mur 307 (a nuisance case).

[56] At 312, per Moncreiff, Dean of Faculty, addressing the jury.

[57] Note that this is subtly different from the standard formulation of homologation which existed, prior to the Requirements of Writing (Scotland) Act 1995, for setting up informal writings: where the point was that the acts to constitute homologation were those of the person seeking to deny the obligation.

[58] Stair, *Institutions*, 1.10.15.

such as "put up with" or "having no or little option". The blurring of meaning is particularly apparent in that, despite the fact that it was orig-inally coined to deal with something other than homologation, there are cases in the nineteenth century where it is treated as being the same thing.[59] The problem is not one of confusion of words only: it is that it equates, by drawing on the doctrine of homologation, the whole of per-sonal bar with the law of contract implied from facts and circumstances.

(2) *Consent as Contract: Homologation*

Now that the issue of setting up bargains where formal writing is required is removed from the law of personal bar and regulated by its own distinct statutory rules, there is an opportunity to revisit homologa-tion as a concept operating in other situations. It could even be argued that homologation has always been the core of this area of law in Scotland. One suspects that if lawyers had continued to use the simpler, alternative word, "approbation",[60] then on the one hand homologation would have been more frequently referred to as an idea, and on the other it would have been more difficult to separate from other concepts in this area of law. It is, however, possible to strip away later accretions and find a relatively clear doctrine of contractual consent, called "homologation", in the institutional writers before Erskine. Stair, for example, wrote:

> The last kind of contracts are these, which are by sole consent . . . and this consent may be either expressed by word, writ, or fact, by doing deeds importing consent, which therefore is called homologation.[61]

This gives rise to "acceptance". The same sort of approach is repeated in this context as an "exception" (i.e., a distinct defence) in the form of:

> acknowledging or approbation of the defender's right, directly and expressly by consent thereto, or ratification thereof, or indirectly, and tacitly by doing deeds importing the same, which is called homologation . . .[62]

[59] For example, *Hall* v. *McGill* (1847) 9 D 1557, at 1561 per Lord Cunninghame who repelled "the plea of homologation or acquiescence"; *Hill* v. *Dixon* (1850) 12 D 808; *Moir (Clerk to the Ochil Road Trustees)* v. *Alloa Coal Co.* (1849) 12 D 77.

[60] That this term is a synonym for homologation is trite in Erskine, *Institute*, III.3.47: "every act done by the granter . . . which implies approbation".

[61] Stair, Institutions, I.10.11. See, however, Stair, at II.11.24, for rather looser phrase-ology in a technical feudal law context: "The superior's consent by homologation, is as sufficient to avoid recognition, as if it were an express consent . . . the superior acknow-ledges [the] vassal".

[62] *Ibid.*, IV.40.29.

More opaquely, though briefly, it is described with reference to the law of proof by way of confession;[63] and homologation is referred to as "a kind of confession or acknowledgement of the right homologated".[64] Bankton is even clearer:

> Consent may be either *express*, by Word or Writing; or *tacit*, by Signs or Deeds importing Consent; when it is inferred from such deeds, the act importing the consent is termed Homologation, which is an "implicit approbation of a former deed, or of another's right".[65]

In contexts where homologation was relevant to setting up informal writings this contractual model started to dissolve into a more generalised idea of approbation. In Erskine it is still consent based:

> [E]very act done by the granter after their date which implies approbation supplies the want of an original legal consent.[66]

In Bell the emphasis shifts away from any question of contract implied from circumstances to an "implied confirmation of a previous obligation, contract or deed".[67]

The Reliance on Representation Model

An extremely commonly encountered statement of a rule that is alleged to sum up the law of personal bar is that the essential elements are: (a) a representation by the defender to the pursuer; and (b) the pursuer acting in response to that representation to his or her prejudice. This, in essence, is the English law of estoppel by representation. The representation may be by conduct, whether in the form of action or inaction. It has recently been put by one Outer House judge that:

> [B]efore the pursuer could rely on personal bar he would require to establish that he relied upon the representation and that he consequently incurred prejudice.[68]

Although this sort of formulation has the attraction of simplicity, both aspects of it are inadequate. First, it cannot be the case that any old

[63] *Ibid.*, IV.45.5: "the next extraordinary manner of probation".
[64] *Ibid.*, IV. 45.7.
[65] Bankton, *An Institute of the Laws of Scotland* (Edinburgh, 1751–1753), 1.11.64.
[66] *Ibid.*, 3.3.47.
[67] Bell, *Commentaries*, I, 141.
[68] *Gordon* v. *East Kilbride Development Corporation* 1995 SLT 62, at 65A, per Lord Caplan.

representation by a person will be enough: even if the other party has acted to his or her detriment. Sometimes the other party will be negligent, or imprudent, or simply bone-headed in acting on it. Secondly, and more seriously, while most cases of personal bar involve detriment, some do not, or at least not in an economic sense. Many of these situations may, on one view, be removed from this area of law by treating them as either (a) variations of contract; or (b) unilateral promises; or (c) waivers. But not all cases can be thus removed and one example is the standard encroachment case. It is possible that an encroachment may result in the owner of the property encroached upon being, in an economic sense, made *lucratus* by the encroachment; and, of course, some unjustified enrichment actions take the form of a claim for recompense by the encroacher. The only detriment suffered is the property lawyer's, which does not proceed from an economic viewpoint. The viewpoint is that the person whose property is encroached upon has suffered detriment to his or her unfettered right of dominium (to decide to be poorer financially by getting rid of the encroachment). In some cases bordering on the law of enrichment there is also a difficulty.[69]

The Equity Model

One argument for a good faith model of the law of personal bar is that aspects of what may be called the "equity model" can be incorporated into it. However, this model is, strictly speaking, different. An equity model is rather crude because its focus is more generalised. It has frequently been expressed that some generalised idea of equity lies at the heart of the law of personal bar. The following, for example, is a statement by the most distinguished conveyancer of the last generation:

> Since the core of the doctrine of personal bar in any of its forms is that it would be inequitable in the circumstances to permit a particular right to be enforced, it is not a field of law in which absolute general rules can be expected.[70]

Sometimes such statements are expressed in respect of only parts of the area of law. The editor of Bell's *Principles*,[71] rejecting the notion that the

---

[69] See *Connelly* v. *Simpson* 1991 SCLR 295, at 298D–299D, per Lord Cowie.

[70] J.M. Halliday, "Acquiescence, Singular Successors and the Baby Linnet", 1977 *Juridical Review* 89, 92.

[71] W. Guthrie. See, *Principles*, para. 27a.

acts required to constitute homologation must cause prejudice, states rather that these acts are "such as make it unfair or contrary to good conscience to hold that [the homologator] is not bound" by them.

The problems with this sort of generalised equitable principle are well-known, not just in Scotland but elsewhere. In the context of estoppel in English law, particularly as it has developed in the British Commonwealth, the role of equity, and in particular "unconscionability" (as in the reference by Bell's editor to "good conscience"), is currently a matter of active debate. As has been observed in England[72] in considering whether or not the person able to benefit from an estoppel arising from the conduct of another is or is not confined to reliance damages (i.e., the delictual approach), analysis of the problem is made more difficult because one frequently applied judicial dictum refers to "justice and equity . . . unjust or inequitable".[73]

A Good Faith Model

An initial hurdle has to be faced right at the start. There is some, or some apparent, authority against the idea of using good faith as the basic principle of a model for the law of personal bar. In one Scots source there is a direct quotation, taken from an English case,[74] to the effect that good faith and bad faith is not the point:

> This doctrine [i.e. estoppel by representation] is not confined to cases where the original representation was fraudulent . . . Even where a representation is made in the most entire good faith, if it be made in order to induce another to act upon it, then *prima facie* the party making the representation is bound by it, as between himself and those whom he has thus misled.[75]

However, it will be seen immediately that even in this statement the crucial matter is the meaning of the phrase "in order". A good faith doctrine of personal bar would comprehend not only active attempts to mislead, or even just turning a blind eye inappropriately, but also being put on one's enquiry objectively and failing to take responsibility in certain

---

[72] E. Cooke, "Estoppel and the Protection of Expectations", (1997) 17 *Legal Studies* 258, 260.

[73] I.e., *Moorgate Mercantile Co. Ltd* v. *Twitchings* [1976] 1 QB 225, at 241, per Denning MR.

[74] *West* v. *Jones* (1851) 20 LJ Ch 362, at 363, per Lord Cranworth.

[75] G. Watson (ed.), *Bell's Dictionary and Digest of the Law of Scotland* (Edinburgh, 1882) *s.v.* "Personal Bar".

circumstances. All of these things are covered in Scots case law in this area.

Negligence

Some situations which have been described as personal bar have been so because the defender was negligent. This has nothing to do with delict but, arguably, something to do with good faith: although this approach seems to have been affected by English authority.[76] In one case, for example, where an agent for trustees forged their signatures, the trustees were held liable on the document under a rule that a forged document is valid if there is negligence on the part of the person whose signature is invalid. It is:

> evidence of that *species* of negligence which alone would warrant a jury in finding that the plaintiffs were disentitled to insist on the transfer being void. . . . [it] must be negligence in or immediately connected with the transfer itself.[77]

Some "duty" language is used of this sort of "negligence": e.g., "a duty lies upon a party whose name is forged not to do or say anything that may mislead a bank".[78] The background of good faith is suggested in one judgement by the phrase "moral duty",[79] and the relevance of conflicting duties has been recognised in this area.[80]

The idea of a person being liable if he or she is put on enquiry has also been contemplated as having a much wider role in personal bar. In the context of rejecting, on the facts as averred, a claim that insurers were not entitled to take a defence under a marine insurance policy that the vessel which sank was unseaworthy, it was said:

> [T]here may be circumstances in which parties may be personally barred from founding upon a breach about which they did not have full knowledge,

---

[76] In *Wallace's Trs* v. *Port-Glasgow Harbour Trs* (1880) 7 R 645 a range of English and Irish authority is relied on.

[77] *Ibid.*, at 648, per Lord Mure. Emphasis added.

[78] *Mackenzie* v. *British Linen Co.* (1881) 8 R (HL) 8, at 15, per Lord Blackburn.

[79] *Mackenzie* v. *British Linen Co.* (1880) 7 R 836 (Inner House), at 846, per Lord Deas.

[80] *Boyd* v. *Robertson* (1854)17 D 159, at 162, per Lord Ivory. A case argued on the grounds of "homologation or adoption". Here an endorser was not barred when, attempting to protect his brother, he had taken no notice of intimations of dishonour of previous bills.

if they were put on their inquiry at the material time, failed to follow it up, and thereafter acted as if the matter was concluded.[81]

Fraud

It has long been the law that a person is barred from pleading his or her own fraud in order to avoid an obligation that would be valid but for that fraud.[82] In some old authority that rule is associated with questions of unjustified enrichment.[83] But notions of "wrongdoing", other than fraud in the technical sense, have been brought within the concept of personal bar by what, it is submitted, is the use of good faith as the ultimate tool of analysis. In one case[84] a woman who owed money to a third party arranged with the latter that her son would pay the money to the third party's agent. The agent, in turn, was to remit the money to the third party: which was done. She also owed the third party a larger sum in rent and it was held that the third party was not entitled to take the son's gift to satisfy that debt. The third party, it was said, was "in *mala fide* to oppone the compensation [i.e. set-off the two sums]". There was no fraud here in the classic sense of a machination to deceive; merely a form of bad faith in seeking to take advantage of the transaction. Such cases can be argued to be extended applications of the *exceptio doli* (as outlined at the beginning of this essay). But they do provide material that is still easier to understand within the concept of good faith than under any of the other competing models for our law of personal bar.

The Instinctual Nature of Good and Bad Faith

Some Scottish judges have expressly treated the law of personal bar as being about good faith or bad faith. In one case, concerning liability on a bill of exchange, Lord Deas said of a party receiving intimation of dishonour:

[81] *Murray* v. *Scottish Boatowners Mutual Insurance Association* 1986 SLT 330J, per Lord Murray. The case itself may have been one of "waiver", but the proposition enunciated relates to personal bar.
[82] *Jacob Serra* v. *Earl of Carnwath* (1723) Mor 10449.
[83] *Buchan* v. *Forbes and Others* (1683) Mor 10440. Here a person had obtained lands under the Cromwellian usurpation. It was said (at 10441) that *nemo debet lucrari ex suo dolo vel culpa* ("no one should benefit from his own wrongdoing or from his own fault"). The benefit would have been getting security against his debtor.
[84] *Young* v. *Representatives of Charles Fall* (1745) Mor 10455.

[He] is not . . . entitled, if his name be a forgery, to mislead the bank by preserving silence *in mala fide*, until the forger shall have made his escape, carrying with him, it may be, all the means he had of making payment of the debt . . . The question, whether a party receiving such intimation was or was not *in mala fide* in making no answer to it . . . [depends on] the whole surrounding circumstances, and as tending to shew whether the suspender acted in good faith or in bad faith.[85]

The concept of blame appears not only in bills of exchange cases but also in other types.[86] Furthermore, the courts have looked at "relative" blame on both sides.[87] Where, for example, the question was whether statutory road trustees were barred only with respect to the past or also to the future by their actings towards a railway which had been built, one judge observed:

We have, however, no specific averments as to the *bona fides* of the defenders, and the other points which it would be necessary to investigate before we could decide such a question.[88]

Consistent with his approach in bills of exchange cases, Lord Deas used principles of good faith to deal with questions of bar in a case of encroachment and interference with a servitude. Thus, where the proprietor of a servitude right stands by and permits the erection of buildings which encroach upon that right, he has:

acquiesced in their being carried on and completed, and would not have been in good faith afterwards to have demanded their demolition.[89]

Moreover, he made it quite clear that this was an extended concept of good faith since, specifically, the person barred was "not entitled to shut his eyes".[90] In one case dealing with the proper conduct of auctions, where the question of *bona fides* in contract law was referred to, the judge coupled his reference to good faith with a reference to personal bar.[91]

---

[85] *Warden* v. *British Linen Co.* (1863) 1 M 402, at 405, per Lord Deas (dissenting). The other judges relied on the more narrow doctrine, specific to the law relating to bills of exchange, that the bill had to be "adopted".

[86] See in particular, *Brown* v. *British Linen Co.* (1863) 1 M 793, at 795, per Lord President McNeill; *Hill* v. *Wood* (1863) 1 M 360, at 369, per Lord Cowan.

[87] *Hill* v. *Wood*, n. 86 above.

[88] *Moir* (*Clerk to the Ochil Road Trustees*) v. *Alloa Coal Co.*, n. 59 above, at 84, per Lord Mackenzie. Lord Mackenzie, who wrote on Roman Law, also makes reference to it; a highly unusual, if not unique, reference in this area of Scots law.

[89] *Muirhead* v. *Glasgow Highland Society* (1864) 2 M 420 at 427.

[90] *Ibid.*

[91] *Wright* v. *Buchanan* 1916 2 SLT 259, at 268, per Lord Skerrington.

One writer, Hume, who says surprisingly little on the topic of personal bar in his *Lectures*, uses a good faith model when referring to encroachment after oral permission was given to encroach on heritable property:

> In good faith, my conduct here is a tacit renunciation, *rebus ipsis et factis* of the privilege of resiling.[92]

Some judges, at least prior to *Gatty* v. *Maclaine*,[93] place emphasis on intention that actings would be relied on.[94]

Three Party Cases and their Resolution[95]

One severe problem with most of the models of personal bar is that these fail to do justice to cases where there are more than two parties involved in the events. Of course, there are situations where bar in a question between A and B will be irrelevant in a question with C: where that bar is irrelevant to the creation of the right which then accrues to C. An old case gives the example where A was barred by quarrelling a defect in a court decree but it was accepted that a third party would still be able to attack it.[96] However, there are three party situations where justice cannot readily be done without the use of the idea of good faith, since all other ideas that can be employed are to some extent fictions.

(1) *Offside goals and duplicated personal rights*

It is notable that one type of three party situation constitutes the best known use of the good faith/bad faith concept in Scots law generally.[97] These are cases where B obtains a personal right from A, and C also

---

[92] G. Campbell H. Paton, *Baron Hume's Lectures 1786–1822* (Edinburgh, 1952), Stair Society, vol. 15, 263.

[93] See n. 45 above.

[94] See, for example, *McKerachar* v. *Anderson* 1893 SLT 238 (failed attempt to establish personal bar against the running of a prescriptive period), at 238, per Lord Kinnear.

[95] The number three is used for convenience and should be taken as meaning "three or more".

[96] *Wallace of Ingliston* v. *Creditors of Spot* (1710) Mor 10444.

[97] This example from property law was utilised, in the absence of any pertinent material relating to contract law, to introduce a concept of good faith in pre-contractual situations in *Smith* v. *Bank of Scotland* 1997 SC (HL) 111.

148   *John W.G. Blackie*

obtains the same personal right from A, but C converts that personal right into a real right before B does.

All Scots lawyers are familiar with this as the *Rodger (Builders) Ltd* v. *Fawdry*,[98] or "offside goals", situation. That case concerned two contracts to sell the same heritable property.[99] But it applies whatever the form of "property". Put simply, the law is that if C acts in bad faith, meaning that he or she turns a blind eye, or has not given value, his or her real right is reducible. There are dicta using the phrase "personal bar" in some modern cases of this sort,[100] but these were probably stated without much thought. The editors of Gloag and Henderson, however, go so far as to include the offside goals cases under this heading as a separate category of personal bar by notice. They summarise the law in the following manner:

> But if he knew, or, as a reasonable man, should have known, that the latent claims existed, he is barred from asserting a right resting merely on the ostensible or apparent facts. So while a purchaser of lands is in general entitled to rely on the title as it stands on the Register of Sasines, if he knows that the subjects have already been sold to a third party he will be personally barred from asserting, in a question with that third party, his author's ostensible capacity to sell.[101]

In sharp contrast, the leading treatment of these cases rejects the classification as being within this area of law, stating that:

> Sometimes, too, the offside goals rule was seen, not perhaps very convincingly, as a development of the law of personal bar.[102]

The difference between the approach which sees this issue as being about personal bar, and the other approach, which sees it as distinct rule within property law, reflects two distinct ways of characterising the claim made against the person who has scored an offside goal in getting the real right before his or her opponent who has the chronologically prior personal right. The personal bar approach proceeds on an analysis that, where the real right is challenged, that challenge is based on a lack of capacity on the part of the person granting it, and the personal

---

[98] 1950 SC 483.

[99] For a complete examination of these situations see K.G.C. Reid, The *Law of Property in Scotland* (Edinburgh, 1996), paras 690 and 695–700.

[100] *Trade Development Bank* v. *Warriner and Mason Ltd* 1980 SC 74; *Trade Development Bank* v. *David W Haig (Bellshill) Ltd* 1983 SLT 510.

[101] See n. 39 above, para. 3.12.

[102] Reid, n. 99 above, para. 695: referring to *Petrie* v. *Forsyth* (1874) 2 R 214, at 223, per Lord Gifford and to Rankine, n. 27 above, 39.

bar operates to prevent the holder of the real right from defending by asserting that there was such capacity. The other approach would deny that it has anything to do with capacity. There is a perfectly good real right. It is not void. There was no lack of capacity in the sense that one might find in a void transaction. So if things have proceeded to this stage, the right of the person with the first personal right is better seen as a distinct rule in property law enabling a real right to be annulled, so that the person with the first personal right can then proceed to turn his or her right into a real right.

However, where the matter arises for consideration before the real right has passed, personal bar does, it is submitted, form the correct category. Where the person never scored the "offside goal", but was tackled when working his or her way up the pitch with a view to doing so, then these situations are more readily classifiable under this heading. This is because at this stage the claim would be by the person with the later personal right and is met by a defence that there is an earlier personal right. Amongst these situations is one that could arise with the sale of specific goods, or, indeed, in a transaction relating to heritage at the point before the disposition is given. It might, for example, be the case that A, having contracted to sell to B, then contracts to sell to C—with an earlier date for the transfer of ownership than that contracted for with B. (The example is even simpler if that date is, on the facts, the same time as the time for delivery.) A is then met with a demand, at the date contracted with C, for the transfer of ownership. A refuses that demand, having now realised the significance of his being contracted to B. C then raises an action against A for specific implement.[103] C's action must fail. It fails because C is now barred. Another example might arise in the context of assignations of debts (a four party situation). Suppose, for example, that A assigns to B a debt owed by D to A. A then assigns the same debt to C. D gets to know of the situation and pre-empts C's intimation of the assignation by giving notice to C that D knows of the earlier assignation—although it has not yet been intimated to him. In such a case it may be that C is personally barred from attempting to intimate to D.

That there has been this dispute about classification may, however, be relatively unimportant. What stands at the core of these situations is the fact that they involve three (or more) parties and can be solved only by the use of the idea of good faith and bad faith.

---

[103] C will in some situations have a perfectly good damages action against A.

Another type of three party situation giving rise to protection on the ground of good faith is one where A has made payment *bona fide* to C, although B in fact has the legal right to payment from A. Early cases of this sort typically deal with payments to the wrong person in the context of assignations, and can be seen as simply part of the law relating to them.[104] Moreover, the question of equity in many cases under this head focuses only on the behaviour of the party who has paid the wrong person and not also on the behaviour of the party who had the legal right. In one early case,[105] for example, though B had the right to be paid as heir, A, in good faith, had paid C as younger brother of B: since B, "in respect of his long absence off (*sic*) the kingdom", was held to be dead. The rule of *bona fide* payment was applied to prevent B claiming against A on his return: although it is not apparent that B could have avoided the situation. However, there are examples where the behaviour of the person with the legal right to be paid was also considered relevant.[106] Following this approach, in one case the defence of *bona fide* payment was expressly linked with a pleading that the person who had the legal right was personally barred through knowing that the payments had been made to the wrong person.[107] While it would seem to be correct to maintain the doctrine of the defence of *bona fide* payment to a third party, as something distinct from the doctrine of personal bar, since it can apply where the only issue is the equity when considering the payer's side, using good faith as a doctrine within personal bar itself, means that the interface with this defence can be handled with coherence.

(2) *People whose rights are linked to the obligations of another*

Cautioners constitute the paradigm constituent of this group. Joint obligants may also fall into this category and there may be other examples still. Nowhere does there appear to be any discussion of the position even of cautioners where the creditor of the person whose

---

[104] For example, *Lyon* v. *Law* (1610) Mor 1786; *Hume* v. *Hume* (1632) Mor 848; *Lawrie* v. *Hay* (1696) Mor 849.

[105] *Tersie* v. *Burnet and Forbes* (1711) Mor 1783.

[106] For example, *Garden* v. *Lindsay* (1757) 5 Brown's Supp 9—paying the former landlord in a situation where an adjudger seemed not to be going to take possession.

[107] *Alexander* v. *Pinkerton* (1826) 5 S 185: payment of contributions to a schoolmaster's salary over a number of years to the wrong parish. The defence failed on the facts.

obligations they are cautioners for is personally barred from claiming from the debtor. This may be a problem soluble from within the law of caution on an analysis of the nature of cautionary obligations. But that may turn out to be based on good faith. The question of co-obligants with joint and several liability still requires analysis in the future.

(3) *Delicts of intention affecting property*

The cases in the books all deal with heritable property where a delict of intention, such as encroachment or nuisance, is committed against it when owned by A and where the property is then sold to a singular successor B. The factual possibilities are, however, wider than this. The problem might also arise with corporeal moveables. If, for example, B has been throwing stones at A's potted geraniums without let or hindrance for the last six months and C, the next door neighbour, buys the flowers as a preliminary to buying A's house, leaving the geraniums where they are, is C barred in a question of future stone throwing?

As briefly mentioned above, the law in this area presents two rules that seem to be in conflict. The general rule in encroachment cases is probably that the singular successor is not bound by any personal bar that may affect his or her predecessor in title.[108] In nuisance cases the rule is the exact opposite.[109] In England it may be the other way round.[110] Moreover, with regard to the English rule that estoppel in respect of an encroachment binds what we would call a singular successor, it has been stated in the leading case, which first recognised it in clear terms, as being a rule that all "civilized countries" would have.[111] However, it is fair to note that the rule in English law was built on the analogy of the transfer of a tenant's interest in a lease and applying those cases to ones where there was a demise of freehold. In Scotland it may well be the case that a tenant under an assigned tenancy is bound by the personal bar of the assignor on the principle *assignatus utitur jure auctoris*. These problems are to some extent problems of the conflict between the (rightly) mechanistic rules of property law and the more

---

[108] See the cases discussed in Halliday, n. 70 above. But note also *Michael* v. *Carruthers*, n. 17 above.

[109] *Charity* v. *Riddell*, n. 19 above; *Colville* v. *Middleton* 27 May 1817 FC.

[110] In the English law of nuisance the way in which common law nuisances become unchallengeable is principally through the law of positive prescription of easements, and applies only to those nuisances capable of becoming easements.

[111] *Taylor* v. *Needham* (1810) 2 Taunt 278, at 283, per Mansfield CJ.

flexible rules of the rest of the law. However, the offside goals" rule is
a flexible one and has been accommodated within property law, so in
this area some sort of flexible rule might also by analogy be incorporated. Gloag sought to develop a rule of notice to cover this.[112] But one
of the cases he relies on deals with nuisance, and the other is one where
independent actings on the part of the purchaser gave rise to personal
bar anyway.[113]

To follow the logic of the law, and to make singular successors bound
on a flexible understanding of good faith as applied to these situations,
would not mean that all third parties are bound by all actings of their
predecessors. For example, the rule that concessions given to a tenant
by his or her landlord do not bind for the future a singular successor of
that landlord would remain unaffected.[114]

Good Faith Shields Have Spikes

If a sophisticated doctrine of good faith/bad faith were seen to be a general controlling principle of the law of personal bar, it would be easier
to blur the line between personal bar as a defence and the same types
of matter as a source of rights.

(1) *Procedural Artificiality*

The first argument for facts that typically constitute a defence of bar
amounting to a source of a right is that in some situations it is proce-
durally artificial to make a distinction. The law relating to the ostensi-
ble authority of an agent acting for an undisclosed principal is the
clearest example of this.[115] On the other hand, the fact that Scots law
has received this rule directly from English law might be argued as
meaning that it forms part of an English doctrine allowing rights to arise
from estoppel that we have not received in any other respect. There are,
however, other examples where not to recognise personal bar as a source
of rights can result in a court having to recognise, as a second best, a

---

[112] W.M. Gloag, *The Law of Contract—A Treatise on the Principles of the Law of Contract in Scotland* (Edinburgh, 2nd edn, 1929), 170.
[113] *Muirhead* v. *Glasgow Highland Society*, n. 89 above, at 426, per Lord Curriehill, and at 427, per Lord Deas.
[114] *Hall* v. *McGill*, n. 60 above.
[115] See *Bank of Scotland* v. *Brunswick Developments (1987) Ltd* n. 42 above.

particular right that is less full than the right that the facts point towards. An example of this could have arisen on slightly different facts in *Hamilton District Council* v. *Lennon*:[116] where a local authority raised an action of ejection from one of its houses against a man who was in possession following the death of an aunt for whom he had been caring. He raised a defence of personal bar, arguing that certain actings of an officer of the authority precluded it from taking this action. The case failed on the grounds that the actings referred to did not (and they would not have on any model of personal bar) form the basis of that defence. However, if those actings had been different, and, instead of the local authority raising an action of ejection, the man himself had raised an action of declarator, what the court would have wanted to do was declare the man to be a statutory tenant. However, to do so would have required the actings in bar to be the source of such a right; either directly, or by forcing the authority to complete some further procedure necessary under the statute. If the action was the other way round, and treated as negative personal bar, the authority could simply have been deprived of their right to bring an action of ejection, but the man's possession, while then lawful, would lack the status of a local authority tenancy and the consequences that would follow under statute.

(2) *Leading People On*

Conduct relied on reasonably, which is clearly at least an element of the core of the law of personal bar, can result in losses and is of great significance. One class of such a situation comprises cases dealing with losses which have occurred as a result of reasonable reliance on the pre-contractual conduct of a party to an anticipated contract (the "Melville Monument" cases). Hector MacQueen argues elsewhere in this volume that these lie within the concept of good faith and qualify as such under a principle of *culpa in contrahendo*.[117] It can, however, be argued that one can go beyond this and, by extension, give remedies in a wider range of situations involving leading on by applying a good faith based understanding arising from personal bar.[118] It is important to emphasise that the issue here is not about promises: although a question may one day have to be answered as to the scope of our law of unilateral

[116] *Hamilton District Council* v. *Lennon*, n. 15 above.
[117] See ch. 2, 20–22.
[118] Some cases are, of course, dealt with by the law of negligent misrepresentation.

promises.[119] Rather, the question in cases of leading on is tied up with conduct, reliance and good faith.[120]

The Melville Monument case, *Walker* v. *Milne*,[121] was itself characterised by a judge (admittedly in a dissenting judgement) in a later case as an example of personal bar:

> The doctrine . . . recognised by the Court is . . . based on considerations of equity. It may also . . . be deemed to be based on the principle of personal bar, in accordance with which one who represents a certain state of facts as existing may be precluded from maintaining that it is different, and may be liable in damages for the representation which he has made.[122]

Although not made clear in the rather brief printed law report, there is material in the Session Papers for *Walker* v. *Milne* that lends some support to this idea. The pursuer's case was pled in the form that the defender's were liable "in damages, the consequence of their conduct . . . founded upon principles of the most unquestionable expediency and justice".[123] Later, with reference to the facts, it is stated that there should be liability "in justice, and in consequence of "the conduct" of the defenders, by their writings, by the use, or rather the *abuse*, of the petitioner's property".[124] There is a reference to the defenders' *bona fides* at one point, although it is oblique: "Now, with what *bona fides* can they maintain, in this question, that it strictly and legally refers to a contract relating to heritage?"[125] Some of the cases cited certainly involve pre-contractual situations. On the other hand, there are two[126] instances where the pursuer was induced by the defender's conduct into thinking that she was married, when in fact it turned out this was not so. Despite the defenders' attempts in *Walker* v. *Milne* to distinguish these as cases of breach of promise to marry, they clearly were not, since the allega-

---

[119] For example, where a business conducts itself in a way from which it can be inferred that it is promising something, now that writing is not required to establish or prove the promise in such cases: see the Requirements of Writing (Scotland) Act 1995, s. 1.

[120] This sort of approach in English and Commonwealth law, typically, has been from within the theory of "promissory estoppel". However, see in particular *Walton Stores (Interstate) Ltd* v. *Maher* (1990) 170 CLR 394 (especially per Mason CJ at 413–16), where there is authority that conduct based "estoppel by representation" gives rise to the same approach. See further, Robertson, n. 50 above, 360, 362.

[121] (1823) 2 S 379.

[122] *Gray* v. *Johnston* 1928 SC 659, at 676, per Lord Justice-Clerk Alness.

[123] Petition for the pursuer at 30.

[124] At 32. Emphasis added.

[125] At 33.

[126] *Grahame and Erskine* v. *Burn* (1685) Mor 8472; *Lynn* v. *Gordon* Fountainhall 20 July 1699; *Drummond* v. *Hope* 2 August 1764 (Commissary Court, Edinburgh) (Unreported) (cited in Petition for pursuer at 31).

tion was not that marriage was promised, but rather that the person thought she was married, and thought so reasonably, albeit wrongly.

In one of the later cases, *Bell* v. *Bell*,[127] the Court applied the approach in *Walker* v. *Milne* to the effect that a son had a good claim when he had spent money on a building on the father's land which the father had orally promised to dispone to him but which he then disponed to a daughter. The judgments contain references to "fraud",[128] which, in the circumstances, must be fraud in the extended sense (considered above) of bad faith. The pleadings suggest that, though not perhaps fully developed, counsel were thinking in the context of personal bar. There was an averment by the defender that his inspecting the house was "not as homologation of the bargain with the pursuers".[129] At the same time, however, counsel referred to the claim that was being made "as in equity", which may possibly be distinct. In a subsequent case, Lord Deas explained *Bell* v. *Bell* as being based on a broad principle that "no man is entitled, *mala fide*, to enrich himself at the expense of another":[130] a proposition reminiscent of early statements of the law of personal bar. This is consistent, of course, with the observations of the same judge in what are definitely personal bar cases considered above. In another Melville Monument case, Lord Deas refers to the claims as being "for actual loss sustained in consequence of the unjustifiable representations and inducements made and held out by the one party to the other, contrary to all good faith".[131] The Lord Ordinary in *Bell* referred to the behaviour as *mala fide* and drew on a case (which is not a pre-contractual situation one)[132] where a man had led his younger brother's creditors to believe that the younger brother owned the family land, when in fact he had nothing. The creditors then claimed against the elder brother when the younger brother went insolvent.

These cases (and others later) are so full of references to good faith and bad faith that it is clear beyond a peradventure that this is what they are about. What the above attempts to show is that they may go beyond pre-contractual arrangements in their implications; although this does not mean that those in the context of pre-contractual arrangements cannot, consistently with this, be considered as an aspect of good faith in contracting.

[127] (1841) 3 D 1201.
[128] At 1204, per Lord Gillies; at 1204, per Lord Mackenzie.
[129] Defences Article 5.
[130] *Allan* v. *Gilchrist* (1875) 2 R 587, at 592, per Lord Deas.
[131] *Ibid.*, at 591, per Lord Deas.
[132] *Dougall* v. *Marshall* (1833) 11 S 1028.

Conclusion

The law of personal bar still awaits a comprehensive study that will give rise to a fully worked-out taxonomy. This essay seeks only to be part of the preparation of the necessary groundwork. What is clear, however, is that the case law contains a variety of approaches, and many interacting and sometimes potentially conflicting models can be found within it. The variety of approaches cannot be resolved by going back to find an original, simple model that has become overlaid by confusion. At the same time, it is submitted that the good faith model has much support in the material considered. As such, it constitutes an existing model and one that could reasonably be developed as a fundamental element of a taxonomy of this area of law. Such a model would also enable the interface with property and obligations law to be more clearly mapped and would then enable a structured approach to be taken to the question— whether personal bar can ever create rights, be a sword as well as a shield, or at any rate a spike in the middle of one?

8

Good Faith: A Principled Matter

Scott Crichton Styles*

Introduction

The general principle of good faith, contained in the general clauses of the *BGB*, and, in particular, the provisions of paragraph 242, is one of the most important aspects of German contract law. By contrast, English and Scots law contain no such explit general principle of good faith, although arguably they do have an implict or undisclosed principle of this sort. In this essay I will first of all briefly consider the reasons for the existence in Germany of a general principle of good faith and its absence, at least in an explicit form, from English and Scots law. I will next consider the main arguments against the introduction of a general principle of good faith, and lastly discuss what effects, if any, the introduction of such a general principle might bring.

Existence and Absence of a Good Faith Principle: Institutional Reasons

There are two, interconnected, reasons why good faith has come to occupy a prominent place in Continental law, especially that of Germany,[1] and a correspondingly less prominent place in the law of England and Scotland. These are (a) institutional and (b) legal cultural. The institutional reason for the importance of good faith in German contract law

* Lecturer in Law, University of Aberdeen.

[1] The most comprehensive modern account in English of the German principle of good faith is to be found in B.S. Markesinis, W. Lorenz, G. Dannemann, *The German Law of Obligations Volume I: The Law of Contracts and Restitution: A Comparative Introduction* (Oxford, 1997), ch. 7. For a more concise account see W.F. Ebke, B.M. Steinhauer, "The Doctrine of Good Faith in German Contract Law" in J. Beatson, D. Friedmann (eds), *Good Faith and Fault in Contract Law* (Oxford, 1995), 171.

is a direct result of the position of the courts in a codified system. The purpose of a code, as opposed to mere legislation, is, of course, to encompass the entire law over a given subject matter within one document. The aim is to create a gapless system of law. Closely connected with the very idea of a code is a suspicion of judicial power. As Wieacker said of the *BGB*:

> The *BGB* is a proper Code, that is, it is intended to regulate the matters within its purview completely and exhaustively, in line with the positivist ideal that the judge should be bound to the enacted and gapless text.[2]

A code, in a sense, is an attempt to "freeze" the law at one particular moment in time but, of course, society does not stand still. The problem then arises as to how the judiciary, faced with an apparently comprehensive code and a prohibition, or at least deep suspicion, of judicial law-making, can find the necessary leeway to develop the law so as to take into account both individual circumstances and general changes in society at large. The answer to this lies partially in the irredeemable ambiguity of the language of code. No matter how hard the draftsman tries to bind the hands of the judges, the latter will always be able to develop the law by interpreting particular provisions in ways unforeseen by, or even contrary to the wishes of, the draftsman. But there is also a second way in which the German courts have found a legislative basis for the necessary freedom to develop the law and interpret contacts, and that is by use of the famous "general clauses":

> These general clauses of the *BGB* have operated as a kind of safety valve, without which the rigid and precise terms of the *BGB* might have exploded under the pressure of social change.[3]

The general clauses of the *BGB* have proved to be of particular importance in Germany precisely because the courts there are faced with such a well thought-out and comprehensive code which *prima facie* greatly reduced their freedom for creative development of the law. Discussing the bland generality of the concept of good faith in paragraph 242 it has been said:

> [I]t is in this generality that we find the first clue of the importance of [paragraph 242]. For its blandness allowed it to become the peg on which numerous value judgements of German courts could be attached, thus acquiring

[2] F. Wieacker, *A History of Private Law in Europe* (Oxford, 1995), T. Weir (trans.), 376.
[3] K. Zweigert, H. Kötz, *An Introduction to Comparative Law* (Oxford, 3rd edn. 1998), 153. The general clauses are paras 138, 157, 242 and 826.

legitimacy in the eyes of jurists who are accustomed to justifying their decisions by reference to a written legal text.[4]

Some of the freedom given to the judges by the general clauses may well have been foreseen by the drafters. For example, the *contra bones mores* provision of paragraph 138, declaring that a legal transaction which "offends against good morals is void" was presumably left deliberately vague by the drafter because "good morals" is something that is hard to define and obviously changes through time. However, other general clauses, such as paragraphs 242 and 826, do not seem to have commanded attention when being drafted[5] and few lawyers of 1900 could have foreseen that paragraph 242 would eventually be recognised as " 'a principle of legal ethics", which dominates the entire [German] legal system".[6] Such fertile ground did the general clauses prove to be that, as Zimmermann remarks, in a standard commentary on the *BGB* the legal development of paragraph 242 alone occupies 1400 pages, predominantly in small print, which are devoted "to the compilation, classification and analysis of the rules and institutions derived from it".[7] The statutory peg of paragraph 242 thus supports a very long coat of case law.

The institutional reason why neither English nor Scots law has seen the need for any explicit, general principle of good faith is because of the relatively more prominent part which the common law courts play in the law-making process. In a largely case driven system with no code, and in the area of contract law, with only limited (though increasing) statutory intervention, the courts have the freedom to develop the law as and how they see fit. In the absence of a code there is no need to ground the judicial development of the law in the "statutory interpretation" of a general clause. Rather in a common law system it is accepted that judges can make and develop the law and that such a role is inherent in their judicial function.

[4] Markesinis *et al*, n. 1 above, 511.

[5] J.P. Dawson, *The Oracles of the Law* (Michigan, 1968), 461.

[6] N. Horn, H. Kötz, H.G. Leser, *German Private and Commercial Law: An Introduction* (Oxford, 1982), 135.

[7] R. Zimmermann, "An Introduction to German Legal Culture" in W.F. Ebke, M.W. Finkin (eds), *Introduction to German Law* (The Hague, 1996), 17.

Existence and Absence of a Good Faith Principle: Legal Cultural Reasons

The second reason for the existence of a good faith principle in German law and for its absence in English and Scots law is to be found in the basic attitude or style of judicial law-making in these jurisdictions, an element which, for want of a better term, I call reasons of the legal culture.

German law has long placed much importance on notions such as rationality and logical coherence. The law is understood as a coherent system and not as a mere sum of its parts. So, for example, the drafters of the *BGB* had an explicit instruction to test "the private law now in force in Germany for appropriateness, internal consistency, and coherence".[8] The lasting legacy of the Pandectists and of the ideal of a *Begriffsjurisprudence*, is embodied in statute by the *BGB* and also by the style of the German judiciary. German courts value and promote the very idea of general principles as important organising devices within a legal system. Whilst the *BGB* is not without its defects, most notably its complex structure and over abstraction, Wieacker nonetheless praises the general clauses as one of the most successful elements of the *BGB*:

> A better way of avoiding the twin pitfalls of colourless abstraction and clumsy detail is offered by *general clauses*, guidelines in the form of maxims addressed to the judge, designed both to control and to liberate him.[9]

In marked contrast, both the English judiciary and legal profession have long delighted in their scorn for general principles and internal coherence, an attitude memorably described by Zweigert and Kötz:

> On the Continent, the system is conceived as being complete and free from gaps, in England lawyers feel their way gradually from case to case. On the Continent lawyers delight in systematics, in England they are sceptical of every generalisation.[10]

The point is also made by McKendrick in this volume:

> English lawyers generally, and English contract lawyers in particular, have a deep-seated distrust of general principles.[11]

---

[8] See Wieacker, n. 2 above, 372.
[9] See n. 2 above, 377.
[10] Zweigert and Kötz, n. 3 above, 69.
[11] See McKendrick, above, 6.

This hostility to general principles is indeed a marked feature of English law and it manifests itself it what I term the "fractured formalism" of English law. It is fractured in the sense that, instead of adopting a wide general approach to legal problems, English law prefers to use "piecemeal solutions in response to demonstrated problems of unfairness".[12] It is formalist in the sense that formal reasons are often preferred by the courts to substantive ones.[13]

The reasons why English law has this hostility to general principles are largely historical and cultural and also beyond the scope of this essay. Here I want to examine, critically, the arguments against the adoption of the *specific* general principle of good faith. In so doing, it appears to me that there are four possible arguments against the introduction of a general principle of good faith into English law. Firstly, there is the argument that if general principles are needed, then their creation is a task for Parliament and not the courts. Secondly, there is the view that it is a violation of contractual freedom that parties should be bound by terms other than those explicitly agreed to. Thirdly, a general principle of good faith may be said to introduce non-legal criteria, such as ethics and morality. Fourthly, and perhaps most fundamentally, that such a general principle introduces uncertainty into the law.

Parliamentary or Judicial Law Reform?

Of all the arguments deployed against the introduction of a principle of good faith, by far the weakest is the one that it is for Parliament and not the courts to do so. For example, in *National Westminster Bank plc* v. *Morgan*[14] Lord Scarman argued against the need for a general principle of relief against inequality of bargaining power and stated that:

Parliament has undertaken the task—and it is essentially a legislative task— of enacting such restrictions upon freedom of contract as are in its judgement necessary to relieve against the mischief: for example, the hire-purchase and consumer protection legislation, of which the Supply of Goods (Implied Terms) Act 1973, Consumer Credit Act 1974, Consumer Safety Act 1978,

[12] *Interfoto Picture Library Ltd* v. *Stiletto Visual Programmes Ltd* [1989] QB 433, at 439 per Bingham MR.
[13] This distinction is made by P.S. Atiyah, *Essays on Contract* (Oxford, 1986), ch. 5, "Form and Substance in Contract Law". A formal reason is one based solely on complying with the appropriate procedure, a reason of substance is an ethical evaluation based on the rightness of the rule.
[14] [1985] AC 686.

Supply of Goods and Services Act 1982 and Insurance Companies Act 1982
are examples. I doubt whether the courts should assume the burden of formulating further restrictions.[15]

But surely it is unsatisfactory to have judges lamenting the state of the
law and then leaving the law as it stands? A good example of this is to
be found in *Lambert* v. *Co-operative Insurance Society Ltd*[16] where,
although the Court of Appeal lamented the state of the law regarding
the duty of disclosure in insurance contracts, it nevertheless found for
the insurance company.

The argument in favour of leaving reform to Parliament is unconvincing. Put simply, if a law reform is worth making, this should be
achieved as quickly and efficiently as possible. If the task is left to
Parliament it will be postponed, often for years, simply because of pressure on the legislative timetable of Parliament. The interests of justice
may dictate a swifter response.

Good Faith: Imposition or Implied term?

Despite various critiques, English and Scots contract law still retain
many of the presumptions of the nineteenth century classical contract
law.[17] *Chitty on Contracts*, for example, still states:

> There may be said to be three basic essentials to the creation of a contract:
> agreement, contractual intention and consideration.[18]

Agreement and consent are, of course, aspects of the will theory of contract law: the notion that the very essence of a contract is the concur-
ring wills of the parties.[19] The "positive liberty" to contract is often
generally understood as also implying a "negative liberty" from the
imposition of any terms other than those consented to.[20] The belief that

---

[15] At 708.

[16] [1975] 2 Lloyd's Rep 485.

[17] "In the nineteenth century the common law defined its conception of a just market
order in a remarkably rigorous set of doctrines. Its architecture was so elegant that it merits the title of the classical law of contract": H. Collins, *The Law of Contract* (London,
1986), 8.

[18] *Chitty on Contracts* (London, 27th edn, 1994), para. 2–001.

[19] This is not to say that modern contract law analysis is solely based on consent. The
importance of other notions, most notably reliance, has been increasingly recognised.

[20] The terms positive and negative liberty were popularised in recent time in Isaiah
Berlin's well known essay "Liberty" in I. Berlin, *Four Essays on Liberty* (London 1969).
The distinction is not unproblematic: see S.J. Heyman, "Positive and Negative Liberty"
(1992) 68 *Chicago-Kent Law Review* 81.

parties should enjoy a negative liberty lies behind the notion that the introduction of a general principle of good faith would be an unwarranted imposition upon the contracting parties:

> [I]f there is one thing which more than another public policy requires, it is that men of full age and competent understanding shall have the utmost liberty of contracting, and that their contracts when entered into freely and voluntarily shall be held sacred and shall be enforced by Courts of justice.[21]

In a similar vein McKendrick asks:

> What justification is there for imposing on the parties a greater obligation than the obligations they themselves have voluntarily assumed? The broad invocation of good faith should not suffice to trump a legally binding, but limited promise.[22]

At first sight, the negative liberty argument seems a strong one, but only a moment's reflection shows that much of the law is about imposing duties: most criminal law and much public law is of this form, and, of course, the imposition of duties is the very essence of the law of tort and delict. Nor does the law allow unfettered positive freedom to contracting parties. Contracts may be struck down because they are illegal, or immoral, or contrary to public policy. An important current example of a legally implied term is the good faith requirement imposed by virtue of the 1994 Unfair Terms in Consumer Contracts Regulations,[23] and the importance of legally implied contractual conditions is now widely recognised:

> On the theoretical level, the approach which attributes the main body of contract law to the parties' intention has been largely abandoned. It is now openly recognized that a substantial part of contract law derives from *ex lege* rules although the parties are, in many instances, free to deviate from them.[24]

Consequently, a general principle of good faith only seems like an anomalous interference in contractual liberty if one ignores the existence of other *ex lege* rules. Furthermore, there is a wider point which needs to be made here, namely, that the classical theory of contract is a nineteenth century, will-centred, individualistic conception of a contract.

---

[21] *Printing and Numerical Registering Co.* v. *Sampson* (1875) LR 19 Eq 462, at 465 per Sir George Jessel MR.
[22] See McKendrick, above, 60.
[23] Which implemented into UK domestic law the EC Directive on Unfair Terms in Consumer Contracts: Council Directive 93/13/EEC, 5 April 1993, OJ L95/29.
[24] Beatson and Friedmann, "Introduction: From 'Classical' to 'Modern' Contract Law", n. 1 above, 3, at 16.

The classical contract is seen as subsisting between the parties and only the parties: the existence of the rest of society and of the state is simply ignored. Human potential, however, can only be realised within the community. Law is "simply a means to the end of a rational ordering of communal life"[25] and this applies to contracts as much as to statutes. Contract is one aspect of our autonomy within community.

The classical approach ignores the fact that in a very real sense the state is the "invisible partner" or environmental background to every contract. As Durkheim put it:

> A contract is not sufficient unto itself, but is possible only thanks to the regulation of the contract which is originally social.[26]

What differentiates a contract from a mere agreement between parties is that a contract is an agreement which is ultimately enforceable by invoking the power of the state. It is the existence of the state, with its vital monopoly of internal forms of physical compulsion, initially in the form of the courts and ultimately in form of bailiffs, sheriff officers and, if necessary, the police, which makes contracts possible. The state, the legal embodiment of society, is the ultimate guarantor of contracts. It therefore follows that society will not be willing to enforce a contract if its terms are in some way repulsive to the values of society. The most obvious way in which this is done in the common law is by using the doctrines of illegality, immorality or of being contrary to public policy to strike down unacceptable contractual terms. But the debate about the possible introduction of a general principle of good faith is also a debate about the values which society upholds.

When one understands a contract *solely* as an exercise in the granting of consent by the individual parties, then it is easy to conceive of a general doctrine of good faith as being essentially an imposition upon the parties, a violation, as it were, of their consent. If, however, one understands a contract as being an exercise in autonomy, within the limits set by the wider community, then this problem largely vanishes. Instead of seeing the principle of good faith as an imposition against the will of the parties, it can be viewed rather as merely making explicit the background assumptions of parties. Moreover, since most parties do in fact contract in good faith, a general principle of good faith can be seen not so much as an unwarranted imposition but rather as an implied term.

---

[25] Zweigert and Kötz, n. 3 above, 146.
[26] E. Durkheim, *The Division of Labour in Society* (1933), quoted in A. Hunt, *The Sociological Movement in Law* (London, 1978), 85.

Admittedly there may be a few rogues and scoundrels who might claim that good faith is indeed an imposition upon them, in which case the law might indeed be said to impose good faith contrary to the parties' will, but this is no more problematic than the law refusing to enforce a contract for the sale of heroin or for the provision of a prostitute's services. We do have freedom of contract it is true, but that freedom is, quite naturally, only to be exercised under the law.

Contracts and Community Values

The third possible objection to the introduction of a general principle of good faith is that such a principle is a moral or extra-legal principle and, therefore, has no place in legal reasoning: the old positivistic argument that morality and the law should be kept separate. The argument that law has nothing to do with morality is one that became dominant in the nineteenth century at much the same time as the will theory was becoming the dominant conception of contract law in both the common and civil law worlds. Indeed, arguably, the two doctrines reinforced each other. As Gordley has pointed out, the reduction of the theoretical basis of contract law to that of the pure will theory is a nineteenth century phenomenon.[27] The ancients and Scholastics[28] had seen the exchange of consent as only one factor in the making of a contract: the Aristotelian virtues of promise-keeping, liberality and commutative justice, together with equality in exchange, were also considered to be vital factors in the interpretation and enforcement of contracts by the courts. These principles had remained important in the seventeenth and eighteenth centuries[29] and were only disregarded in the systematic reformulation of legal doctrine which occurred in the nineteenth century and which only gradually assumed its present, will-centred, individualistic form. The classical contract law assumption, that it is the task of the courts to administer the "pure positive law" uninfluenced by such extraneous factors as the moral values of society, leads naturally to the argument that the moralistic notions implicit, indeed explicit, in a general principle of good faith must be rejected. However, as already argued above, the classical, positivistic approach is based on a crude and unconvincing notion

---

[27] J. Gordley, *The Philosophical Origins of Modern Contract Doctrine* (Oxford, 1991), ch. 7.

[28] *Ibid.*, chs 2 and 3.

[29] *Ibid.*, chs 4–6.

of the autonomy of the law. The law has never existed in isolation from the rest of society's values and nor do contractual agreements. Morality is used as a controlling device in respect of contracts most notably, though certainly not exclusively, through the concept of public policy. Moreover, the traditional hostility of the English courts to general principles of good faith and fairness seems to rest not so much on a strong positivistic separation of law and morality, but rather on the presumption that those particular general principles are incompatible with the values of society in the broadest sense. The courts for the past two hundred years have held a strong, if often inarticulate, faith in *laissez faire* capitalism. In the nineteenth century, courts and theorists alike largely adopted the perspective of the "Manchester" school of economics.[30] The classical model of contract law presupposes that the self-interest of the parties will determine the market, and the operation of the unfettered free market will in turn, via Adam Smith's invisible hand,[31] lead to the promotion of the common good as understood in utilitarian terms. It is this presumption that the market is sacrosanct, because what is good for the market is good for society at large, which lies behind the unwillingness of the courts to interfere with what may be a manifestly unfair or bad faith contract.

In Germany the principle of good faith proved to be a powerful mechanism for allowing non-legal values to influence the development of contract law. As Zimmermann remarks:

> General clauses like paragraphs 138 and 242 are widely regarded as the most important as well as the most convenient ports of entry for the values of the community, as sanctioned by the catalogue of Basic Rights in the Basic Law.[32]

In England and Scotland the courts have also been willing, in appropriate circumstances, to strike down contracts which in some way offend against morality or public policy. And so they have struck down as unenforceable contracts which are perceived to be immoral, such as the leasing of premises to a prostitute,[33] or in restraint of trade.[34] Given that

---

[30] See further, P.S. Atiyah, *The Rise and Fall of Freedom of Contract* (Oxford, 1979).

[31] *An Inquiry into the Nature and Causes of the Wealth of Nations* (1759), IV.1.10, R.H. Campbell, A.S. Skinner (eds), (Oxford, 1976).

[32] Zimmermann, n. 7 above, 18.

[33] *Girardy* v. *Richardson* (1793) 1 Esp 13.

[34] For example, *Mason* v. *Provident Clothing and Supply Co. Ltd* [1913] AC 724; *Esso Petroleum Co. Ltd* v. *Harper's Garage (Stourport) Ltd* [1968] AC 269. Scots law has been much influenced in the sphere of restraint of trade by the English decisions.

the courts have been willing to interfere with "freedom of contract" for reasons of sexual ethics and commercial utility respectively, it can be seen that there is no general argument against the use of extra-legal criteria in judicial decision making and, therefore, on that ground there can be no argument against the introduction of a general principle of good faith. The fact of the matter is that the courts do apply ethical and other non-legal values in their decision making. One important and welcome example of this value-led approach was the refusal of the eighteenth century courts in both England and Scotland to recognise slavery as an institution.[35] On the other hand, it is surely astonishing that whilst the British courts might strike down contractual terms in restraint of trade, they were still willing, prior to the Unfair Contract Terms Act 1977, to uphold (subject to the doctrines of due notice and interpretation *contra proferentem*) all sorts of extreme exclusionary or limitation clauses[36]—including those against loss of life. Is it not somewhat paradoxical that the courts which would not allow an employer to impose an overly restrictive covenant in restraint of employment, would nonetheless permit a carrier to make a contract of carriage on terms which excused him for any loss or liability to the passenger for the death or injury of that passenger?

It is also perhaps the specifically moralistic flavour of the expression "good faith" which causes some disquiet among the pragmatically minded English and Scottish judiciary. In this context, it is interesting to speculate what might have happened if the *BGB* had spoken of "reasonableness" and/or "fairness" rather than "good faith". If, for example, paragraphs 157 and 242 read respectively:

> Contracts shall be interpreted according to the requirement of *reasonableness and/or fairness*, giving consideration to general usage.
> The debtor is bound to effect performance according to the requirements of *reasonableness and/or fairness*, giving consideration to general usage.

If the *BGB* had been framed in terms of "reasonableness and/or fairness", rather than in terms of good faith, I do not believe that the German courts would have developed the law in any significantly different way. On the other hand, put in this hypothetically amended form, I believe that such a general principle of "reasonableness and/or fairness" would be acceptable to even the most conservative English lawyer.

[35] *Somersett* v. *Stewart* (1772) 20 St Tr 1; *Knight* v. *Wedderburn* (1778) Mor 14545.
[36] *The Stella* [1900] P 161. Here the exclusion clause was broad enough to exclude successfully liability for the death of a ship's passenger even although the stranding was caused by the, admitted, negligence of the carrier.

Yet the difference between a general principle of good faith and a general principle of reasonableness or fairness is, it is submitted, largely rhetorical. In both cases, the judges must interpret a contract in the light of a wide general principle which embodies the values of society at large. Imagine, for a moment, present day counsel appearing in an English case involving pre-contractual expenditure. If counsel argues the case on the ground of "good faith" it is likely that the judge will tell him or her that such a principle is unknown to English law; and add for good measure that he or she for one is glad that English law has no truck with such an abstract and vague concept. If, however, counsel argues the case on the basis of "reasonable expectations" or the "legitimate expectations of persons in that particular line of business" it is likely that the judge will give an argument in this form a much warmer reception. But, in essence, good faith and reasonable expectations amount to the same thing.[37]

Good Faith: An Uncertain Principle?

Perhaps the most fundamental and widespread reason for hostility to a general principle of good faith within some quarters is the belief that general principles promote uncertainty in the law. McKendrick, for example, believes that the reason for this hostility is that:

> When confronted with a broad general principle their (i.e., English contract lawyers') instinct is to object that it is too vague, too uncertain or, otherwise unworkable.[38]

Instead of general principles, English lawyers place their faith in incremental reasoning, adjusting certain pre-existing categories of controlling devices (such as frustration, undue influence and estoppel) to achieve much the same results as the Germans achieve with a broad principle of good faith. The common law seems to prefer narrow "doctrines" to wide principles. Pragmatism and robust common sense are preferred to legal logic and principles. Given the importance of these doctrines, it is therefore worth considering the use of exclusion clauses and the doctrine of undue influence, two of the controlling devices employed by

---

[37] Often by use of the doctrine of implied terms which satisfy the test of "business efficacy". See, for example, *The Moorcock* (1889) 14 PD 64; *Shirlaw* v. *Southern Foundries (1926) Ltd* [1939] 2 KB 206; and *Liverpool City Council* v. *Irwin* [1977] AC 239. Characteristically the courts have developed the doctrine in a fairly restrictive way, stressing that the term should be necessary to give business efficacy to the contract.

[38] See McKendrick, above, 6.

English law, in order to see how these operate. First, however, a few words must be said about the wider issue of uncertainty in the law.

Contractual Certainty and the Limits of Language

Both the English and Scottish courts make much of the need for certainty in the law. But to a large extent, when the courts try to find certainty by relying on the words of the contract *alone*, they are attempting an impossible task. The problem is one, long discussed by philosophers, of the basic ambiguity of language.[39] All language, even that of meticulously drafted contracts, contains an inherent penumbra of ambiguity. Much of this ambiguity is, however, resolved by the context of the words and also by contact and co-operation between the participating parties. As Pinker has pointed out: "people work around its (i.e., language's) limitations by tacitly agreeing on how to use it".[40] The difficulty for legal draftsmen, whether of contracts, statutes or other documents is that, as Pinker further observes: "The law requires language to do something for which it is badly designed: to leave nothing to the imagination".[41] The important point for present purposes is that the meaning of words, including those in contracts, is *always* contextual, and cannot be understood apart from the relevant context.[42] Even the classical approach to contract law recognises that the context of a contract is sometimes essential for its interpretation and, typically, resolves such cases by use of the notion of an implied term.[43] When the

[39] The ambiguity of language was a problem known to the ancient Greeks (*vide* Plato and Aristotle) and has continued to fascinate and perplex in this century: as witnessed by the work of Wittgenstein and Derrida. For a useful philosophical collection of primary sources, see A.P. Martinich, *The Philosophy of Language* (Oxford, 1990).

[40] S. Pinker, "Ins and Outs of the Meaning of 'is' ", *The Independent*, 19 February 1999. Although this quotation comes from a newspaper Pinker has published extensively in the field of socio-linguistics. See Pinker, *Connections and Symbols* (Cambridge, Mass., 1988); *The Language Instinct: The New Science Of Language And Mind* (London, 1994); and *How The Mind Works* (London, 1998).

[41] *The Independent*, n. 40 above.

[42] For a lengthy, if slightly dated, discussion of some of the problems of contractual interpretation, from a reasonably philosophical perspective, see A.L. Corbin, *Corbin on Contracts: A Comprehensive Treatise on the Working Rules of Contract Law* (St. Paul, Minnesota, 1950–64), vol. 1, ch. 4; vol. 3. For the issue approached with a statutory emphasis see W. Twining, and D. Miers, *How to Do Things with Rules: a Primer of Interpretation* (London, 3rd edn, 1991), *passim*.

[43] The classic English case is *The Moorcock*, n. 37 above. See also, *Reigate* v. *Union Manufacturing Co.* [1918] 1 KB 592 and *L. Schuler AG* v. *Wickman Machine Tool Sales Ltd* [1974] AC 235.

principle of good faith is criticised as being "too vague, too uncertain or, otherwise unworkable"[44] this is a vital point which is frequently overlooked. Just because a word needs to be interpreted in context does not mean it is ambiguous or uncertain. Consider the simple example of the word "tall". The actual height described by the word tall will depend on its context. A tall person is a very different height from a tall tree. Indeed, a tall man, say six feet plus, is the same height as a small tree. Nevertheless, we understand the meaning of the word, and do not find it too vague to be unworkable. The concept of good faith (and for that matter the concepts of fairness and reasonableness) works in a similar way. Much of the meaning of good faith will necessarily depend on the context of the contract. This is not a weakness, but a strength, and should alert judges to the need to take into the account the intentions of the parties: intentions which, typically, will be heavily context dependent. In the oil industry, for example, it is common to demand contractual performance "in accordance with good oil field practice". While this may be vague, it is far from meaningless: thus any practice which jeopardises safety or entails prohibitive costs would certainly be deemed to be contrary to good oil field practice.

The problem with the traditional approach of the English and Scottish courts is that they often ignore the actual factual context of a contract and, instead, understand all contracts as being set in the same context: that of the "one-off" deal negotiated in the open market. The paradigm appears to be that of the man or woman in the street market haggling over the price of fruit or an old painting. In this situation the parties are indeed adversarial: the buyer wants a low price the seller a high one. The transaction is a "one-off". The parties will never have dealings with each other again. It is unspoken assumptions predicated on this unidimensional view of contractual context which, I believe, leads to judicial comments of the following sort:

> [T]he concept of a duty to carry on negotiations in good faith is inherently repugnant to the adversarial position of the parties involved in negotiations.[45]

I would argue, however, that in practice most people, in most contractual situations, do not conceive of contracts as being inherently adversarial. Most contracts are in fact seen as "win-win" deals, where the

---

[44] See McKendrick, above, 6.

[45] *Walford* v. *Miles* [1992] 2 AC 128, at 138 per Lord Ackner. For a discussion of this case see P. Neill, "A Key to Lock-out Agreements?" (1992) 108 *Law Quarterly Review* 405.

buyer gets reasonable goods or service and the seller gets a reasonable price. Moreover, as has been well recognised, in many contracts, typically but not only those now generally characterised as "consumer" contracts, there is no negotiation of price or conditions, and the buyer must simply take the contract or leave it. Equally many commercial contracts are essentially "relational" transactions where the parties may be united, generally to their mutual benefit, over a period of many years.[46] One cannot help but speculate that the judiciary's devotion to the notion of the inherently adversarial nature of all contracts is actually a reflection of the influence of their own experiences, initially, as counsel and, subsequently, as judges. It is courts, not contracts, which are inherently adversarial, and it may be that the necessarily atypical range of cases which comes before the courts gives those who spend their working lives there a distorted impression of the reality of ordinary commercial and contractual life. After all, by definition, if contractual parties have reached the stage of suing each other, the relationship between them will indeed be adversarial. However, the vast majority of contracts are never litigated upon.

Exclusion Clauses

An example of the negative consequences which flow from a lack of general principles is to be seen in the attitude of the English and Scottish courts to exclusion clauses before the enactment of the Unfair Contract Terms Act 1977. According to the classical notion of freedom of contract, parties can bind themselves in any way whatsoever (subject to the restraints based on public policy and illegality) and are, therefore, free to agree any terms, including an indemnity or exclusion clause, no matter how unreasonable. The theory, however, ignores that in reality contractual life often involves unequal bargaining, standard terms, monopoly suppliers and the like. Such unequal circumstances allow the stronger party to impose terms which may be highly disadvantageous to the weaker party. Because of the fear of general principles, the English and Scottish courts failed to develop a coherent substantive approach to

---

[46] There is a growing literature on relational contracts, perhaps the most prominent writer in this field is I.R. MacNeil, *Contracts: Exchange Transactions and Relations* (New York, 2nd edn, 1978). A full list of MacNeil's writings is given in D. Campbell, "The Social Theory of Relational Contract: MacNeil as the Modern Proudhon" (1990) 18 *International Journal of Sociology of Law* 75.

exclusion clauses, such as that which would be embodied in a general
principle of good faith, or even in a general principle of "unreasonable"
or "unfair" terms. Instead, the British courts chose to deal with this
problem by employing such indirect controlling devices as the requirement of due notice and the interpretation of contract terms *contra proferentem*. Naturally, the courts only invoked doctrines such as due notice
or interpretation *contra proferentem* when they considered that the contract was in some sense unfair, but through fear of general principles the
courts could not bring themselves to admit that their underlying concern was really with basic contractual fairness. The approach is fractured
because there is no general principle, it is indirect because it addresses
collateral issues rather than the main problem, and it is formalist in the
sense that notice is often understood formally rather than substantively.
Many of the problems in this area were of course resolved by the introduction of the Unfair Contract Terms Act 1977, which introduced a
(general principle!) basic standard of reasonableness for exclusion
clauses in business contracts. If the English judiciary had had a legal culture which was happier with general principles, then the problems in
this area could have been resolved many years earlier by the development of an indigenous general principle of good faith or unfairness. A
general principle of good faith would have resolved such problems in a
direct and substantive manner. This example of the negative consequences which may result from a lack of general principles in English
law can be contrasted with the German judiciary's development of paragraph 138 to combat unfair standard contract terms. So effective was
this judicial use of paragraph 138 that much of the content of the subsequent German Standard Terms Act 1976 was merely a statutory
embodiment of the principles laid down by the courts.[47]

Undue Influence and Duress

Another of the controlling devices used by English and Scots contract
law is the doctrine of undue influence. As with doctrines such as due
notice and *contra proferentem*, the approach is largely an indirect one: a
contract is struck down not because its terms are unfair or lacking in
good faith but because of a deficiency in consent.

[47] Zimmermann, n. 7 above, 17. For details see O. Sandrock, "The Standard Terms
Act 1976 of West Germany" (1976) 26 *American Journal of Comparative Law* 551. For a
discussion of the pre-1976 German case law see J.P. Dawson, "Unconscionable
Coercion—the German Version" (1976) 89 *Harvard Law Review* 1041.

A striking example of judicial hostility to general principles can be found in the decision of the House of Lords in *National Westminster Bank plc* v. *Morgan*[48] where Lord Scarman firmly quashed the attempt by Lord Denning MR in *Lloyd's Bank Ltd* v. *Bundy*[49] to create a general principle of "inequality of bargaining power" which would cover cases of undue influence. Lord Scarman was critical of the Denning principle, not merely because of its content,[50] but because it was a principle:

> There is no precisely defined law setting limits to the equitable jurisdiction of a court to relieve against undue influence. This is the world of doctrine, not of neat and tidy rules . . . A court in the exercise of this equitable jurisdiction is a court of conscience. Definition is a poor instrument when used to determine whether a transaction is or is not unconscionable: this is a question which depends on the particular facts of the case.[51]

This a remarkably frank, but far from atypical, example of the English judiciary's dislike of definitions, of a judicial culture which, quite unlike that of Germany, resists any attempt to introduce general principles into the operation of the law. However, Lord Scarman's statement contains a paradox which I believe lies at the heart of much English legal reasoning. A *general* principle is criticised because of its alleged uncertainty and, therefore, general principles must be rejected in favour of distinct, but limited, doctrines such as undue influence or due notice. These doctrines, however, remain undefined except to the extent that the courts will announce, in a given case, whether or not a set of facts comes under a particular doctrine. But while this approach maximises judicial discretion to decide a case on its merits, it also maximises uncertainty, since the application or non-application of a doctrine will often seem to be arbitrary. So, for example, the categories of relationships where undue influence (a doctrine which as Lord Scarman stated in the passage quoted above has no precise limits) is presumed may suddenly be

[48] See n. 14 above.
[49] [1975] QB 326.
[50] The general principle argued for by Lord Denning was problematic because he chose to stress inequality of bargaining power which was too narrow a notion, as Lord Scarman said: "The fact of an unequal bargain will, of course, be a relevant feature in some cases of undue influence. But it can never become an appropriate basis of principle of an equitable doctrine which is concerned with transactions not to be reasonably accounted for on the ground of friendship, relationship, charity, or other ordinary motives on which ordinary men act". For a general discussion, see J. Cartwright, *Unequal Bargaining: A Study of Vitiating Factors in the Formation of Contract* (Oxford, 1991).
[51] See n. 14 above, 709.

widened to include spouses, as happened in *Barclays Bank plc* v. *O'Brien*:[52] a development which can hardly be viewed as conducive to certainty in the law, not least because it appears to be based on a view of the relationship between husbands and wives which is completely out of sympathy with modern views of gender equality.[53]

Equity: A Less Certain Principle than Good Faith?

To an outsider, such as a Scots lawyer, the arguments in England against the introduction of a general principle of good faith, on the grounds that it will be productive of uncertainty, sit strangely with the fact that English law contains that eclectic bundle of principles and doctrines known as equity. To cavil at a general principle of good faith, yet accept the principles of equity, is to strain at a civilian gnat, whilst happily swallowing an equitable camel. The breadth of the twelve maxims of equity is quite breathtaking. To cite three of the vaguest: "Equity will not suffer a wrong to be without a remedy"; "Equity looks upon that as done which ought to be done"; and "Equity is equality". Are these equitable maxims inherently any more certain than the general clauses of the *BGB*? When compared with the equitable maxims just cited, the provisions of paragraph 157 ("Contracts shall be interpreted according to the requirement of good faith, giving consideration to general usage".) or of paragraph 242 ("The debtor is bound to effect performance according to the requirements of good faith, giving consideration to general usage".) are of crystalline clarity.

The basic meaning of the term equity is fairness and justice, and, had English legal culture been more favourable to general principles, the notion of equity could have been used as a general principle governing the creation, interpretation and enforcement of all contracts. The actual use of equity is, of course, far from being merely the random application of the Lord Chancellor's foot to whatever problem comes along.[54] In English law equity was tamed in two related ways. First, it has been refined into various rules and doctrines (such as promissory estoppel and

---

[52] [1994] 1 AC 180.

[53] See S.M. Cretney, "The Little Woman and the Big Bad Bank" (1992) 108 *Law Quarterly Review* 534.

[54] *Gee* v. *Pritchard* (1818) 2 Swan 402, at 414 per Lord Eldon: "Nothing would inflict on me greater pain in quitting this place than the recollection that I had done anything to justify the reproach that the equity of this court varies like the Chancellor's foot".

undue influence) which are all controlled by precedent. Second, equity is a remedy which is only available in certain pre-existing circumstances, such as promissory estoppel or undue influence situations. Here we see very clearly the English fear of general principles. When confronted with a patently unfair contract the English judge does not start with a broad principle like good faith or fairness and then apply a specific example of the principle to solve the problem. Instead the judge asks himself if this situation comes under any of the pre-existing grounds for the application of an equitable remedy and, if it does, the remedy may be granted: if it does not, the judge will express regret and find for the other party. Equity is not a remedy of potentially universal application to contracts but is available only in certain limited situations, and affords yet another example of the tendency towards fractured formalism in English law. On the other hand, it cannot be denied that equity continues to develop in new and unforeseen ways.

In contrast, the *BGB* conception of good faith is one of potentially universal application to contracts. The German judge starts with the assumption that if the situation requires it he or she will be able to deploy the principle of good faith to resolve it. That said however, the manner in which the principle of good faith has been developed by the German courts does have some strong parallels with the development of doctrines of equity in England. Much of the potential uncertainty in the operation of equity is resolved by breaking the concept down into distinct doctrines, such as promissory estoppel or undue influence, controlled by precedent. In a similar fashion, the (potentially very wide) scope of the general principle of good faith contained in paragraphs 157 and 242 might be expected to produce uncertainty in the interpretation of contracts: but this is not in fact how the German courts have operated. In their interpretation and development of the general principle of good faith, the German courts have inevitably broken down that wide principle into various smaller, more specific, examples such as *culpa in contrahendo*, impracticability and frustration of purpose, mutual error, and, the doctrine of the destruction of the foundation of the transaction (*Wegfall der Geschäftsgrundlage*).[55] As Markesinis remarks: "In reality . . . it is not the general clause but the case law of the courts which produces the rules".[56] So whilst a general principle of good faith was

---

[55] 112 RGZ 329 (1926), discussed in Dawson, n. 5 above, 474.

[56] B.S. Markesinis, "The Legacy of History on German Contract Law", in his *Foreign Law and Comparative Methodology: A Subject and a Thesis* (Oxford, 1997), 90. See also Wieacker, n. 2 above, 411.

created by the *BGB*, the content or meaning of that general principle was, and is, determined by the exposition of German judges and jurists.

The fact that the broad principle of good faith is, in Germany, largely applied by the mediation of intermediate doctrines, such as the doctrine of the destruction of the foundation of the transaction, might lead one to suppose that the practical, as opposed to the theoretical, differences between English and German law in the area of good faith may be overstated. However, I would argue that whilst there are undoubted similarities between good faith and the controlling devices used by English law, there still remain some important differences.

Good Faith: An Undisclosed but Weak Principle?

Whilst it is true that English lawyers appear happiest when applying discrete categories rather than general principles such as good faith, there is undoubtedly an over-arching concern with fairness and reasonableness in both the English and Scottish courts. MacQueen has argued, elsewhere in this volume, that good faith may be seen as an undisclosed principle in Scots law.[57] With regard to English law, McKendrick seems to distinguish between different conceptions of good faith, one of which English law already has, the other which it does not:

> [I]n so far as good faith incorporates the principle that the expectations engendered by a binding promise must be honoured few problems are likely to arise. Similarly, in so far as good faith is used to explain why wrongs, whether legal or equitable, must be remedied or why unjust enrichments must be reversed few practical problems are likely to arise. But . . . good faith is redundant in these contexts. These principles can stand in their own right and the invocation of good faith is more likely to distract than illuminate. Where good faith comes into its own is when it goes beyond these principles and it is at this point that I begin to have difficulty.[58]

McKendrick then gives two scenarios where good faith gives him difficulties:

> The first arises where good faith is used in an attempt to impose on a contracting party a more onerous obligation than that contained in the contract. The second arises where good faith is used to limit the ability of a negotiat-

---

[57] See Macqueen, above, 13.
[58] See McKendrick, above, 59.

ing party to withdraw from contractual negotiations without incurring any liability for doing so.[59]

The first form of good faith to which McKendrick refers I propose, for convenience, to term the "weak" conception of good faith; the second may be termed the "strong" conception. In its weak guise McKendrick appears to accept that good faith does, in effect, form part of English law; that it is, as MacQueen says of good faith in Scots law, an undisclosed principle. But whilst MacQueen favours the adoption of good faith as an explicit principle of Scots law, McKendrick is opposed to the adoption of good faith as an explicit principle of English law on the ground that it is both unnecessary and potentially confusing:

> [G]ood faith is redundant in these contexts. These principles can stand in their own right and the invocation of good faith is more likely to distract than illuminate.[60]

With respect, I would suggest that McKendrick is mistaken in his reservations concerning a strong good faith principle. An *explicit* principle of good faith, even in its weak form, would have two important advantages over the present position of (depending on one's point of view) either no principle at all or an undisclosed one. Firstly, an explicit principle of good faith would liberate the notion of fairness in English law from the restrictions of the doctrines of equity. Good faith would be a remedy available whenever it was needed and not restricted to those situations where equity applies. Secondly, the adoption of an explicit principle of good faith should result in the judiciary developing an increased self-awareness of the task they perform when dealing with unfair contracts. Too often the courts have consciously or unconsciously hidden their desire for fairness behind the various controlling devices of English law, a situation regretted by Atiyah:

> Unfortunately, the extreme reluctance of courts to acknowledge openly that they are trying to ensure that a contract operates as a fair exchange means that the conceptual apparatus of the law is highly complex and often obscures what is actually going on.[61]

A principle of good faith, simply by making explicit what is presently merely implicit in English law, would result in a more purposive interpretation of contracts. This, in turn, would help to promote coherence

---

[59] *Ibid.*
[60] *Ibid.*
[61] Atiyah, n. 13 above, 337.

in the law of contract, thereby mitigating the tendency of English law to break down into the fractured formalism of distinct doctrines whose underlying rationale or interconnection is often but little understood by practitioners and judges. A principle of good faith would help to promote a rational contract law, where substantive fairness to the parties was achieved within a coherent set of rules.[62] Admittedly, once an explicit general principle of good faith is adopted it might well be hard to stop the principle being extended in the stronger fashion which McKendrick fears. But, rather than being perceived as unwarranted impositions on free agents and creating uncertainty in contracts, these interventions might in fact be welcomed by the business community, and, indeed, by society at large, as merely bringing the law into line with the existing values and expectations of these groups.

Conclusion

Although I believe the adoption of an explicit general principle of good faith in both England and Scotland to be a highly desirable goal, I also believe that the adoption or rejection of such a principle is ultimately less important than the legal-cultural values of the judiciary. Any principle or doctrine can be used for good or ill. In this respect, the history in Germany of the general principle of good faith furnishes vivid examples. In the 1920s, the principle of good faith was used positively to allow commerce, and society at large, to cope with the problems of hyperinflation,[63] but in the 1930s, under the Nazi regime, it was used negatively to promote the anti-Semitic policies of that regime.[64] Had there been an equally anti-Semitic totalitarian regime in power in England at this time, the courts there might conceivably have developed the doctrines of English law in an equally malign fashion: e.g. by developing the doctrine of undue influence to negate contracts favourable to Jewish businessmen.

Regardless of whether or not a general principle of good faith is explicitly adopted by, or imposed (through membership of the European

---

[62] For a stimulating argument in favour of an explicit principle of good faith as a means of promoting legal and moral rationality within contract law see J. Adams, R. Brownsword, *Key Issues in Contract* (London, 1995), ch. 7.

[63] See, for example, the cases RGZ 100,129 and RGZ 103,328. Note also, J.P. Dawson, "Effects of Inflation on Private Contracts: Germany 1914–1924" (1933) 33 *Michigan Law Review* 171.

[64] Markesinis *et al*, n. 1 above, 512.

Union) upon, the English and Scottish legal systems, what really matters is the attitude of the judges. Even if there were to be no explicit
adoption of a good faith principle in the near future, bold English judges
could easily extend the existing doctrines of English law to provide all
of the remedies presently afforded by the German good faith principle.
In many ways a start in exactly this direction was made during the judicial career of Lord Denning. For example, in *Central London Property
Trust Ltd* v. *High Trees House Ltd*[65] he invented promissory estoppel,
thereby transforming the common law doctrine of estoppel, which was
generally understood as concerning misrepresentations of existing facts,
into a new doctrine of reliance on promises. Contrariwise, even if a general principle of good faith is explicitly adopted, or imposed by Europe,
it would be perfectly possible for the English judiciary to interpret that
principle in the most fractured and formalist manner should they wish
to, so breaking down the general principle into sets of distinct doctrines.
This is the view taken by Teubner:

> In Britain, it may well be that "good faith" . . . will trigger deep, long-term
> changes from highly formal rule-focused decision-making in contract law
> toward a more discretionary principle-based judicial reasoning. But it will
> probably move into a direction quite different from German-style dogmati-
> sation. Given the distinctive British mode of episode linkages, good faith
> will be developed rather in forms of judicial activism similar to those other
> common law countries have adopted, combining close fact-orientated case
> analysis with loosely arranged arguments from broad principles and poli-
> cies.[66]

Even more than a general principle of good faith, what would transform
contract law in England and Scotland is a judiciary which embraces, as
a primary legal cultural value, the idea of substantive fairness in the law
and of the internal coherence of the law. Substantive fairness is important because the role of contract law, like all law, should be to promote
the welfare of society at large. It may be said that English judges already
do try to implement fair solutions, it is just that they often try to hide
the fact. As Atiyah comments: "It is my view that in fact the law of contract is today greatly concerned with substantive fairness of exchange".[67]
Internal coherence is important because that is the best way to promote

[65] [1947] KB 130.
[66] G. Teubner, "Legal Irritants: Good Faith in British Law or How Unifying Law
Ends Up in New Divergences" (1998) 61 *Modern Law Review* 11, 20–1.
[67] See n. 13 above, 331.

the comprehensibility and predictability of the law for both lawyers and non-layers alike. As a matter of principle, the law needs to be principled, and the adoption of a general principle of good faith would be an excellent way to promote that goal.

9

Good Faith in Consumer Contracts: Rule, Policy and Principle

Chris Willett*

Introduction

This chapter considers the role of good faith in consumer contracts. It looks at a particular good faith *rule*. It also looks at the possibility of developing a *general principle* of good faith which could be used to shape consumer policy and aid the rational development of the law. The good faith rule under consideration is contained in the Directive on Unfair Terms in Consumer Contracts.[1] This Directive was implemented almost verbatim by the Unfair Terms in Consumer Contracts Regulations 1994.[2] An important aspect of the argument made below is that the good faith rule must be understood in the context of the consumer policy of the European Community. European consumer policy seeks, *inter alia*, to promote market integration by establishing a high level of consumer protection, and by generating consumer confidence. Information is the primary tool to be used in protecting consumers and generating confidence. The idea is to ensure that the consumer has information on all of the matters that affect his interests: or, to put this another way, the idea is that certain things should be transparent to the consumer. The next task is to identify just what it is that should be transparent to the consumer and what form this transparency should take. Following this, we must consider the limits of transparency. Even if a high level of transparency can be achieved, will this be sufficient to ensure consumer protection and confidence? If transparency cannot guarantee protection and confidence, then it has to be supplemented by

---

* Professor of Consumer Law, De Montfort University
[1] Council Directive 93/13/EEC, 5 April 1993, OJ L95/29.
[2] SI 1994/3159.

other measures of procedural fairness, and/or by direct control over the substantive distribution of rights and obligations.

Viewing the good faith rule in this context has certain implications. The rule states that sellers and suppliers must comply with the requirement of good faith in the context of the terms which they offer to consumers. We must interpret the requirement of good faith by reference to the European consumer policy which it seeks to further. This means that the contract terms offered by the seller or supplier to the consumer must be made transparent to the consumer. This necessarily implies that they be available and be in plain and intelligible language. It may also involve the contract being structured in a particular way, and/or the consumer having an extended period to examine the terms, and/or the seller or supplier explaining the meaning and effect of certain terms. These transparency measures are intended to protect the consumer interest by guaranteeing informed consumer consent to the contract terms. This may be enough to establish that the seller or supplier has acted in good faith. However, in some cases more may be required if there is to be a sufficient level of consumer protection and confidence. In the case of some terms it may be that there is only good faith where a choice of terms was available to the consumer. In other cases it may be found that the seller or supplier has acted contrary to the requirement of good faith by taking advantage of his superior bargaining position to impose terms which unduly compromise the interests of the consumer. In yet other cases (perhaps irrespective of questions of transparency, choice, or bargaining imbalance), the substantive terms may be so unfavourable to the consumer that the seller or supplier can be said to have failed to comply with the good faith requirement.

Having dealt with good faith as a distinct rule, I go on to consider the potential for using good faith as a general organising principle. I advance the view that a general principle of good faith, based upon respect for the legitimate interests of the consumer, would make a significant contribution to the rational development of law and policy. The framework for analysis of the consumer interest would be very similar to the framework applicable to the good faith rule already discussed. In other words, transparency would be seen as fundamental but not necessarily sufficient.

I suggest that we would need to proceed cautiously with such a general good faith principle. It could be difficult to transplant it forthwith as a common law concept which can override established rules and principles. Its role in most cases must be as a norm to which we should aspire, and which should guide those who prepare and draft legislation or soft law measures.

The Good Faith Rule: Some Introductory Comments

The Unfair Terms in Consumer Contracts Directive/Regulations (here-inafter referred to as the "Directive/Regulations") apply to terms in contracts between sellers or suppliers, and consumers.[3] All terms must be in plain and intelligible language.[4] Under the Directive/Regulations a term used by a seller/supplier is unfair if:

> contrary to the requirement of good faith [it] causes a significant imbalance in the parties' rights and obligations under the contract to the detriment of the consumer.[5]

If a term is unfair it is not binding on the consumer. However, the rest of the contract continues to be binding if it is capable of continuing in existence without the unfair term.[6] The test of unfairness does not apply to terms which define the main subject matter of the contract or the price.[7]

The first point to note is that the so-called requirement of good faith appears to be the overriding concept in the test of unfairness. It seems that the overriding question is whether the term is contrary to the requirement of good faith. In order to be contrary to the requirement of good faith one condition which must be satisfied is that the term must cause a significant imbalance in the parties' rights and obligations, and this must be to the detriment of the consumer. The point is that significant imbalance causing detriment seems to be a component part of the idea of acting contrary to good faith. Good faith itself seems to be the overriding issue.

It is absolutely necessary that we understand this good faith rule in the context of the European Community consumer policy which the Directive seeks to implement. European Directives are subject to

---

[3] Directive, art. 1(1); Regulations, reg. 3(1).
[4] Directive, art. 5; Regulations, reg. 6.
[5] Directive, art. 3; Regulations, reg. 4(1).
[6] Directive, art. 6(1); Regulations, reg. 5(1).
[7] Directive, art. 4(2); Regulations, reg. 3(2).

purposive interpretation,[8] and it is this European consumer policy
which tells us the purpose of the Directive generally and the good faith
rule in particular. It is important to give primacy to an autonomous
European Community conception of the consumer interest. The good
faith rule is, after all, a European Community rule. The good faith traditions of the national legal systems should, of course, be drawn upon.
However, they must not, simply on the basis of their greater strength of
tradition, be allowed to colonise this new and autonomous community
rule.[9]

European Consumer Policy[10]

The Treaty of Rome as agreed in 1957 contained four explicit references
to the consumer interest. Article 39 lists five objectives of the common
agricultural policy, the fifth of which is "to ensure that supplies reach
consumers at reasonable prices". Article 40 says that the organisation of
agricultural markets shall exclude "any discrimination between producers and consumers within the Community". Under Article 85(3), if an
agreement between firms is to be exempt from prohibition under Article
85(1), the agreement in question must allow consumers "a fair share of
the resulting benefit". Under Article 86 abusive conduct by firms in a
dominant position is exemplified by "limiting production, markets or
technical development to the prejudice of consumers". None of these
Treaty provisions create rights for consumers. They do, however, insist
on certain consumer interests being taken account of. The consumer,
then, is intended to be a beneficiary of the common agricultural policy
and the policies on market sharing and abuse of market power.

---

[8] For another example of a discussion of the good faith rule in its European
Community context see R. Brownsword, G. Howells, T. Wilhelmsson, "Between Market
and Welfare: Some Reflections on Unfair Terms in Consumer Contracts" in C. Willett
(ed.), *Aspects of Fairness in Contract* (London, 1996), 25.

[9] See the discussion by T. Wilhelmsson, *Social Contract Law and European Integration*
(Aldershot, Brookfield USA, Singapore, Sydney, 1995), 100; Roppo, "La nuova disciplina
delle clausole abusive nei contratti tra imprese e consumatori" *Rivista di Diritto Civile*
(1994), 277; S. Weatherill, "Prospects for the Development of European Private Law
through "Europeanisation" in the European Court" (1995) *European Review of Private
Law* 307.

[10] On European consumer policy generally, see S. Weatherill, *EC Consumer Law and
Policy* (London, 1997); and Bourgoigne, "European Community Consumer Law and
Policy: From Rome to Amsterdam" (1998) *Consumer Law Journal* 443.

Consumers are also intended to benefit from the Treaty provisions on free movement of goods, persons and services. These provisions are contained in Articles 30, 48 and 59 respectively. Free movement of goods, persons and services is supposed to aid market integration by preventing market partition. However, free movement is also assumed to generate competition and consumer choice (which choice should be greater in an integrated market which is larger than individual national markets). This, in turn, is assumed to bring to bear market discipline on sellers and suppliers, providing them with an incentive to provide good quality and safe goods and services at reasonable prices. In other words, free movement and closer European market integration are supposed to protect the economic and safety interests of consumers.

However, there are limits on the capacity of free movement and closer integration (operating alone) to protect these consumer interests. One problem is that so much is dependent on consumer choice acting as a discipline upon what is provided by sellers and suppliers. But consumer choice is of limited effectiveness as a discipline if it is not fully informed choice. Consumers are likely to have limited information about the possible quality and safety risks associated with complex goods and services; the terms upon which they are supplied; and the legal framework which determines their rights and obligations as consumers. If consumers do not have information in relation to a given issue, then they cannot make a rational assessment as to their interests in respect of that issue, and whether these interests may be under threat. Unless significant numbers of consumers can make such an assessment, no market signal can be sent to sellers and suppliers as to what consumers regard as being in their interests. As such, sellers and suppliers are not under pressure to compete with each other to act in the interests of consumers.

If free movement of goods and services does not in itself provide consumers with sufficient information, then the obvious response is for the law to insist on disclosure. The idea must be that sellers and suppliers should be required to disclose, or otherwise make transparent, certain information. At the very least, this must include that information which is necessary for consumers to be informed as to the quality and safety risks associated with products or services, and the terms upon which the products or services are supplied. It might also be argued that sellers and suppliers should disclose to consumers those elements of the broader legal framework which affect the consumers rights, obligations and remedies.

Transparency, in the context of these sorts of issues, increases the chance that consumers will make fully informed decisions to enter into contracts. In addition, the aggregate of informed consumer contracting decisions should impose a discipline upon sellers and suppliers, forcing them to offer goods and services which, in substance, come closer to reflecting what an informed consumer market wants. On one view, as long as these information rules are adhered to, this operates as a sufficient protection of the consumer interest. The argument would be that the market failure, caused by lack of consumer information has been corrected, and that the market is now more fully responsive to consumer preferences. Of course, even on this view, there would still need to be the capacity to set standards in relation to the supplier's substantive responsibilities in those cases where the information rules have not been adhered to. For example, if a term has not been made transparent, then the view could be that the law should disallow the seller or supplier from relying upon it if it seems to allocate rights or obligations in a way that the consumer would be unlikely to have agreed to if he or she had been aware of it.

However, there is a more welfarist view which would hold that there should in all cases be a minimum level of substantive protection.[11] On this approach, for example, the consumer should be protected from certain sorts of terms, even although these terms were transparent and the consumer was prepared to agree to them. A welfarist perspective is also likely to wish to take account of the weaker bargaining position of a consumer in deciding what level of protection to give. Welfarism may also be concerned to promote choice. This must be distinguished from a free market conception of choice. For the free marketeer, choice is a desirable (and likely) result of the operation of a free market. It is regarded as likely that free markets will produce choices (in the sense of alternatives) between the products offered, the services offered, and the terms upon which they are supplied. The free marketeer will countenance measures, such as improved transparency, designed to improve the operation of markets. If choices are produced as a result, then the free marketeer will regard this as a good thing. However, if choices are not produced, then the free marketeer may take the view that this is because insufficient numbers of customers insisted upon such choices existing. In the absence of some other market failure the free marketeer will be content with this and regard it as an efficient result.[12] The welfarist on

[11] On welfarism generally, see R. Brownsword, G. Howells, T. Wilhelmsson, *Welfarism in Contract Law* (Aldershot, 1994).

[12] This seems, broadly, to be the approach of M.J. Trebilcock, "An Economic Approach to the Doctrine of Unconscionability" in B.J. Reiter, J. Swan (eds), *Studies in Contract Law* (Toronto, 1980), 379.

the other hand may not be content. The welfarist may take the view that good quality choices should be available even although the market has not produced them naturally.

If this sort of protection is to take place, or even if transparency standards are to be set, then it is clear that there must be the scope for positive regulation. European law recognises this in two ways. First of all there is some scope, within the basic framework of the law on free movement, for member states to protect consumers. Article 30 seeks to prevent trading rules which hinder free movement of goods. This provision is, however, qualified by Article 36. Under Article 36, rules which are restrictive of free movement of goods are acceptable if they are "justified on the grounds of . . . (*inter alia*) the protection of health and life of humans, animals or plants". Under the "*Cassis de Dijon*" principle, national measures designed to protect consumers' economic interests may be allowed despite their restrictive effect upon the free movement of goods and services.[13]

Article 36 and the "*Cassis de Dijon*" principle operate in a permissive fashion in relation to national regulatory rules which protect consumer interests. However, the second way in which European law provides scope for positive regulation is via Articles 100, 100a and 129a. Here the power to regulate in the consumer interest is given to the Community itself. Article 100 and Article 100a are both concerned with harmonisation rules which are necessary for the completion of the internal market. Article 100a was introduced by the Single European Act 1987. Measures can be adopted under Article 100a on the basis of qualified majority voting (QMV), while under Article 100 unanimity is required.[14] As a result of this, Article 100a is becoming the favoured basis of law making in this area. The Unfair Terms in Consumer Contracts Directive was adopted under Article 100a as were various other Directives.[15]

Article 100a provides for the adoption of measures:

> for the approximation of the provisions laid down by law, regulation or administrative action in member states which have as their object the establishing and functioning of the internal market.

---

[13] Case 120/78 *Rewe-Zentrale AG* v. *Bundesmonopolverwaltung für Brantwein* [1979] ECR 649 (*Cassis de Dijon*).

[14] See the discussion of QMV in S. Weatherill, P. Beaumont, *EU Law* (London, 3rd edn, 1999), chs 3 and 5.

[15] See, for example, Council Directive 90/314, OJ 1990 L 158/59 (Package Travel Directive) and Council Directive 94/47, OJ 1994 L 280/83 (Timeshare Directive).

It is, of course, immediately noticeable that there is no explicit reference
either to consumer protection or the consumer interest in Article 100a.
The rationale for adoption of consumer protection measures under
Article 100a is that market integration is hindered by the existence of
variation as between the consumer protection laws of the member states.
In the pursuit of market integration it is, therefore, necessary to introduce some degree of harmonisation of consumer protection laws.

Transparency should be a fundamental element of this protection. As
I have said above, this is necessary to ensure informed consent by consumers and to impose market discipline upon suppliers. It seems that
transparency is in fact a fundamental element of the European
Community conception of the consumer interest. The main evidence of
this comes from the various soft law measures produced over the years;
and the influence these have had on the Directives adopted. By "soft
law" I mean the various resolutions and action plans which have
emanated from the European Commission and the Council of Ministers
in relation to consumer policy. The first of these was the Council
Resolution of 14 April 1975 which contained an Annex entitled a
"Preliminary Programme of the European Economic Community for a
Consumer Protection and Information Policy".[16] Five basic rights were
asserted here: (a) the right to protection of health and safety; (b) the
right to protection of economic interests; (c) the right of redress; (d) the
right to information and education; and (e) the right of representation
(i.e., the right to be heard). This Resolution has been followed by a
series of other Resolutions and Action Plans.[17] These have, in varying
ways, re-asserted the five basic rights from the 1975 Resolution. One
thing which is particularly noticeable, and relevant to our discussion, is
that consumer information and education seem to have been given an
increasingly high priority over the years. The second and third Three
Year Action plans begin by citing information and education as top pri-
orities. Such soft law provisions do not have binding legislative effect.
However, these soft law consumer initiatives, and their particular emphasis on transparency, have had a very direct effect upon the legislative
process. Various Directives have imposed transparency requirements on
sellers and suppliers of goods and services.[18] Most importantly, in our

[16] OJ 1975 C91/2.
[17] Three Year Action Plan 1993–95, Com. (93) 378 and Three Year Action Plan
1996–98, Com. (95) 519.
[18] See Council Directive 87/102, 22 December 1986, OJ 1987 L42/48 (concerning
Consumer Credit) amended by Council Directive 90/88, 22 February 1990, OJ 1990
L61/14. See also the Package Travel and Timeshare Directives, n. 15 above.

present context, the 1975 resolution is cited in the Preamble to the Unfair Terms in Consumer Contracts Directive.[19] The general idea of transparency in European Community law and policy seems to be that it is a fundamental requirement. The consumer should always be "conscious of his rights and responsibilities".[20] The belief is that this will help individual consumers to give informed consent and to enforce their rights; and, further, that it will improve competition between sellers and suppliers.[21]

The next question we must ask is whether the European Community conception of the consumer interest is restricted to the need to ensure this minimum level of transparency in relation to important issues affecting consumers, or, whether it goes further. Is European law also in the (more welfarist) business of giving a degree of protection to the consumer in relation to issues affecting his interests even where the risks in question have been made transparent to the consumer? There is certainly no doubt that, in the context of health and safety, the answer to this is—yes. The General Product Safety Directive imposes a general "safety" requirement,[22] and the Product Liability Directive imposes liability on producers and others for damage caused by a "defect" in a product.[23] Transparency is indeed relevant to the conception of what is safe and what constitutes a defect. For example, the product may be supplied with warnings which serve to better inform the consumer as to how to use it safely.[24] However, transparency is only one factor. A product will not be safe or non-defective simply on the grounds that the risks were made transparent to the consumer. Irrespective of transparency, certain risks will be considered unacceptable.

But what is the position of European law in relation to the economic interests of the consumer? Is transparency sufficient in itself, or is it more welfarist, being in the business of protecting the consumer's economic interests, even where compromise of these interests was made transparent? For example, is the consumer to be protected from certain economic risks *per se*? Is the consumer to be protected against economic risks where he is in a weaker bargaining position than the supplier? Is choice to be insisted upon, or at least promoted, even where it has not

[19] Recital 8.
[20] See n. 16 above.
[21] See the discussion by S. Weatherill, "The Role of the Informed Consumer in European Community Law and Policy" (1994) *Consumer Law Journal* 49.
[22] Council Directive 92/59, June 1992, OJ 1992 L288/24, art. 1.
[23] Council Directive 85/374, 25 July 1985, OJ 1985 L210/29, art. 1.
[24] Directive 92/59, art. 2(b) and Directive 85/374, art. 6(1).

been produced naturally by market forces? In order to give a proper answer to such questions it is necessary to say a little more about the Treaty of Rome and the general trajectory of EC consumer policy. We have already seen that Articles 100 and 100a seek harmonisation of rules in order to further integration. However, Article 100a(3) gives more detailed guidance on the appropriate content of harmonisation measures. It provides that:

> the Commission, in its proposals envisaged in paragraph 1 concerning health, safety, environmental and consumer protection, will take as a base a high level of protection.

This provision is now supported by the new Article 129a of the Treaty which provides that:

> The Community will contribute to the attainment of a high level of consumer protection through:
> (a) measures adopted pursuant to Article 100a in the context of the completion of the internal market.
> (b) specific action which supports and supplements the policy pursued by the member states to protect the health, safety and economic interests of consumers and to provide adequate information to consumers.

Three important observations can be made about these provisions. Firstly, it is noticeable that in Article 129a the protection of the various consumer interests (including economic interests) is mentioned separately from the provision of information to consumers. This in itself suggests that the provision of information cannot be seen as synonymous with, or sufficient for, adequate protection. Secondly, there are the references to a *high* level of consumer protection. This confirms that a high level of transparency should be a fundamental requirement. It also suggests, however, that consumer interests should be protected even where their possible compromise has been made transparent. The third point relates to the reasons for requiring a high level of protection. If we read Articles100a and 129a together, it seems that there is a purely welfarist strand to the approach: in that a high level of consumer protection is seen as something which is thought to be desirable in itself. However, there is also a mixed welfare/market strand, in that the high level of protection is something which is thought to be necessary to aid completion of the internal market. The internal market rationale for a high level of consumer protection seems to be based upon the need to encourage cross-border shopping by generating consumer confidence.

The connection between these two policy strands may be seen by looking at the Preamble to the Unfair Contract Terms Directive itself. Recitals 5 and 6 read as follows:

> Whereas, generally speaking, consumers do not know the rules of law which, in Member States other than their own, govern contracts for the sale of goods and services; whereas this lack of awareness may deter them from direct transactions for the purchase of goods or services in another Member State. Whereas, in order to facilitate the establishment of the internal market and to safeguard the citizen in his role as consumer when acquiring goods and services under contracts which are governed by the laws of Member States other than his own, it is essential to remove unfair terms from those contracts.

It has been argued by Weatherill that:

> This envisages a consumer who is active in the market, not simply a consumer who passively awaits the economic advantages of integration. That activity will be induced only where the consumer has sufficient confidence to treat the market as border-free. That confidence is engendered only where the crossing of a border has no detrimental impact on the consumer's minimum level of legal protection.[25]

So, on this view, we can see the Directive as aiming at creating a confident body of consumers who will make use of and enhance the development of the internal market. The consumer confidence issue has been seen as important since at least as early as the Sutherland Report of 1992. This report saw lack of consumer confidence as being a significant obstacle to the practical achievement of the internal market.[26]

We can conclude, then, that the EC model of the consumer interest is one in which a high level of transparency is a fundamental requirement. However, it is also one in which welfarism and the need to generate consumer confidence may demand that a high level of protection be delivered by means additional to transparency. In the context of consumer contract terms this has the following implications:

(1) *Transparency*

First of all it is clear that if transparency is a fundamental requirement, then terms should be transparent irrespective of value judgements as to

---

[25] Weatherill, n. 9 above, 315.
[26] *The Internal Market After 1992: Meeting The Challenge.*

their substance. It is not, in other words, simply a matter of making terms transparent if these terms are in some way substantively unfair to the consumer. European Community consumer policy, as I have noted, aims to inform consumers of their "rights and responsibilities". This is seen as being fundamentally important in its own right since it promotes informed consent, helps in the enforcement of rights, and also improves competition.

Terms should be available at the time of the contract. They must also be clearly expressed, so that the consumer is in a position to understand what is on offer and to compare this with the terms offered by other suppliers. For terms to be clearly expressed they must obviously be in language which the average consumer can understand. The wording should not be overly verbose or legalistic and should be generally easy to follow. Terms must also be in decent sized and generally legible print. However, account must also be taken of the number of terms involved, the general complexity of the issues and the time available for consideration. The terms should be clearly enough structured under appropriate headings so that a reasonable consumer is able to assimilate the information, and able to understand and distinguish between different issues. The consumer should, in particular, be able to identify key rights and responsibilities.

A regime such as this would be a considerable advance on what either common law or the Unfair Contract Terms Act 1977 have been able to achieve. At common law a term is not binding upon the consumer unless it has been incorporated into the contract. In the case of unsigned documents, the basic common law rule is that the consumer must have reasonable notice of the terms if they are to be treated as having been incorporated into the contract.[27] Constraints on length preclude here a detailed analysis of how this law is applied. However, it is usually thought to be satisfied if there is an acceptable form of notice to the effect that the terms exist.[28] Terms do not necessarily need to be physically available. There is no general requirement that the terms be in plain language or decent sized print; nor is there any general requirement that the contract be structured in a rational and understandable fashion. Things are somewhat different in the case of terms which can be regarded as particularly onerous or unusual: where special steps must be taken to draw these to the attention of the consumer.[29] This means that the consumer will at least be aware of such terms. However, it is

---

[27] *Parker v. S.E. Railway Co.* (1877) 2 CPD 416.
[28] *Ibid.*
[29] *Interfoto Picture Library Ltd v. Stiletto Visual Programmes Ltd* [1989] QB 433.

not clear if it also follows that the term must be in sufficiently plain language that it can be understood. In any event it must be remembered that this special disclosure rule probably only applies to those terms at the extreme end of the unfairness spectrum.

If the consumer signs a contractual document (assuming that there has been no fraud by the supplier), it seems that under the common law he is bound by it, even without reasonable notice that it contains terms.[30] As with unsigned documents there is no requirement of plain language, decent sized print or rational structuring. It is not clear whether the rule about particularly onerous or unusual terms even applies to signed documents, but it is quite possible that it does not.

The Unfair Contract Terms Act 1977 applies a reasonableness test to a variety of exemption clauses.[31] But it cannot be said with confidence that transparency is a prerequisite to a term passing that test. It is true that the Act does expressly mention transparency, but it does not do so in the context of consumer contracts.[32] And in the application of the reasonableness test by the courts there is rarely a mention of transparency.[33] It is also very important to recognise that the Unfair Contract Terms Act only applies to certain positively defined exemption clauses. It does not apply to exemption clauses falling outside these definitions, nor does it apply to other sorts of terms, such as those which impose an obligation or burden of some kind upon the consumer.

(2) *Substance, Choice and Bargaining Power*

As well as demanding transparency, a regime which seeks both to provide a high level of consumer protection and generate consumer confidence will need to be able to take account of the substantive nature of terms in deciding whether to enforce them. This might take place as follows. If a consumer has agreed to a term which is harsh in substance, the law might ask whether a choice (in the sense of a reasonable alternative) was available from the seller or from a local competitor. It might be, for example, that a term excludes all liability for consequential loss and a consumer agrees to this term. However, this seller, or another

[30] *L'Estrange* v. *Graucob Ltd* [1934] 2 KB 394.
[31] Section 11.
[32] See Sched. 2, para. (c).
[33] When the House of Lords set out criteria which should always be considered they did not include transparency. See *Smith* v. *Eric S. Bush* [1990] 1 AC 831.

local seller, may offer a more expensive product or service, but one in
which some or all liability for consequential loss is accepted. If this other
package is viewed as a reasonable alternative, that may help to justify
the harsh exclusion to which the consumer nevertheless chose to agree.
Equally, if no alternative package exists, then this may help to confirm
the unfairness of the exclusion to which the consumer had no choice but
to agree. Substance may also interact with an analysis of the bargaining
positions of the parties. If a term is harsh in substance, then it may be
further condemned by the fact that the consumer was not in a strong
enough bargaining position to persuade the seller to offer anything better. Equally the term may be justified if the consumer was in fact in a
strong bargaining position but chose not to take advantage of this to
obtain a better term. Substance might also have its own independent
dynamic. Terms may, for instance, be so harsh in substance that they
cannot be justified either by the existence of consumer choice or by
strong consumer bargaining strength. Equally, there may be terms
which are mildly, but not grossly, unfair in substance and which are
compensated for by other more favourable terms.

This kind of regime was never adopted by the common law. At common law the lack of a reasonable alternative is relevant in the context of
the duress doctrine. Here, however, the lack of a reasonable alternative
must have been brought about by an illegitimate threat of some kind
emanating from the other party: e.g., a threat to break a contract, or
commit a tort or a crime.[34] It is not sufficient that the lack of an alternative was brought about (as in the typical seller-consumer relationship)
simply by market forces. English equitable rules may have some scope
to take account of gross abuse of a superior bargaining position,[35] however, this has not been regarded as generally applicable to the seller-consumer relationship. Finally, some terms are controlled at common law
purely on the basis of their substance. Here, however, we are talking
about closely defined categories of terms, such as penalty clauses. There
is no generally applicable control which has been applied to the terms
in consumer contracts.

As already mentioned, the Unfair Contract Terms Act applies a test

[34] See *Universe Tankships Inc. of Monrovia* v. *International Transport Workers'
Federation* [1982] 2 All ER 67 (HL). See also the discussion in H.G Beale, W.D. Bishop,
M.P. Furmston, *Contract Cases and Materials* (London, 3rd edn, 1995), ch. 34.
[35] See N. Bamford, "Unconscionability as a Vitiating Factor" (1995) *Lloyd's Maritime
and Commercial Law Quarterly* 538.

of reasonableness. And that test does take account of the substantive nature of the terms, the choices available to consumers, and the bargaining strengths of the parties.[36] But as I have already noted, it only applies to certain positively defined exemption clauses and related devices.

The Good Faith Rule Revisited

The good faith rule, as it is expressed in the Directive/Regulations, would appear to accommodate the approach to contract terms which I have said is necessary. The preamble to the Directive seems to sum up the concept of good faith by referring to an obligation on the seller or supplier to take into account the "legitimate interests" of the consumer.[37] A key interest in entering into a consensual arrangement must surely be the ability to give informed consent. All aspects of transparency must, therefore, be relevant to good faith. Indeed it must surely be the case that if a term is unfair in substance, then transparency is a necessity if the term is to stand any chance of satisfying the good faith requirement. The next question, however, is whether there is a precondition that term be transparent *per se*. In other words do terms have to meet a certain standard of transparency irrespective of their substantive content? I have made the point above that this is what is demanded by European Community consumer policy. However, there is some doubt as to whether the Directive/Regulations do in fact require comprehensive transparency in the case of all terms irrespective of their substantive content.

The Directive/Regulations do however say, in a separate provision from the good faith test, that all terms must be in plain and intelligible language. However, rather ironically, it is not clear what sanction is available if a term is not in plain and intelligible language. The provision reads as follows:

> A seller or supplier shall ensure that any written term of a contract is expressed in plain, intelligible language, and if there is doubt about the meaning of a written term, the interpretation most favourable to the consumer shall prevail.[38]

It must be assumed that whether terms are plain and intelligible is to be

---

[36] See *Smith* v. *Eric S. Bush*, n. 33 above.
[37] These criteria originated in Recital 16 of the Preamble to the Directive.
[38] Directive, art. 5; Regulations, reg. 6(1).

judged by the standards of the average consumer. But if terms fail this test, what is the sanction? If there is doubt as to their meaning they will be interpreted favourably to the consumer. This can be seen as a sanction of sorts. The problem, though, is that it is not at all clear that a term which is not plain and intelligible will always have a doubtful meaning. It depends on what it means to say that there is doubt about the meaning of a term. If this is also judged by the standards of the average consumer, then it may be that whenever a term is not plain and intelligible by these standards, there will always also be doubt as to the meaning of the term. However, if the question of doubt as to meaning is to be judged by the standards of lawyers, then the interpretation rule will not always be an effective sanction where terms are not plain and intelligible. The term in question may not be plain and intelligible by the standards of the average consumer, whilst by the standards of a lawyer there may be no doubt as to its meaning.

Even if doubt as to the meaning of a term is judged by the standards of the average consumer, so that the interpretation rule serves as a useful sanction where terms are not plain and intelligible, we still have a problem. Plain and intelligible language is only one aspect of transparency. A term may well be in plain and intelligible language. This, however, does not necessarily mean that it was physically available for inspection. Moreover, even if the term was available for inspection and consideration, it is arguable that it might be found to be in plain and intelligible language despite being in small print and, also, despite being hidden in a complex set of terms which lack a rational structure.

There is, however, another way of looking at the plain and intelligible language requirement. It could be argued that, rather than being a separate rule, the requirement is, in fact, supportive of the good faith rule. There is some support for this approach in the opening provisions of the Directive. The scope of the Directive is said to be the control of "unfair terms".[39] Nothing is said of the distinct and separate control of terms which are not in plain and intelligible language. Given that terms are said to be unfair if they are contrary to the requirement of good faith, it could be concluded that the plain and intelligible language requirement only exists to support the requirement of good faith. It is true that neither of the specific provisions cross-refer to each other. This, however, could simply be an example of the rather loose approach to drafting which is sometimes found in EC Directives. Perhaps the

---

[39] Article 1(1).

intention is that good faith incorporates the plain and intelligible language requirement as well as those other aspects of transparency which, I have suggested, are not necessarily covered by the plain and intelligible language requirement, namely: availability; opportunity for consideration; decent sized print; and a rationally structured contract. It seems that the Office of Fair Trading, in discharging their regulatory functions under the Regulations, may support this analysis. They seem to take the view that transparency covers all of these sorts of issues.[40] But this simply brings us back to where we were before: all aspects of transparency are relevant to good faith. It does not tell us whether a term can be unfair, and therefore not binding, purely upon grounds of intransparency.

The wording of the good faith test does, in fact, leave some room for doubt as to whether a term can be contrary to good faith, and consequently be unfair, purely upon the basis that it is intransparent in some way. A term is unfair if:

> contrary to the requirement of good faith it causes a significant imbalance in the rights and obligations of the parties under the contract to the detriment of the consumer.

Even assuming that good faith is the overriding issue, it seems fairly clear that for a term to contravene the good faith requirement it must cause a significant imbalance in the parties' rights and obligations. Most of us would probably assume that the reference to "rights and obligations" is a reference to the substantive nature of the terms of the contract. If this is the case, then surely an imbalance in rights and obligations is something which results from the fact that the substantive features of a term favour the seller or supplier, and that the substantive features of any terms which are favourable to the consumer are insufficiently favourable to strike a fair balance. It then seems to follow that in order for a term to contravene the good faith requirement it must, in its substance, contain some feature which is unfair. On this approach it would seem to be impossible that a lack of transparency could, in itself, cause an imbalance in rights and obligations. The lack of transparency may well have caused the consumer to agree to the term. But if that term is not substantively unfavourable, then no imbalance in rights and obligations has been caused.

There is, of course, another way of reading the good faith test which would allow a term to fail it (and, consequently, be unfair) purely on the

---

[40] *OFT Bulletin on Unfair Contract Terms*, Issue No. 4, 13.

basis of lack of transparency. Perhaps an imbalance in "rights and obligations" *can* be caused by a term which, though intransparent, is not
substantively unfair to the consumer. The argument could be that a consumer's rights under a contract go beyond the substantive rights allocated by the express and implied terms of that contract, and include the
procedural right to be fully informed as to all of the terms of the contract. On this approach intransparency, of itself, causes an imbalance in
rights and obligations. I would submit that the good faith test should be
read in this way, so as to meet the demands of European Community
consumer policy.

Whether or not the good faith test does have the effect of making
transparency a fundamental requirement, it must surely be the case that
it is, very important to good faith. In particular it must be that if a term
is at all unfair in substance, then it must be transparent in order to stand
any chance of satisfying the good faith requirement. But what if such a
term is indeed transparent? Is it possible that the term can still be contrary to good faith on the basis of its substantive makeup; on the basis
of lack of choice; or on the basis of the weak bargaining position of the
consumer? I have argued above that the high level of protection required
by European consumer policy may necessitate transparent terms being
found to be unfair on these other grounds. I have also argued that there
should exist a regime in which the law takes account of the substantive
nature of the terms of the contract, the choices available to the consumer, and the relative bargaining strengths of the parties. I have further argued that these factors should be able to operate for or against
enforceability. They should, in other words, be able to confirm the fairness of a term which causes significant imbalance but which is transparent. Equally they should be able to confirm that, despite the
transparency, the term is unfair. The test does seem to have the capacity to facilitate such an approach.

When assessing good faith it is relevant to consider generally whether
the seller or supplier has dealt fairly and equitably with the consumer.[41]
This seems to involve an assessment of all of the interests of the consumer, both substantive and procedural. So, for example, it may be that
the degree of significant imbalance and detriment caused by the substance of the term is so great that it fails to satisfy the good faith
requirement. It may also be that the existence (or lack) of a choice is
seen as confirming or denying the existence of good faith. Choice is not

---

[41] Regulations, Sched. 2, para. (d).

mentioned explicitly. However, choice is certainly an important factor in the German good faith concept,[42] and it is generally believed that this concept was strongly in mind when the Directive was drafted. As far as bargaining strength is concerned, the Directive/Regulations say explicitly that this is relevant to good faith.[43] It must be, therefore, that this can be a determining factor.

Objective or Subjective Good Faith?

Based on the analysis so far, we can conclude our discussion of the good faith rule by dealing with a perennial good faith issue. This is the question as to whether we are talking about subjective or objective good faith. By subjective good faith I mean "honesty in fact", the sort of issue which is under scrutiny in the "good faith purchase" scenario in transfer of title cases.[44] By objective good faith I mean a legally imposed standard of behaviour which is not constructed by reference to the subjective perceptions of the party in question.[45] It is clear that our good faith rule is an example of objective good faith. What matters, for example, is whether the terms are transparent, not whether the supplier believed them to be. Any significant element of subjectivity would clearly undermine the general goals of EC consumer law and policy which the rule is supposed to serve. We cannot obtain a high level of protection and confidence if the approach is dictated to by the subjective perceptions of the supplier.

A General Principle of Good Faith

Finally, I would like to suggest the need for an underlying general principle of good faith in consumer contracts. In the space available here I cannot provide a comprehensive analysis of the issues involved.

[42] See H.W. Micklitz, *"La Loi allemande relative au régime juridique des conditions générales des contrats du 9 décembre 1976. Bilan de onze années d'application"* (1989) 41 *Rev. Int. Droit Comparé* 101.

[43] Regulations, Sched. 2, para. (a).

[44] On subjective good faith, see E.A. Farnsworth, "The Concept of Good Faith in American Law" *Centro di Studi e Richerche di Diritto Comparato e Straniere, Saggi, Conferenze e Seminare 3*, Rome, April 1993; and S. Waddams, "Good Faith and Reasonable Expectations" (1995) *Journal of Contract Law* 55.

[45] Farnsworth, n. 44 above. The subjective/objective debate is considered in more detail elsewhere in this volume by Forte and MacQueen.

However, I would like to adumbrate some general proposals which will hopefully serve as a stimulant to debate. For more than forty years there has been growing, sometimes heated, academic debate as to whether there should be a general principle of good faith in contract law and, if so, what form such a principle should take.[46] It has, in fact, been in the context of commercial contracts that many fear good faith might do harm. There are, for example, concerns that good faith would cause commercial uncertainty. There are also concerns that good faith would undermine party autonomy and the unbridled pursuit of self interest.[47] There are those who believe that, in the context of commercial contracts, such values are not only important in themselves, but are vital if the market economy is to flourish. It is probably fair to say, however, that even those who are most sceptical about good faith are less worried about its potential effects in the context of consumer contracts than in the purely commercial sphere. This diminished concern may be explained partly because of a lack of interest in consumer contracts. It is also because less money tends to be at stake in consumer contracts, so that the implications of uncertainty are less significant. There is probably also a sense that those who buy goods or services in a private capacity are genuinely deserving of some protection.

However, it is one thing to say that consumers should be protected. It is another thing to say that this protection should take place by a reference to a general principle of good faith. Even if such a principle would be relatively harmless, we should know what its positive benefits would be. Howells has approached the issue from one angle.[48] He notes the limitations of the good faith rule in the Unfair Terms Directive/ Regulations. The rule does not apply to purely pre-contractual or post-contractual relations.[49] Clearly a general principle of good faith would have at least something to say about these issues. The most significant observation made by Howells is that if good faith is to be pervasive and effective, then private law is a wholly inadequate vehicle for its achievement. There must be an emphasis upon public, collective and reflexive

---

[46] For a seminal 1950s discussion see R. Powell, "Good Faith in Contracts" (1956), 9 *Current Legal Problems* 16.

[47] For an excellent overview of the good faith debate, see R. Brownsword, "Positive, Negative, Neutral: the Reception of Good Faith in English Contract Law" in R. Brownsword, N.J. Hird, G. Howells (eds), *Good Faith in Contract: Concept and Context* (Aldershot, Brookfield USA, Singapore, Sydney, 1999), 13.

[48] G. Howells, "Good Faith in Consumer Contracting" in Brownsword *et al*, n. 47 above, 91.

[49] *Ibid.*, 96–7. See also Directive, art. 4(1); Regulations, reg. 4(2).

regulation.[50] I certainly agree with these views. However, I would argue that the whole fabric of control must be underpinned by an organising good faith principle which could aid the rational development of the law. This principle would be based upon the idea of respect for the legitimate interests of the consumer.

We must identify the range of ways in which the interests of consumers are affected. Transparency must be emphasised as the primary requirement. The ways in which consumer interests are affected must always be transparent to consumers. We must then consider to what extent the protection of the consumer interest should go further than this. This sort of approach would help us to focus on developing a rational and comprehensive framework of consumer interests. We have talked, for example, about the economic interests of consumers, and about how it is in the economic interests of consumers that there be protection from unfair contract terms. But the economic interests of consumers are affected by *all* of the ways in which the law shapes the relationship (e.g., via rules on formation and remedies), *and* by the ways in which the law allows the parties to shape the relationship. We must think about the extent to which these rules fairly balance the interests of the parties; and whether features which are unfavourable to the consumer should be amended substantively or at least made more transparent to the consumer.

The law relating to insurance contracts provides a good example of the potential application of such an approach. Here the consumer must disclose to the insurer all facts of which he is aware and which are also material to the underwriting of the risk, even if the consumer does not appreciate that they are material facts. If the consumer fails to disclose such facts to the insurer, and this failure has induced the insurer to enter the contract, then the insurer may avoid the contract, even although the fact which has not been disclosed is unconnected with the circumstances giving rise to the claim.[51] This duty of disclosure arises by virtue of insurance contracts being viewed as contracts of the "utmost good faith". This good faith principle also requires the insurer to disclose material facts to the insured consumer. However this does not really take proper account of the consumer interest. There is usually very little or nothing in the way of fact for the insurer to disclose to the consumer.

---

[50] Howells, n. 48 above, 102–10.
[51] See the discussion in C. Willett, N.J. Hird, "Consumer Protection in Insurance Contracts" in Cartwright (ed.), *Consumer Protection in Financial Services* (The Hague, London, Boston, 1999), chapter 10.

The real problem for the consumer is the broad and onerous nature of his own legal duty of disclosure, and the surprisingly draconian consequences of his failure to meet this legal duty. At the least, the consumer must surely have a legitimate interest in being told of the nature of his duty of disclosure and the highly detrimental consequences which will ensue if he is in breach. This approach has in fact been taken by the Statements of Insurance Practice where it states:

> If not included in the declaration, prominently displayed on the proposal form should be a statement:
> (1) drawing the attention of the proposer to the consequences of failure to disclose all material facts, explained as those facts an insurer would regard as likely to influence the acceptance and assessment of the proposal.
> (2) warning that if the proposer is in any doubt about facts considered material he should disclose them.[52]

The Statement of Practice also goes beyond this transparency based approach, and actually limits the substantive right of the insurer to avoid the obligation. The insurer is not supposed to repudiate for non disclosure of any material fact which a policy holder could not "reasonably be expected to have disclosed".[53] We must now consider putting this sort of approach onto a legal footing.[54]

Insurance contact law is, of course, only one area in which my general principle of good faith might require a rethink and reform. There are other ways in which the law may compromise (or permit compromise of) the economic and other interests of consumers. Many, although perhaps not all, of these are already adequately regulated. However, there are also new ways in which traditional consumer interests may be compromised; and new types of consumer interest which might be recognised. Genetically modified foods provide a good example of something which may be a *new* threat to consumer health and safety interests. The first priority must obviously be the most rigorous transparency, so that consumers may know whether a product contains any genetically modified material. There is already a European Community Regulation on this subject and improved national rules are

---

[52] Association of British Insurers, Statement of General Insurance Practice (1986), s. 1(c).

[53] *Ibid.*, para 2(b).

[54] For a discussion of reforms of this nature in other jurisdictions, see D. Friedmann, "The Transformation of 'Good Faith' in Insurance Law" in Brownsword *et al*, n. 47 above, 311.

currently under preparation.[55] However, there must obviously be a debate as to whether the risks are so considerable or uncertain as to demand going beyond transparency to an outright ban.

A good example of a *developing* consumer interest arises in relation to the environmental impact of products. Consumers are increasingly keen to buy products which do not have a negative impact upon the environment. Retailers and manufacturers, however, are inclined to make vague claims about the "environmentally friendly" or "ozone friendly" nature of their products, and such claims may well encourage consumers to buy the product. These claims may have very little substance to them and yet they may not actually be false: so that they avoid attracting civil liability for misrepresentation or criminal liability under the legislation relating to trade descriptions. At the very least, consumers have an interest in the introduction of some form of proactive transparency in this context. Some work has already been done on this by the Code of Advertising Practice, according to which, advertisers should be able to substantiate claims, and should not make vague environmental claims.[56] Again, we must think about putting this rule onto a legal footing.

Concluding Comment

I have argued for the introduction of a general principle of good faith which could aid the rational development of the law. We could work towards transplanting such a general good faith principle into the common law of consumer contracts. However, we must proceed cautiously in this regard, thinking carefully about the way in which it would interact with established rules and concepts. In particular, we must avoid causing "irritancy" to perfectly good rules and concepts.[57] In the main we should see good faith as a norm to which the law should aspire and which should guide those who prepare and draft legislation or soft law measures.

---

[55] See the EC Regulation on Genetically Modified Soya and Maize Labelling, 1139/98, 3 June 1998, OJ 1998 L159/4. Note also the draft Food Labelling (Amendment) Regulations 1999.

[56] Committee of Advertising Practice, Briefing, 1993.

[57] On legal transplants and their potential for causing irritancy, see G. Teubner, "Legal Irritants: Good Faith in British Law or How Unifying Law Ends Up in New Divergences" (1998) 61 *Modern Law Review* 11.

INDEX

Location references are to page numbers, with any footnote references in brackets after the page number.

Index

Index